THE TOWNSHEND DUTIES CRISIS

THE
TOWNSHEND DUTIES
CRISIS

The Second Phase of the
American Revolution
1767–1773

PETER D. G. THOMAS

CLARENDON PRESS · OXFORD
1987

Oxford University Press, Walton Street, Oxford OX2 6DP

Oxford New York Toronto
Delhi Bombay Calcutta Madras Karachi
Petaling Jaya Singapore Hong Kong Tokyo
Nairobi Dar es Salaam Cape Town
Melbourne Auckland

and associated companies in
Beirut Berlin Ibadan Nicosia

Oxford is a trade mark of Oxford University Press

Published in the United States
by Oxford University Press, New York

© Peter D. G. Thomas 1987

British Library Cataloguing in Publication Data

Thomas, Peter D.G.
The Townshend duties crisis: the second
phase of the American Revolution, 1767–1773.
1. United States—History—Revolution,
1775–1783—Causes
I. Title
327.41073 E210
ISBN 0–19–822967–4

Library of Congress Cataloging-in-Publication Data

Thomas, Peter David Garner.
The Townshend duties crisis.
Bibliography: p.
Includes index.
1. United States—Politics and government—Revolution,
1775–1783. 2. Townshend, Charles, 1725–1767.
3. Great Britain—Colonies—America—Economic policy.
4. United States—History—Revolution, 1775–1783—
Economic aspects.
I. Title.
E215.3.T46 1987 973.2'7 86-28467
ISBN 0–19–822967–4

Set by Hope Services, Abingdon
Printed in Great Britain
at the University Printing House, Oxford
by David Stanford
Printer to the University

Preface

THE years between the Stamp Act Crisis of 1765–6 and the Boston Tea Party of 1773 are usually seen as a lull separating the two major storms in the coming of the American Revolution. This book seeks to remedy the comparative neglect of that period, and to demonstrate that much of what happened after 1773 had already been anticipated. Primarily a study of the British response to the colonial resistance to Charles Townshend's taxes and other American defiance of British rule, it shows that attitudes on both sides of the Atlantic were already hardening into a sense of confrontation before the catalyst of the Tea Party.

Among my debts to other students of the period I am especially grateful to those who have made available unpublished research. Huw V. Bowen has given unstintingly of his immense knowledge of the East India Company. I also thank the authors of the theses listed in the bibliography for permission to consult them: two of them, M. T. Hamer and P. Marshall, kindly lent their personal copies.

No such study would be possible without the generosity of owners of manuscripts. I am grateful to the following for permission to cite and quote from manuscripts in their possession or in public repositories: the Earl of Dartmouth; Olive, Countess Fitzwilliam's Wentworth Settlement Trustees and the Director of Sheffield City Libraries; the Duke of Grafton, the Earl of Harrowby, and Lord Rayleigh. Permission to use their manuscript holdings was given by the William L. Clements Library, University of Michigan, and by the Henry E. Huntingdon Library. I have also received much assistance from the staff of the History of Parliament Trust; the British Library; the Public Record Office; the National Library of Wales; the Institute of Historical Research; Sheffield City Library; the County Record Offices for Essex, Kent, Staffordshire, and West Suffolk; and the Library of the University College of Wales. Margaret White and Dora Burroughs typed the manuscript with their customary expertise and expedition.

P.D.G.T.

Contents

I

America in British Politics

I shall always consider that this country, as the parent, ought
to be tender and just; and that the colonies, as the children,
ought to be dutiful. A system of arbitrary rule over the
colonies I would not adopt on this side, nor would I do
otherwise than strenuously resist when attempts were made
to throw off that dependency to which the colonies ought to
submit, not only for the advantage of this country, but for
their own real happiness and safety.[1]

LORD ROCKINGHAM'S letter of 11 May 1767 to the Speaker of
the Massachusetts Assembly reflected the broad consensus of
opinion in Britain as to the subordinate status of the American
colonies, and it was an interpretation of the British Empire
accepted then by the great majority of Americans. Yet within a
few years this was not to be so, for the colonists did not share the
British assumption that Britain's sovereignty over America was
and should be exercised through Parliament. This fundamental
point of difference had been at the heart of the Stamp Act Crisis
dispute of 1765–6 over taxation of the colonies by Britain. Its
revival in what may be called the Townshend Duties Crisis was to
lead to a deepening gulf, that became too wide to be bridged,
between the maximum concessions that any Parliamentary
politicians were willing and able to envisage, and the minimum
demands of the colonial leadership. The crisis was to end in the
American Revolution.

Assumptions within Britain meant that the political debate
over America was not conducted at that level of argument. Only a
few radicals, mostly in London, supported the developing colonial
challenge first to the authority of Parliament and ultimately to
that of the Crown. In that sense, as colonial observers in Britain
soon came to perceive, there was no foundation for an American
party in Britain, or at least at Westminster. The dispute within
Parliament was merely about whether it was wise and expedient
to tax and pass other laws for America, and not over whether

[1] *Grenville Papers*, IV, 13 n.

Parliament had the right to do so. Men like George Grenville and Lord North saw themselves as defending what they believed to be the great victory won at the Glorious Revolution of 1688–9, the supremacy of Parliament in the state. The denial by the colonies of Parliament's authority and their attempt to put themselves directly under the Crown therefore had sinister implications in British eyes. It is only within this context of consensus on the basic issue of Parliamentary sovereignty that any validity may be attached to such comments on the British political scene as the one made on 8 August 1767 by the most famous American in Britain, Benjamin Franklin.[2]

America . . . is now made one of the distinctions of party here; those who in the last two sessions have shown a disposition to favour us, being called by way of reproach *Americans*; while the others . . . value themselves on being true to the interest of Britain, and zealous for maintaining its dignity and sovereignty over the colonies.

This observation exemplifies what was for long the conventional interpretation, both contemporary and historical, of the British side of the coming of the American Revolution: a clear distinction being drawn between the political factions headed by William Pitt, Earl of Chatham, and the Marquess of Rockingham, and deemed sympathetic to colonial aspirations and demands, and those led by George Grenville and the Duke of Bedford, both portrayed as hardliners. The Stamp Act Crisis was the foundation of this simplistic analysis. In 1766 the Rockingham administration, supported by Pitt and his followers, had carried the repeal of that American taxation against the opposition of the Grenville and Bedford groups, who had constituted the Grenville ministry responsible for the measure in 1765. Such a scenario is accurate only at the surface level of politics. There were certainly differences of attitude over America between British politicians that created discord and disagreement. But to some extent these had been caused by the sheer accident of who had happened to be in government and in opposition between 1763 and 1766 when the policy of taxation was enacted and then reversed. Any politicians in office in the years immediately after 1763 would have acted towards America in much the same way as Grenville and his colleagues did. Pitt himself that year had not commented on, let alone challenged, the first announcement of the intention to tax America.[3] Even the recent political record of the various parties

---

[2] *Franklin Papers*, XIV, 229.   [3] Thomas, *WMQ*, 38 (1981), 110–12.

was not as clear-cut as the assumptions based on it. The followers of Rockingham had not opposed the Stamp Act either vigorously or on principle while it was being enacted in 1765, and Pitt had been absent. The next year the Rockingham ministry had accompanied its repeal with a Declaratory Act that affirmed Parliament's right to legislate for America 'in all cases whatsoever'. And although this had then been challenged on the issue of internal taxation by Pitt and his followers, they had subsequently come to accept it as enacted law. The Townshend Duties Act of 1767 was a colonial revenue measure passed with the full support of the Chatham ministry.

Nor did all British politicians and American observers accept that insistence on taxing the colonies was necessarily the sole criterion of a hard line towards America. Both George Grenville and Lord Hillsborough, when the first Secretary of State for America, regarded as more reprehensible for this very reason the Chathamite emphasis on economic control, as voiced by Pitt in the House of Commons on 14 January 1766. 'We may bind their trade, confine their manufactures, and exercise every power whatsoever, except that of taking their money out of their pockets without their consent.'[4] In 1768 Grenville recalled that Pitt had threatened to fill 'their towns with troops and their ports with ships of war' if this should prove necessary to stop manufacturing in the colonies. Such a step, Grenville thought, 'would be most violent and unjust as well as impracticable'.[5] And when Benjamin Franklin visited Hillsborough in Ireland during 1771 his host, fired by Franklin's analogy between Ireland and America, vehemently attacked Chatham's position as more tyrannical than mere taxation.[6]

The Chatham administration formed in the summer of 1766 on the dismissal of Rockingham comprised an informal coalition of Pitt's followers with a few men still regarded by Rockingham for some time as his supporters. Pitt himself declined to undertake either the Leadership of the House of Commons or any important executive post, becoming Earl of Chatham and Lord Privy Seal. Ill

[4] Almon, *Debates*, VII, 77. This is the most publicized contemporary version of what Pitt is supposed to have said. There are variant wordings. He said something similar on 21 Feb. 1766: *Ryder Diary*, p. 309.

[5] Grenville Letter-Books, 2. Grenville to William Knox, 27 June 1768, printed *HMC Knox MSS*, pp. 95–6.

[6] *Franklin Papers*, XIX, 48–9.

health soon caused his role as head of the ministry to become largely formal, the Duke of Grafton taking over that task as the one normally appertaining to his post as First Lord of the Treasury. Other key posts went to two Chathamites who had opposed the Declaratory Act, Lord Camden as Lord Chancellor and Lord Shelburne as Southern Secretary, whose sphere of responsibility included the colonies. The Northern Secretaryship and Commons Leadership were retained by General Henry Conway, the man deemed to be the most pro-American among the leading Rockinghamites. A more junior member of the outgoing ministry, that notorious political weathercock the brilliant and erratic Charles Townshend, was promoted to Chancellor of the Exchequer. Otherwise Chatham's projected takeover of the previous administration after the removal of Rockingham was largely a failure. Loyalty to the Marquess and Chatham's high-handed disregard of other men's susceptibilities led to a spate of dismissals and resignations both immediately and during the next few months. The sole effort to broaden the base of the ministry, by an approach to the Duke of Bedford, proved abortive, with Bedford pointedly reminding Grafton of their differences on American policy. 'It can't be unknown to you how much the measures pursued in the last session of Parliament by the late, as well as the present, administration, were opposed in the totality by myself and my friends.'[7] Before the end of 1766 the Chatham administration faced an opposition of three distinct political groupings.[8]

The biggest was that headed by the displaced Prime Minister, Lord Rockingham. This faction considered itself as the Whig party in the sense of being the political heir of Prime Ministers Sir Robert Walpole and Henry Pelham. Until his death in 1768 the veteran Duke of Newcastle provided a personal link with their administrations through his record thirty-eight years as a cabinet minister, eight as successor himself to his Pelham brother and more recently as Lord Privy Seal under Rockingham. Strict examination of the Parliamentary personnel of this group casts doubt on the boasted Whig lineage. It had been purged by loss of office in 1762 and 1766 of many ambitious men, as the party changed from a governing to an opposition role, and so attracted men hitherto deemed independent or even Tory. But belief in its Whig tradition was a cherished bond. The party was formidable

---

[7] *Bedford Papers*, III, 343–4.
[8] For the formation of the ministry see Brooke, *Chatham Administration*, pp. 6–19; and Thomas, *British Politics and the Stamp Act Crisis*, pp. 283–7.

in both Houses of Parliament, with the young and energetic Duke of Richmond, Southern Secretary in the last months of Rockingham's ministry, well to the fore in the Lords. A phalanx of peers, about thirty strong, was matched by a substantial following in the Commons, perhaps around 100 in July 1766, but dwindling in a couple of years to a hard core of little more than half that number.[9] The acknowledged leader of the Rockingham party there was William Dowdeswell, a surprising and successful recruit by Rockingham in 1765 from among the independent members to be his Chancellor of the Exchequer. 'Dull Dowdeswell' was a man regularly consulted and trusted by Rockingham and a respected figure in the Commons, where between 1766 and 1774 he made some 500 speeches on all manner of subjects, as befitted the spokesman of the main opposition party. Eloquence was supplied to the full by Edmund Burke, who spoke as often and usually at greater length. And the party, though weak in lawyers apart from Rockingham's former Attorney-General Charles Yorke, never lacked a cohort of speakers, men like Lord John Cavendish and Sir George Savile.[10]

Already in opposition for a year were the two groups dismissed in 1765 to make way for the Rockingham ministry. George Grenville, Prime Minister for the previous two years, was the man identified by his brother-in-law Chatham as the most formidable opponent in the Commons. Obsessed with Parliamentary rights and financial economy, Grenville was not likely to lose sight of the issues raised by the Stamp Act Crisis. A man of tenacity and probity, and highly regarded by independent opinion in the House, he had built up a Commons following that in 1766 was around forty, prominent among whom were the able and eloquent lawyer Alexander Wedderburn and Thomas Whately, Grenville's former Secretary to the Treasury and now his political man of business. In the Lords his brother Lord Temple and Lord Lyttelton led a small group, among them the young Earl of Suffolk.[11] The Duke of Bedford's party, a group dating from the 1740s, had hitherto trodden the same path as Grenville through the political vicissitudes of the 1760s, in office until 1765 and thereafter in

[9] O'Gorman, Rise of Party, p. 191.

[10] Much has been written on the Rockingham party in this period. See O'Gorman, ibid., pp. 197–314; Hoffman, The Marquis, pp. 133–200; and Langford, 'The Rockingham Whigs and America 1767–1773', Statesmen, Scholars and Merchants, pp. 135–52.

[11] Lawson, Thesis, is the fullest survey of the Grenvillite party in the later 1760s. See also his George Grenville, pp. 227–88.

opposition. Contemporaries sometimes tended to link them together, but the two factions retained their separate identities. The Bedfordites numbered less than twenty in the Commons, with Richard Rigby as their spokesman. Their more effectual strength lay in the Lords, with Gower, Sandwich, and Weymouth providing a vociferous part of the opposition there.[12]

All calculations of the size of such party groups must necessarily be vague and tentative. They were constantly changing in personnel, and all had soft edges of fluctuating and uncertain membership around an inner core.[13] In any case these factions comprised only a limited proportion of the Commons membership of 558 MPs, about a quarter to a third, and a minority of the House of Lords of some 200 peers. Opposition politicians were confronted not only with their rivals in office but also with a corps of office-holders of one sort or another, from holders of sinecures in the royal household to army colonels. The estimated size of this court party varies according to definitions, but in this period may conveniently be numbered at about 150 in the Commons; and their regularity of attendance provided any ministry with an almost invariable majority. The political battle at Westminster was for the hearts and minds of the independent MPs, who held the balance of power if they could be persuaded to attend. Any hope of success for critics of the administration depended on the emergence of contentious issues of policy and an opposition able to exploit them. It so happened that these conditions existed in the Parliamentary session of 1766–7, when India and America provided ample ammunition for a talented and vigorous opposition to fire at an administration singularly ill-equipped to cope with such a predicament. Chatham soon absented himself from the fray; cabinet ministers differed among themselves on policies; and the position in the Commons was confused and complicated by the circumstance that neither of the leading administration figures there was a personal follower of Chatham himself. Conway was highly rated by both Rockingham and Chatham as a Commons leader, and could be an effective speaker when roused:

---

[12] In this brief survey of the political scene I have omitted any discussion of the role of Lord Bute, even though contemporary political thinking and behaviour was affected by a mistaken belief in his secret influence on George III. He was no longer an active politician and had stopped seeing the King privately on political matters early in 1765: BL Add. MSS 51379, ff. 175–6.

[13] Brooke, *Chatham Administration*, pp. 241–7, demonstrates how at this time contemporary political leaders could not even identify their own followers.

but in 1767 he was indecisive, and unhappy about official policy. The lead in the House was usurped by the forceful Charles Townshend. The man whom many contemporaries regarded as Chatham's real voice there—William Beckford, wealthy West Indies sugar planter and prominent City of London politician, a devoted Pittite for the last decade—was not in office. Another belligerent speaker on the same side was Colonel Isaac Barré, the Commons mouthpiece of Lord Shelburne, and a master of savage invective who made some 400 speeches during the next eight years: but he was happier in opposition, and of little use to government in 1767.

A variety of factors combined to create a situation in which the Chatham administration suffered a severe Parliamentary battering from a powerful and well-organized opposition. The most famous setback was the ministry's Commons defeat on 27 February 1767 over its chief tax proposal. When Townshend moved for the customary land tax rate of 4s., or 20 per cent, a sensationally successful opposition amendment for 3s. was carried by 206 votes to 188, involving a loss of £500,000 in revenue.[14]

Greater difficulty and embarrassment for the Chatham administration than this temporary humiliation arose out of the long-running sagas of India and America, and in both instances the ministry to some extent brought trouble upon its own head. India, not America, was the political topic uppermost in Parliamentary minds. By 1766 it was widely believed in Britain that the territorial revenues recently acquired there by the East India Company would produce a net income of £2,000,000, equivalent to about one-quarter of Britain's total national budget. Chatham was one of many who believed that these possessions, acquired in the recent war, should belong of right to the state and not to a private trading company. The prospective revenue brought the issue to the forefront of British politics. Before the end of 1766 Chatham instructed William Beckford to launch a Parliamentary inquiry, with the intention that this would be followed by a declaration on the state ownership of the Indian territory: presumably the intention was then to appropriate all or most of the revenue, but it is unclear how far Chatham and his adherents had formulated any such proposals in detail. What seemed to be a general Chathamite attack on the Company's property and

---

[14] It is now apparent that there was no connection, as was long thought, between this event and Townshend's decision to tax America: Thomas, *EHR*, 83 (1968), 42–3.

chartered rights roused the three opposition groups of Rockingham, Grenville, and Bedford to united hostility; Conway and
Townshend led resistance within the ministry; and Chathamite
hopes of a Parliamentary declaration on the ownership of the Indian
territories were frustrated. Beckford's expectation of an Indian
revenue that would pre-empt the case for an American tax was
disappointed.

American matters came before Parliament infrequently in 1767.
The issue of colonial defiance centred on the continuing refusal of
New York to contribute towards the cost of soldiers stationed in
the colony as required by the 1765 Mutiny Act. That specified the
provision not of food but of a number of items that included fuel,
bedding, cooking utensils, and alcoholic beverages. The controversy
both within the ministry and in the House of Commons was not
over whether New York should be coerced, but how. The cabinet
accepted Townshend's proposal that the colony's assembly should
be prevented from functioning until it paid the requisite army
costs, and the administration carried this policy in the face of
opposition demands for sterner action. The whole discussion
proved to have been unnecessary. New York voted the money
before news of the decision, but without any reference to the
Mutiny Act. The colony's Governor Moore gladly reported what
he deemed to be this compliance, but Grenville, ever a stickler for
technicalities, had not forgotten this episode the next year.
Opposition was well beaten in the Commons on this issue, but
pressed the administration hard in the Lords on two North
American questions: its allegedly too soft handling of a Massachusetts Act which while providing compensation for victims
of the Stamp Act riots in Boston had also encroached on the royal
prerogative of pardon by granting an indemnity to everyone
involved; and the lack of any policy decision on Canada.[15]
Contemporaries were seemingly unaware that the most significant
American measure of the session was the one that was discussed
almost incidentally in a couple of debates on the cost of the
American army, in the Budget debate, and in the main debate over
New York. By the time Townshend's American taxes were
formally brought before Parliament in June it was the end of the
session and most MPs had already gone home.

The outcome of the Stamp Act Crisis had generated in Britain a
feeling of annoyance and indignation that the colonists had by

[15] Thomas, *British Politics and the Stamp Act Crisis*, pp. 293–329.

determined resistance, based on violence and an apparently successful trade boycott, defeated the attempt to tax them. It is evident that almost any British politicians in office during 1767 would have made a new effort to do so, in the belief that such a policy was equitable and in the certainty that it would be a popular move. Even the Rockingham ministry that had repealed the Stamp Act had been contemplating some sort of trade duties for purposes of taxation and had converted the molasses duty to that end. The Chatham administration had made up its mind to tax America before the end of 1766. Yet those were the two political factions that by repute, word and deed were the most sympathetic towards the colonies![16]

For contemporaries determined to tax America there was an obvious line to take, exploitation of the distinction supposedly made in the colonies between internal and external taxation. The mode of doing so by customs duties required no special perspicacity on the part of Charles Townshend, who bluntly said that he thought the distinction nonsense, but proposed to exploit it to get round colonial objections to taxation. Internal taxes were those that had their impact on everyday life within the colonies, as stamp duties on newspapers, legal documents, and so on would have done. External taxes were revenue duties levied on goods entering American ports in the same way as duties already imposed for the regulation of trade. This distinction was generally and genuinely believed in Britain to be the American interpretation of taxation within the British Empire. The Rockingham ministry had deliberately conveyed that impression to Parliament and to a wider public opinion; and Benjamin Franklin had categorically said so when a witness before the House of Commons on 13 February 1766. There were several other reasons why it should be credible in Britain that the Americans had made such a distinction. Their assemblies already levied taxes within the individual colonies, whereas external taxes could only be imposed by an outside body with overall authority, such as Parliament. Franklin had added the argument that such taxes were optional, being dependent on the purchase of the relevant items.[17] There had been no colonial protest about the molasses duty which in 1766 had made the final transition into a revenue duty, pure and simple, from its original role as a trade regulation.[18] And, after all, in

---

[16] Ibid., pp. 265, 296–8. Chaffin, *WMQ*, 27 (1970), pp. 90–121.
[17] Thomas, op. cit., pp. 215–33.
[18] Ibid., pp. 270–1.

Britain itself customs duties were a major source of revenue. They were an obvious method to exploit in America.

The point at issue in the Stamp Act Crisis had been the American challenge, albeit in a limited manner, to the authority of Parliament over the colonies, one answered promptly and explicitly by the Declaratory Act of 1766. Gradual awareness of the implications of the controversy led to a more fundamental change in British attitudes than that legislation or even the renewal of taxation in 1767, one that became apparent that year. This reaction was to make greater use of Parliament in imperial matters and to rely less on the prerogative of the Crown. It might explain why an Act of Parliament was passed to establish an American Customs Board, although such an essentially executive decision would usually have been regarded as within the scope of the royal prerogative. The reaction is more clearly seen with respect to the evolution of a policy for Canada. In 1763 a Proclamation by the King in Council had been deemed appropriate for governmental and boundary decisions for North America: and in 1766 the Rockingham ministry did not intend to use Parliamentary legislation to implement their proposed measures for Canada. But in 1767 the Chatham ministry decided that that would be the correct procedure, and the eventual Quebec Act of 1774 was to enact decisions similar to those in the 1763 Proclamation.[19] This change in imperial procedures was probably deliberate policy; and in 1771 Governor Thomas Hutchinson of Massachusetts urged upon the North ministry a general strategy of regular legislation for the colonies as an end in itself.[20]

Every act of Parliament carried into execution in the colonies tends to strengthen government there. A firm persuasion that Parliament is determined at all events to maintain its supreme authority is all we want ... If Acts were passed more or less to control us every session we should soon be familiarised to them and our erroneous opinions would die away and peace and order would revive.

The shift in British attitudes was matched in America by a similar and quite deliberate response to the changing situation. In the later 1760s the colonies increasingly began to direct their petitions to the King and not to Parliament: and while at first they put forward as the reason that this was because of the seemingly disdainful manner in which Parliament treated their complaints,

[19] Ibid., pp. 40–3, 279–81, 334–6.
[20] DAR, III, 32–3.

the underlying implication was that they regarded themselves as subject only to the Crown and not to Parliament.

History and tradition were on their side, with Parliament a belated intruder on the imperial scene. The colonies were royal colonies, except for three originally granted to proprietors, Pennsylvania, Delaware, and Maryland. Their governors were appointed by the King, but for the two elected governors of Rhode Island and Connecticut, and of course in the proprietory colonies: and orders, instructions, and information were dispatched to them in the King's name. All had their own assemblies, regarded in America as mini-Parliaments, with powers of internal legislation and taxation. They were defended by the King's army, commanded in America by General Thomas Gage between 1763 and 1775: and by the royal navy, the Commodore of the American Squadron being Captain Samuel Hood from 1767 to 1771 and then Rear-Admiral John Montagu. Their trade was regulated by the King's Customs, a miniscule organization incapable of fulfilling the demands made upon it.

By the 1760s this royal framework of empire was long outmoded. The colonies accepted Parliament's regulation of the economic system. It was Parliament that voted the finance for defence and other purposes of government. Decisions were taken by British politicians who, though appointed by the King, were also dependent upon Parliament for their success and survival. But the formal structure of the British Empire gave credence to the colonial case, and it was by no means entirely archaic. The Privy Council, 'the King in Council', in form the key institution in imperial government, did still retain a useful function, and one not confined to routine matters. The controversial 1772 decision over the proposed Ohio colony of Vandalia was made there, initially by the Council's Committee on Plantation Affairs. In practice the Privy Council or its Committee usually referred colonial matters to the Board of Trade and Plantations for advice and information. A department solely concerned with the colonies and commerce, the Board in 1766 had been demoted to 'a mere board of report upon reference' and deprived of any more positive role.[21]

Whatever the actual mode of procedure employed, whether a resolution in the Privy Council, an act of Parliament, or instructions from the Secretary of State, the course of political evolution in

[21] Thomas, op. cit., pp. 21–8, 287–9.

Britain had by now placed the real power of decision-making in the small group of ministers who comprised the cabinet. The unofficial Prime Minister was usually the First Lord of the Treasury, though Chatham was merely Lord Privy Seal, by now a post of formal business and whose holders were not always in the cabinet during the years after his resignation. If a commoner, the First Lord was also Chancellor of the Exchequer, who in any case sat in the cabinet from 1766. The other members included the Secretaries of State, Northern, Southern, and also, from 1768, American; the First Lord of the Admiralty, and sometimes the head of the army, as Lord Granby, its Commander-in-Chief from 1766 to 1770; the Lord Chancellor, as head of the law, and the Lord President of the Council, who chaired the Privy Council and its Committees. It was customary for each cabinet minister to propose policy concerning his own department. Responsibility for the colonies, apart from financial business, rested with Southern Secretary Shelburne until the beginning of 1768, and thereafter with the successive American Secretaries, Lords Hillsborough and Dartmouth. Their views might be modified or rejected, for the cabinet took decisions if necessary by a majority vote, but they had the initial responsibility for devising colonial policy.

The cabinet was remarkably free to make its own decisions, and policy was usually settled there, despite the constitutional roles of the King and of Parliament, and occasional outside pressures from lobbyists and interest groups. George III was not a man to play a passive role in politics, but he acted in accordance with accepted contemporary constitutional practice. While he frequently informed ministers of his opinions, and was indeed sometimes consulted by them, that was as far as royal influence on policy went. Lord Hillsborough, American Secretary from 1768 to 1772 and so a man in a position to know from the inside how things were done, told former Governor Hutchinson in 1775 that the King 'will always leave his own sentiments and conform to his ministers, though he will argue with them, and very sensibly; but if they adhere to their own opinion, he will say, "Well. Do you choose it should be so? Then let it be." '[22] That this 'small efficient cabinet', as historians have sometimes termed it, should decide policy was a recent development and not one, apparently that met with George III's entire approval. It had had the effect, perhaps deliberately under Grenville and Rockingham, of reducing his personal influence, for

[22] *Hutchinson Diary*, I, 480. For a discussion of the King's role see Thomas, *History*, 70 (1985), 16–31.

royal pressure on individual ministers could more easily be resisted by such a collective decision. A small cabinet did not in fact necessarily mean an efficient one, and George III informed Grafton on 18 February 1768 of the dejection of the newly appointed Hillsborough at a recent cabinet failure to come to a decision on an important matter of policy within his department.[23]

He fears the same spirit of procrastination will appear on every other measure he may have to lay before them. I have directed him for the future to lay open his ideas to you and the Chancellor previous to the summoning a cabinet, that matters may be digested and nothing required there but approbation, which till of late years was the established method of transacting business.

It should be borne in mind that the easy acceptance of cabinet decisions over America by King and Parliament doubtless owed much to compatibility of opinions. Most British politicians shared the same attitudes and instinctive responses concerning the colonies, and ministers were aware of the need to tailor their policies so as to meet a favourable reaction. Their measures were sufficiently in accordance with the general desire of George III and of the great majority of both MPs and peers for a firm line with the colonists as to encounter few obstacles to their enactment. And on the other hand it is improbable, to put it no higher, that any ministry could have carried through Parliament a soft-line measure such as complete repeal of the Townshend taxation. The combination of circumstances that had enabled the Rockingham administration to carry repeal of the Stamp Act in 1766 was not likely to recur.

It is a moot point how far the lobbying of colonial agents and British merchants and manufacturers had contributed to that event. Their activity was a weapon used by the ministers to assist the success of their policy. But if administration opinion was not sympathetic towards the demands of agents and merchants it was unlikely to be altered by their efforts. Throughout the Townshend Duties Crisis British merchants played a far less active and important role than in 1766, and the manufacturers barely stirred at all. Merchants had little incentive to intervene in the dispute, and even had motives of resentment not to do so. In June 1767 Benjamin Franklin reported back to America his concern that London merchants were complaining that they had spent nearly £1,500 in their efforts to obtain repeal of the Stamp Act and had

[23] Grafton MSS, no. 510.

received no thanks from any of the colonies except Rhode Island.[24] There were more substantial reasons for mercantile inactivity. The general trade depression coincidental with the Stamp Act boycott was coming to an end, and Britain found markets in Europe that would compensate for any loss in American trade. In 1768 total British exports were, at over £15,000,000, higher than in any year since 1764.[25] The second colonial boycott, in the later 1760s, was spasmodic and incomplete, reducing American imports from Britain by an amount equal only to about 5 per cent of Britain's total exports. Mercantile opinion was unworried, cynical as to the boycott's effectiveness and duration; and London merchants could find no support elsewhere for their own rather half-hearted efforts.

Only the support and assistance of the merchants could give weight to the lobbying of agents. The merchants would be asking favours for Britain, the agents only too obviously for America. Lord Hillsborough when American Secretary put further obstacles in their path by insisting that correct accreditation of an agent chosen by an assembly meant approval by the colony's governor and council. This had always been the formal position, but in the 1760s the position had become confused and complex, with several colonies having more than one agent. So Dennis De Berdt, a London merchant chosen by the Massachusetts Assembly, was repeatedly informed by Hillsborough that he was 'no agent at all', and in September 1768 reported that the American Secretary had made 'objections of the like nature to several other agents and seems to think the correspondence would be best carried on with the governors directly'.[26] Certainly in November he asked Governor Moore of New York to recommend to his assembly adoption of the correct procedure of appointing agents as followed in the West Indies, Virginia, the Carolinas, and Georgia.[27] De Berdt, always on bad terms with Hillsborough, continued to act as agent until his death in 1770; while the Massachusetts Council blandly ignored the British Government's attitude by appointing William Bollan as its own separate agent in 1768. Hillsborough's insistence on formality, and his dislike of the whole system of agencies,

[24] *Franklin Papers*, XIV, 183.
[25] Schumpeter, *English Overseas Trade Statistics*, p. 15.
[26] *De Berdt Letters*, pp. 333–4, 341. The Board of Trade had stipulated the required procedure in 1761, and the campaign against De Berdt had been begun by Shelburne: *JCTP 1759–1763*, p. 249; *JCTP 1768–75*, pp. 9–10.
[27] *NYCD*, VIII, 108.

rendered even more difficult any effective role of the colonial
agents in the renewed quarrel with Britain.

Colonial agents so circumstanced had one obvious recourse, an
attempt to influence public opinion. The press was a burgeoning
new political phenomenon that they could exploit. Newspapers
capitalized on the political excitement of the 1760s, expanding in
numbers and circulation and making the important gain of
Parliamentary reporting as the centre-piece of their political
coverage. By the middle of 1770 there were being published in
London four daily, eight tri-weekly, and four weekly papers, all
carrying political news. Since controversies sold copies, the same
newspapers often printed news items and political essays, usually
couched in the form of pseudonymous letters, on all sides of any
political argument.Circulation as well as constitutional principle
was the spur to Parliamentary reporting. The columns of many
newspapers frequently contained the same news paragraphs and
polemical items, for copying was rife. The best-known personality
in the contemporary publishing world was John Almon, reporter,
writer, editor, publisher, pamphleteer, and bookseller. Almon's
sympathies were anti-government and pro-American, but his
commercial instincts led him to publish on both sides of the
colonial argument, with thirty-six pamphlets on America in 1768
alone. It was Almon who published a reply by William Knox to
Philadelphian John Dickinson's *Farmer's Letters*:[28] and at Lord
Temple's behest he ran the monthly *Political Register* as a
Grenvillite paper between May 1767 and July 1768.[29]

The daily newspapers tended to be moderate in political tone. In
terms of prestige and circulation the way was led by the *Public
Advertiser*, managed by H. S. Woodfall. It was therefore the choice
of Junius as the vehicle for his polished anonymous invective.[30]
Also with a daily circulation of around 5,000 was the *Gazetteer*, a
paper soon to develop radical connections. If the *Daily Advertiser*
had little concern with politics, William Woodfall soon gave the
Morning Chronicle, founded on 28 June 1769, a reputation for
reporting Commons debates. In the tri-weekly press the government side of any argument always received short shrift in the
London Evening Post, an opposition paper since its foundation in
1734 and which now became radical under John Miller and his ally

---

[28] Bellot, *William Knox*, pp. 81–91.
[29] Lawson, *George Grenville*, pp. 236–41.
[30] The letters were published between 1769 and 1772. For a superb modern
edition see Cannon, *Letters of Junius*.

John Almon. Not quite as virulent was the *Middlesex Journal*, founded on 4 April 1769 by William Beckford, the Chathamite and City radical. Of the other tri-weekly papers *Lloyds Evening Post* was generally pro-government, and so was the *London Chronicle* from 1770: whereas the *General Evening Post* was middle-of-the-road, and the *St. James' Chronicle* inclined to opposition.[31]

The political excitement that had stimulated the growth of the newspaper press was generated not by America but by the activities of that radical gadfly of government John Wilkes: and for two years from early in 1768 the controversial ramifications of his election for Middlesex dominated the political scene in Britain to the virtual exclusion of America and every other issue. The press nevertheless provided an obvious vehicle for the opinions of both critics and friends of the colonies. Although pamphlets were used for major statement of views, political arguments were increasingly conducted in newspapers between pseudonymous protagonists, many of whom remained unidentified. Until 1771 James Scott, Lord Sandwich's clerical polemicist, attacked America under such pseudonyms as Anti-Sejanus and Old Slyboots. Benjamin Franklin used at least forty-two different pseudonyms in his unofficial role as press officer for the colonies.[32] How much more than a propaganda exercise this was must be very doubtful. America was too far away to engender much spontaneous interest. Only one cartoon relating to the Townshend Duties Crisis was published, as compared with hundreds concerning Wilkes and even a dozen about the earlier Stamp Act Crisis.[33] Even major incidents, like the burning of the *Gaspée* in 1772, received little attention in London newspapers. Franklin and other agents and Americans like William Bollan and Arthur Lee, who wrote as Junius Americanus, spared no effort to propagate the colonial cause by placing in the press American news and views: but they were contending against the bias and ignorance concerning the colonies about which Americans in London incessantly complained. And on the key issue of Parliamentary sovereignty over America, British opinion was inflexible and virtually monolithic. Despite Franklin's frequent self-congratulations on his journalistic activities,

[31] Much has been written about the newspaper press of this period. J. P. Thomas, Thesis, supersedes but does not replace Rea, *English Press in Politics, 1760–1774*; Hinkhouse, *Preliminaries of the American Revolution*; and Haig, *The Gazetteer*, pp. 57–133. For Parliamentary reporting see Thomas, *EHR*, 74 (1959), 623–36.

[32] Crane, *Benjamin Franklin: Letters to the Press.*

[33] Thomas, *The American Revolution*, pp. 21, 68–9.

all his and similar endeavours counted for little in influencing British attitudes.

But the cut and thrust of debate in Parliament was now of double significance. This was genuine argument at the political nerve-centre of the nation, with a real impact on decision-making in the sense that ministers took cognizance of Parliamentary opinion. From 1769 onwards reports of Commons speeches began to fill press columns. Westminster debating now for the first time had a direct impact on public opinion, one with which anonymous journalists and pseudonymous correspondents could not compete. Only Junius could vie for attention with purportedly authentic pronouncements of Lord North, George Grenville, and Edmund Burke. Westminster became the centre of the British political stage.

2

Charles Townshend Taxes America[1]

TEA provided a fortuitous link between the two major policy issues confronting the Chatham administration in 1767, India and America. It was both the main target in Townshend's taxation of the colonies and the source of around 90 per cent of the East India Company's trading profit. By law the Company had had since 1724 a monopoly of the tea market in Britain and in the colonies, the tea being sold to wholesalers at half-yearly Company auctions in London. In practice both in Britain and in America smugglers, mainly from Holland, which had its own East India Company, undersold the legal traders retailing the Company's tea. Smuggling constituted an important part of contemporary economic life, and tea was a favourite commodity in clandestine trade, being a profitable cargo and easy to render unidentifiable. The East India Company, with considerable justification, believed that government taxation was jeopardizing its tea markets. Since 1745 the tax was a duty of 25 per cent of the Company's auction sale price; and tea sold within Britain also paid an inland duty of 1s. a lb., but since 1748 not tea exported to America or elsewhere.[2] These were heavy burdens when the auction price was already higher than the Dutch wholesale price, 3s. a lb. in London during 1766 as compared with 1s. 11d. in Amsterdam.[3]

Estimates of contraband trade in the eighteenth century are notoriously difficult to make; but it is probable that at least half of the tea consumed in Britain and three-quarters of that in the colonies was illicitly imported, some contemporary guesses being significantly higher. Even so, the legal trade was substantial enough for tea to be the fourth most important export from Britain to America, where tea drinking was widespread and increasingly popular. The natural growth of the market, together with stricter

---

[1] Some aspects of this subject are more fully discussed in Thomas, *British Politics and the Stamp Act Crisis*, pp. 337–63.

[2] *Statutes at Large*, V, 488–92, 602–5.

[3] Labaree, *Boston Tea Party*, pp. 6, 332. The internal tea duties alone produced an average annual return of £500,000 in the early 1760s. *Jenkinson Papers*, p. 252.

enforcement of the trade laws and a reduction in smuggling profit margins caused by a fall in the London price, had led in the 1760s to a substantial increase in legal tea sales to America.[4] In negotiations with the Chatham administration over its future, the East India Company sought to gain the actual monopoly of the tea market in Britain and America which legally belonged to it, while tea was the most important feature of Charles Townshend's taxation plans for America. The scheme devised by the Chancellor of the Exchequer did reconcile these two objectives in financial terms, but foundered on the political rock of colonial objections to taxation.

Removal or reduction of the existing duties was obviously the way in which the administration could assist the Company to expand its tea sales, and during the second half of 1766 Charles Townshend was turning his mind towards this solution. On 20 October Thomas Whately, who had had a long conversation with Townshend the previous day, reported to Grenville his views on the East India Company. 'As to his own schemes in the finances, he is reserved.' But Whately had picked up rumours about ideas currently being canvassed. 'To increase the consumption of tea is one object, with which view the duty retained on the exportation to America and to Ireland is to be given up, and some say sixpence to be taken off from the home consumption.'[5] At about the same time Townshend was advised by his predecessor and friend William Dowdeswell that there was a national interest involved in helping the East India Company to sell its tea in the colonies. 'Cut off the smuggling of teas in America and you cut off the smuggling of many other commodities.'[6] This additional benefit from the elimination of a very profitable part of the smuggling trade was another reason for the ministry to welcome the approach made by the Company towards the end of 1766. It was after discussions that Grafton and Townshend had in December with Company Directors that the East India Company formally submitted to Grafton on 8 January 1767 a list of proposals that included these two suggestions: 'for an alteration in the inland duty on tea, with a view to prevent smuggling, and thereby to increase the legal consumption; for allowing a drawback on the exportation of tea of the whole custom paid thereon'.[7]

[4] Labaree, *Boston Tea Party*, pp. 6–8, 12, 331.
[5] *Grenville Papers*, IV, 334.
[6] Quoted from the Dowdeswell MSS by Forster, *Charles Townshend*, p. 135. He suggests October 1766 as the probable date.
[7] *Chatham Papers*, III, 163–6.

By that date, before his famous promise on American taxation in the House of Commons on 26 January, Charles Townshend's plans for an American revenue were well advanced, and they doubtless already included tea. The surviving documentary evidence, often undated, does not make possible any clear assessment of the timing of Townshend's various ideas for colonial taxation, but he evidently gave top priority to tea, one memorandum stating that 'the most necessary duty which ought to be immediately put into execution is the article of *tea*'.[8] A colonial tea tax was not a novel idea. At the time of the 1764 Revenue Act Charles Jenkinson, then a Secretary to the Treasury under Grenville, had calculated that a revenue of £75,000 could be obtained from a duty of 1s. a lb. on tea entering colonial ports.[9] And in January 1766, when the Rockingham ministry was embarking on repeal of the Stamp Act, an unidentified George Spencer suggested to the Treasury Board that to replace it there could be a 1s. duty on tea exported to America.[10] In addition, at least two colonies had themselves recently taxed tea for revenue. Import duties imposed in Massachusetts included 1s. a lb. on tea, and there was also a heavy inland excise duty of 4s. a lb. Low consumption or extensive tax evasion is reflected in the small yield: this import duty in 1756 raised £636, the excise £344 in 1755 and £1,446 in 1762, being discontinued in 1763. New York imposed a tea excise in 1756, which in 1764 raised £1,200.[11]

When Townshend decided to include a tea duty in his schemes for American taxation is not known, but by the end of 1766 his general tax proposals were being formulated. There is firm evidence that at least some of his later ideas were already under consideration. He obtained information from the Customs Board on china exports, and he was examining the possibility of a duty on salt going to America. He must also have been aware of a plan during the Rockingham ministry for permitting direct trade in wine and fruit from Spain and Portugal to the colonies, on payment of an import duty in America.[12] By the time of his Parliamentary announcement about colonial taxation on 26 January Townshend evidently had import duties in mind, although he did not disclose his proposed method to MPs and had not informed even his cabinet colleagues: for Shelburne, when

[8] Forster, *Charles Townshend*, p. 135 n.
[9] Ritcheson, *British Politics and the American Revolution*, p. 19 n.
[10] Labaree, *Boston Tea Party*, pp. 20, 270.
[11] Gipson, *British Empire*, X, 54–6, 58, 61, 79–80.
[12] Chaffin, *WMQ*, 27 (1970), 95.

reporting the incident to Chatham on 1 February, added this public rumour in explanation: 'I have heard, indeed, from general conversation, that Mr. Townshend has a plan for establishing a Board of Customs in America, and by a new regulation of the tea duty here, and some other alterations, to produce a revenue on imports there'.[13] By 12 February Connecticut agent William Samuel Johnson believed the plan was to put duties on 'tea and china ware'.[14]

Charles Townshend's Parliamentary statements on American taxation in early 1767 were merely a premature public affirmation of an existing ministerial decision to raise money from America, and not an unwarranted and irresponsible commitment of the Chatham administration to such a policy. Differences of opinion within the ministry concerned methods and not aims. Not until later was Townshend to alter the purpose of the proposed American revenue from the maintenance of the army in the colonies that was the original motive behind the Chatham administration's search for an American revenue, as it had been also during the ministries of Grenville and Rockingham. One source widely favoured and closely investigated was quit-rents. These were annual payments for land granted for settlement, and on the face of it a promising basis for a substantial and growing income. Shelburne was to urge this as an alternative to Townshend's plans for customs duties well into 1767, despite discouraging information and advice from officials in America.[15]

In the House of Commons on 26 January Secretary at War Lord Barrington presented to the Committee of Supply the enormous estimate of £405,607 for the cost of the American army. Grenville called on the administration to disclose any plans that there were to make the colonists bear this burden. Since it must have been known in informed political circles that the ministry already had such an intention, Grenville was merely asking for details and not attempting to extract a public commitment, even though Townshend's announcement may have been a shock to some MPs and agents. After stating that there would be an American tax for this purpose, Townshend evaded an attempt by Lord George Sackville to make him promise that this would meet the entire cost. Townshend also refused to accede to Grenville's request for

---

[13] *Chatham Papers*, III, 185. [14] *Trumbull Papers*, p. 218.
[15] Chaffin, *WMQ*, 27 (1970), 91–7. Thomas, *British Politics and the Stamp Act Crisis*, pp. 296–8. There is no evidence of Chatham's own views at this time on colonial taxation. He was not attending cabinet.

information, as agent Charles Garth's report to South Carolina made clear: 'He should bring into the House this session some propositions that he hoped might tend in time to ease the people of England upon this head and yet not be heavy in any manner upon the people in the colonies, but of which nature those propositions are he did not disclose.'[16]

The ministerial plan for American taxation was now a matter of public knowledge, and Townshend had hinted at his proposed method by a scornful attack on the distinction between internal and external taxation made in 1766 by Chatham himself among others, and generally believed to be the American interpretation of Parliamentary sovereignty over the colonies. He followed this by a clearer statement in the next Commons debate over American army finance on 18 February, when a supplementary account brought the total of American army bills to be paid in 1767 to about £570,000, a sharp contrast to the original 1763 estimate of £225,000.[17] Diarist Ryder recorded Townshend as speaking of 'the distinction between internal and external taxes as not founded in reason but proper to be adopted in policy'.[18] By the time of the next cabinet meeting concerning America on 12 March Townshend knew that there had been an unsuccessful attempt to replace him as Chancellor of the Exchequer by Lord North. He turned the tables by threatening resignation unless he obtained approval of his American import duties. Shelburne, when informing Chatham that Townshend had asserted 'that he had promised this to the House and upon the authority of what passed in the cabinet', did not deny or even comment on this claim.[19] No evidence has been found of the cabinet discussion of this matter, but Sir George Colebrooke, MP and East India Company magnate, in his later memoirs made this statement about Lord Mansfield, Lord Chief Justice of King's Bench: 'This Lord in 1767 had declared himself explicitly against the absurd and dangerous measure of imposing duties, in which he was followed by three cabinet ministers.'[20]

During the next few weeks, while Townshend was preparing a schedule of import duties, he changed the purpose of his American taxation. Hitherto the declared intention, in the Commons debates of 26 January and 18 February and in the cabinet of 12

---

[16] *SCHGM*, 29 (1928), 132. For a fuller account of this debate, with documentation, see Thomas, *British Politics and the Stamp Act Crisis*, pp. 338–42.

[17] Ibid., pp. 38, 339, 344 n. [18] *Ryder Diary*, p. 331.
[19] *Chatham Papers*, III, 232–6. [20] *Colebrooke Reminiscences*, II, 49.

March, had been to use the revenue towards the cost of the army in North America. Now Townshend decided instead to pay the costs of civil government in the colonies, an idea he had conceived as early as 1753 when a junior member of the Board of Trade and had put forward on several subsequent occasions.[21] He made no secret of this change of plan even though he had not obtained cabinet support for it: on 11 April Benjamin Franklin reported to Pennsylvania 'that a project is on foot to render all the governors and magistrates in America independent of the annual support they receive of their several assemblies'.[22]

Townshend completed his first schedule of American import duties by early May. He included the proposals American John Huske, an MP since 1763, had made to the Rockingham ministry the previous year for duties on foreign wines, olive oil, dried fruit, and citrus fruit.[23] Townshend anticipated a revenue of £7,000 from £7 a ton on foreign wine; £2,500 from 2s. 6d. a hundredweight on dried fruit; £3,000 from 4d. a hundred on oranges and lemons; £9,920 from £5 a ton on olive oil; and £1,000 from small duties on capers, olives, and corkwood. Townshend also had other duties in mind. His papers show that he hoped to obtain £5,000 a year from small duties on glass sent to America; £2,000 from duties on painting materials, described as 'red and white lead and painters' colours'; and £5,000 from a 9 per cent duty on paper of all kinds. His idea to raise money from china exports to America was not an import duty but the cancellation of the existing export rebate of duty in Britain, worth about £8,000. Altogether he expected a total revenue of £43,420 from these measures.[24]

There were two significant omissions from this list. Nothing could be decided about a tea duty until a general agreement was reached with the East India Company, and Townshend had already abandoned his early idea for a salt duty. John Huske warned him on 9 April that 'a more fatal imposition to both Great Britain and her colonies could not be devised'.[25] Townshend had explained that he intended to levy a duty of 6d. a bushel on salt imports, to be offset by a bounty on fish and salt-meat exports. He asked Huske for his objections, and Huske enlisted the help of Benjamin Franklin, who soon produced arguments that the duty would be unpopular, productive of only a trifling net revenue, and

[21] Namier and Brooke, *Charles Townshend*, pp. 40, 140.
[22] *Franklin Papers*, XIV, 109.
[23] Namier and Brooke, op. cit., p. 187. Huske sent him the details on 9 April.
[24] Ibid., pp. 189–91.   [25] Ibid., p. 188.

obstructive to trade.[26] The campaign by colonial agents and London merchants against the salt duty was successful, but on the general point of import duties Townshend stood firm. Barlow Trecothick, who led the merchants, told the House of Commons on 8 February 1769 his recollection of the circumstances. 'After beating about for taxes upon salt, and such taxes, after consulting with the merchants, the merchants offered to pay the taxes here. We remonstrated against the taxes as likely to involve America in disputes. But America was to be taxed at the expense of the commerce of Great Britain, as well as America.'[27] Certainly agent Johnson at the time told Governor Pitkin of Connecticut of Townshend's evident determination to carry out his taxation plan.[28]

The Chancellor of the Exchequer (who is at present in great estimation, is the principal manager in the House of Commons, and bids fair to conduct the counsels of the nation) declared at one of those meetings that although he did not in the least doubt the right of Parliament to tax the colonies internally, and that he knew no difference between internal and external taxes, (which by the way, is a doctrine very generally adopted here,) yet since the Americans were pleased to make that distinction he was willing to indulge them, and chose for that reason to confine himself to regulations of trade, by which a sufficient revenue might be raised in America.

Townshend did not announce the American taxes in his Budget on 15 April, presumably because he was not ready: but Grenvillite James Harris noted that he pledged himself to make up a deficit of £33,000 'by an American tax'.[29] Such a declaration was misleading, for Townshend was meeting the popular demand for a colonial tax without fulfilling the implicit purpose of transferring part of the British tax burden to America: since most colonial officials were already paid from American sources, Townshend was merely changing the mode of payment rather than the incidence of taxation. If Townshend's misrepresentation was not deliberate, he either misunderstood the existing situation or hoped that the American taxes would more than suffice for the costs of colonial government.

[26] *Franklin Papers*, XIV, 119, 184.
[27] Cavendish Diary, BL Egerton MSS 217, f. 268.
[28] *Trumbull Papers*, p. 229.
[29] BL Add. MSS 35608, ff. 14–15. Neither of two other reports of the speech mentions American taxation: *Ryder Diary*, p. 340; BL Add. MSS 32981, f. 175 (James West).

Four weeks later, on 13 May, Townshend chose to reveal his American tax plans to MPs during the speech when he was proposing the coercive measures against New York for disobedience to the Mutiny Act. He stated what he had told the agents, that he was adopting the method of import duties because of the colonial distinction between internal and external taxes, even though he did not accept it. He then announced the duties already decided upon, but estimated the total revenue below his actual calculation at under £40,000. Townshend also publicly stated for the first time the way he now meant to use this American revenue. Diarist Ryder noted only the general purpose, 'that the judges and magistrates who are now in many colonies dependent every year for their salary or at least part of it on the assembly ought to be made independent'.[30] Two agents recorded more details. William Johnson could report only from hearsay, since for the first time in that session all strangers, even colonial agents, were excluded from an American debate: he understood that Townshend had said 'that the governor and chief justice in the King's governments should be rendered more independent by giving the first £2,000 and the latter £500 per annum, to be paid out of the American revenue'.[31] Charles Garth, present as an MP, sent this report to South Carolina:[32]

The Chancellor of the Exchequer did likewise in the Committee open a plan for improving the system of government in the colonies in order that the authority of the executive power might carry with it in the several departments the weight and respect essentially necessary to answer the ends of its institution, and for that purpose after showing in what manner the civil officers of the Crown were provided for and the extent of such provision, he should propose that, out of the fund arising from the American duties now, or to be imposed, His Majesty should be enabled to establish salaries that might be better suited to support the dignity of the respective officers, and for which to be no longer dependent upon the pleasure of any assembly.

In the ensuing debate only George Grenville commented on Townshend's tax proposals. Grafton was told by his Treasury Secretary Thomas Bradshaw that he denounced them as quite insufficient, suggesting that pressure from within the administration had prevented more extensive measures; and that he attacked the plan for duties on wine, fruit, and oil as subversive of the Navigation Acts that sought to give Britain a monopoly of her

[30] *Ryder Diary*, pp. 344–5.
[31] *Trumbull Papers*, pp. 230–1.   [32] *SCHGM*, 29 (1928), 223–6.

colonial trade. James West told Newcastle that 'Mr. Grenville scouted Mr. Townshend's taxes', while diarist Ryder noted that he 'does not much approve of Townshend's taxes'.[33] This weight of eyewitness reporting shows that the absent Johnson was mistaken in informing Governor Pitkin that 'Mr. Grenville, on his part, concurred in the taxes mentioned by Mr. Townshend'.[34] Grenville's attitude towards the Townshend Duties was to be a subject frequently discussed in later debates on American taxation. Contemporary evidence clearly shows that he was scornful of their inadequacy, and that Dowdeswell was quite correct when on 19 April 1774 he challenged the claims by administration speakers for Grenville's support of the taxes. 'If Mr. Grenville were now alive, he would not have supported the tax now before you. He had not the idea of bringing on this contest for the sake of this paltry tax. He objected to the sentence of the tax in that very session in which it was laid.'[35]

Townshend replied to Grenville's comments later in the debate. He denied that he had given up any taxes because of cabinet pressure on him. The salt tax had been dropped as impractical, and there would be a tea duty, but the details depended on an agreement with the East India Company.[36]

What exactly was agreed upon between the East India Company and the Chancellor of the Exchequer about the American tea trade became a matter of subsequent acrimony. On 28 April Grafton, Townshend, and Conway held a meeting with three Directors of the Company: Henry Crabb Boulton, as Chairman of the Company's Committee of Treasury, and two members of that Committee, George Dudley and Sir George Colebrooke. These three reported to the Court of Directors on 30 April that their general proposals had been the basis of an agreement that, among other provisions, effectively gave the Company what it had requested concerning the tea duties in its first proposal of January.[37] There would be a complete drawback or rebate of the 25 per cent duty on all tea exported to America and to Ireland; and also the removal of the inland duty of 1s. a lb., leaving only the 25 per cent duty on tea sold within Britain. In return the Company was to reimburse the

---

[33] Simmons and Thomas, *Proceedings and Debates*, II, 465, 467, 472.
[34] *Trumbull Papers*, p. 231.
[35] Simmons and Thomas, op. cit., IV, 199.   [36] Ibid., II, 465, 472.
[37] I owe this information to Dr Huw V. Bowen, who obtained it from the Company's Court of Directors Minutes (volume B/83, pp. 25, 29) in the India Office Library.

government for the loss of revenue on the export trade and also for any loss of duty if increased sales at home did not make up for the revenue lost by the reduction of duty. This compensation was to be based on the average tea sales during the previous five years. The ensuing legislation enacted these provisions for a period of five years.[38]

Discussions over the tea duty formed only part of the general negotiation between the ministry and the East India Company, in which interest centred on the compensation to be paid by the Company for retention of the territories in India, without any decision being made on the question of ownership. The final arrangement was that the Company should pay £400,000 a year. An agreement was concluded by 20 May, when the Company submitted to the House of Commons a petition covering all the points at issue. The petition was considered by a Committee of the House on 22 May, when, as diarist Ryder noted, the rebate of the tea duty on exports to America 'was objected to by Mr. Grenville but agreed to at last without a division'.[39] The resolution on the tea duties was subsequently referred to the Committee of Ways and Means, whose function was to consider methods of raising revenue.[40]

Future controversy concerned not this arrangement but Townshend's imposition of a duty on the tea imported into America, the political repercussions of which were to destroy the Company's hope of a greatly expanded colonial tea market. After this consequence had become apparent, opposition MPs and Company spokesmen were to accuse the administration, and Townshend in particular, of gross deception, on the ground that the Company would never have agreed to the arrangement about the British tea duties, notably the compensation for lost revenue, if informed beforehand about the tea tax plan. Here is the subsequent recollection of Sir George Colebrooke.[41]

Such a retraction of promise with regard to the India Company was not unusual. It had been practised by Mr. Townshend more than once. Parliament had engaged to take off the duty of 25 per cent on teas. Who could have thought that Parliament, plighting its faith, would lay on immediately a duty in another shape? Mr. Townshend never in his treaty with the Company discovered his intention.

[38] *Statutes at Large*, VI, 778–80.
[39] *Ryder Diary*, p. 350.   [40] *CJ*, XXXI, 377–8, 381–2.
[41] *Colebrooke Reminiscences*, II, 27 n. For a complaint in Parliament see Simmons and Thomas, op. cit., III, 216.

It is unlikely that the truth of this matter will ever be ascertained. One possible explanation for the later grievance is that in 1767 there was an interval of over four months between the dates when the Indemnity Act came into operation in Britain, on 4 July, and the commencement of the Townshend duties in America on 20 November. British merchants doubtless took full advantage of this chronological loophole, for more tea was legally shipped to America in 1767 than in any previous year. Human memory being fallible and biased, this episode may in recollection have subsequently become a basis for the charge of government deception. But the case against Townshend is not convincing. His plan to levy an American import duty on tea was a matter of public knowledge long before the agreement with the East India Company, and Colebrooke himself was a close personal associate of Townshend: he was one of two men dining with the Chancellor of the Exchequer prior to his famous champagne speech of 8 May.[42] It is conceivable that Townshend, not a man above deceit, did at some time mislead the Company representatives into thinking that the arrangements made over the British tea duties, involving compensation for lost revenue, obviated the need for his American tea duty. If they thought that, they were certainly credulous, and also oblivious to the wider political situation of the popular demand for American taxation.

Townshend's speech on 13 May clearly signalled that there would be an American import duty on tea, and there is no reason to believe that he ever changed his mind. He expected that the lower price of the Company's tea exported to America, which would be much cheaper than in Britain itself, would knock out most smugglers from the colonial market, and he intended to exploit this increase in trade to obtain a substantial revenue. Legal tea exports to America had been 489,180 lbs. in 1764 and 515,477 lbs. in 1765, falling to 358,392 lbs. in 1766, no doubt as a consequence of the boycott during the Stamp Act Crisis.[43] But a memorandum among Townshend's papers shows that he anticipated an American market of 1,500,000 lbs. 'upon a supposition that the duty is omitted here', if he imposed a duty of 6d. a lb., to give a revenue of £37,500.[44] When introducing his actual duty of 3d. a lb. Townshend told the Commons that he anticipated a yield of £20,000, implying a legal trade of 1,600,000 lbs. He was

---

[42] *Colebrooke Reminiscences*, I, 119–20.
[43] Labaree, *Boston Tea Party*, p. 331.
[44] Forster, *Charles Townshend*, p. 135 n.

sacrificing almost half the original anticipated revenue from tea, presumably as a concession to the East India Company. Even with the Townshend tax the Company's tea in America would cost significantly less than before, since the customs rebate in Britain was worth between 7d. and 1s. a lb., depending on the auction prices. Townshend's expectation was mirrored in such contemporary reactions as this report by agent Johnson to Governor Pitkin of Connecticut on 9 June, after the announcement of the 3d. duty.[45]

Notwithstanding the duty upon tea, yet, as you see, all the present duties are to be taken off upon exportation (and to be made good to government by the East India Company). It must be much cheaper in America than it has usually been, and as there will be very little, if any, temptation to run it from Holland, etc. it is expected that America will in future be entirely supplied from hence, and the consumption be increased, so that the trade will be beneficial to the East India Company and at the same time produce a very considerable revenue.

The Committee of Ways and Means which was planned for the American taxes was postponed four times,until 1 June.[46] Another reason for this delay, apart from the tea tax, was the reluctance of the cabinet to approve Townshend's plan to use the revenue for the salaries of colonial officials instead of for the original purpose of paying army costs. Grafton's correspondence contains the following undated letter from Townshend, probably written on 25 May.[47]

He sincerely laments that the opportunity has not been taken of soliciting his Majesty's assent to the proposition of independent salaries for the civil officers of North America, especially as he had pledged himself to the House for some measure of this sort, and had the assurances of Lord Shelburne in the last cabinet for the whole extent of the establishment, and the Duke of Grafton on Saturday adopted the idea at least as far as New York. In this distress Mr. Townshend does not think he can with honour move the resolutions this day, and therefore hopes either to have the authority or that some means may be found of postponing the matter for a day or two till he can receive it.

Townshend had apparently obtained the authority of King and cabinet for his idea by 1 June, for he formally proposed his American taxes that day, so late in the session that only ninety

---

[45] *Trumbull Papers*, p. 236.   [46] *CJ*, XXXI, 370, 381, 384, 388, 392.
[47] Grafton MSS no. 445. For a discussion of the dating see Thomas, *British Politics and the Stamp Act Crisis*, p. 355 and n.

members were present at a vote immediately before the debate.[48] These taxes differed significantly from his ideas of 13 May. He announced the tea duty, to produce £20,000, and reminded MPs of the duties on glass, paper, and painting materials, and of the cancelled rebate on china exports, measures that would produce a further £20,000.[49] These were now the only duties, for Townshend announced that because of complaints he had dropped those on fruit, wine, and oil. These objections had come not from the American agents, who favoured the idea as ending one restriction on colonial commerce, but from 'the merchants trading to Portugal and Spain', who were opposed to any direct trade between those countries and America.[50]

Grenville dismissed as 'trifles' these long-awaited taxes, a meagre £40,000.[51] To counter this obvious criticism Townshend had already said his duties were only a beginning. Strictly contemporary evidence of this statement does not survive, apart from a note by Sir Roger Newdigate on 26 January that Townshend had then announced that he would 'plan by degrees'. But on 5 March 1770 George Grenville asserted that Townshend had stated 'repeatedly, in this House, this is a beginning only': and Edmund Burke recalled on 9 May 1770 that 'he did declare that this was but the beginning of the revenue'.[52] No colonial agents appear to have picked up these ominous remarks.

Grenville misunderstood Townshend's purpose, which was not simply or merely to obtain as large a revenue as possible from America. His aims were political rather than financial, the re-establishment of the practice of colonial taxation and the making of Parliamentary provision for the costs of civil government and the administration of justice in the colonies: the latter was clearly stated in the ensuing legislation.[53] This proposed use of the new revenue aroused belated concern among some colonial agents. William Johnson sent an alarmist letter to Connecticut, forecasting that the assemblies would never meet, and Charles Garth more circumspectly expressed similar fears to South Carolina.[54]

Cool and deliberate policy is not a sufficient explanation for

---

[48] *CJ*, XXXI, 392.
[49] Only Charles Garth recorded them, but he misunderstood some of the figures. *SCHGM*, 29 (1928), 295–6. For the correct estimates see Scott, *Econ. HR*, 6 (1935–6), 89.
[50] *Franklin Papers*, XIV, 184.   [51] *Ibid.*, 181.
[52] Simmons and Thomas, *Proceedings and Debates*, II, 410; III, 222, 306.
[53] *Statutes at Large*, VI, 768–71.
[54] *Trumbull Papers*, p. 239; *SCHGM*, 29 (1928), 299–300.

Townshend's American taxation. It must also be seen as a
response to the popular desire for a colonial revenue. After the
storm of the Townshend Duties Crisis had broken his cousin
Thomas Townshend reminded the House on 8 February 1769 of
the political atmosphere less than two years before.[55]

It was not the opinion of one man, but of numbers. It had pervaded the
nation that it was absolutely necessary to do something. It was the
opinion of that gentleman. He exerted all that ability which made him the
delight of the House and all who knew him. He desired taxes agreeable to
the Americans themselves. He flattered himself too far. In those hopes he
was misled by the Americans themselves, who told him, take the tax, let
it but bear the appearance of port duties, it will not be objected to. A
Chancellor of the Exchequer at that time who had not attempted
something of the kind would have been looked upon as blameable.

The mood of the moment swept all doubts aside. That no
Parliamentary opposition to the American Revenue Bill was
voiced is virtually certain from the complete absence of any
information on either debates or divisions in Commons or Lords.[56]
Only at the Commons Committee stage on 15 June was some
opposition threatened, from the Rockingham group. On 12 June,
Frederick Montagu reported to Newcastle a rumour that Dowdeswell and the veteran London politician Sir William Baker intended
to attack the proposed duties on glass.[57] No evidence has been
found as to why that should have been thought a point of criticism
or whether any such challenge was made. The report stage was on
16 June, when James West told Newcastle 'there has nothing
happened material in the House of Commons today . . . There
were not above fifty members in the House at any one time.'[58] The
bill received the royal assent on 29 June. Never could a fateful
measure have had a more quiet passage.

Later there were to be some astonishing admissions and
recollections. Conway, Leader of the House of Commons at this
time, told MPs on 5 March 1770 that 'at the first laying . . . the
present tax . . . he had been of opinion that they were an unjust
burden on the Americans, as they were not represented'. Yet,
whether or not Conway raised any opposition in cabinet, he
certainly made none in Parliament. In the same debate Thomas
Townshend, himself a junior member of the Treasury Board in

---

[55] Cavendish Diary; BL Egerton MSS 217, ff. 267–8.
[56] Simmons and Thomas, op. cit., II, 511, 515.
[57] BL Add. MSS 32982, ff. 317–18.   [58] BL Add. MSS 32982, f. 346.

1767, declared that 'if there had been a vote or division upon the question, I should have opposed those duties . . . It was not the humour of the time to oppose them.'[59] What made this passive Parliamentary acceptance all the more remarkable was that subsequently some MPs claimed that an obvious flaw in the measure had already been perceived. This was not that the duties would provoke colonial resistance, but that all except the one on tea were uncommercial in the sense that they were effectively a tax on the export of British manufactured goods: for it so happened that Charles Townshend had for one reason or another dropped all those that were not liable to this objection. Welbore Ellis, defending the retention of all the duties in the debate of 5 March 1770, admitted 'that those taxes being laid upon the produce and manufactures are against commercial principles. Were this House ignorant at the time they made them?' Edmund Burke more forthrightly claimed on 9 May 1770 that it had always been known that the duties were uncommercial. 'You submitted the principles of commerce to the principles of policy, in order to establish the civil government.'[60]

Within the context of the British understanding of the imperial relationship there was no ground of political or constitutional argument on which any opposition to the Townshend duties could have been based. The Rockinghamite party when in office had endorsed the principle of Parliament's right to tax America by passing the Declaratory Act, and can have seen no reason to oppose the duties on the ground of impolicy: the colonists were thought not to object to this method of taxation, and the taxes themselves could not be considered an onerous burden. The Townshend duties, too, were in accordance with the official Chathamite line adopted during the Stamp Act Crisis of the distinction between internal and external taxes: but in any case Chatham's acceptance of the Declaratory Act as statute law implied an abandonment of that distinction, and this is what Thomas Whately told American customs official John Temple had taken place.[61]

The distinction between internal and external taxes frequently occurs, not now as a subject of debate, but as a matter of reproach to those who maintained last year that Parliament had not a right to lay the former as well as the latter. . . . Those who defended it then disclaim it now, by

[59] Simmons and Thomas, op. cit., III, 227, 238.
[60] Ibid., III, 225, 306.
[61] Bowdoin–Temple Papers, p. 83.

alleging that the Declaratory Act has put an end to the question, and determined the law.

The acceptance of Townshend's tax proposals was shared by men more obviously 'friends of America' than these Parliamentary factions. MP John Huske, himself an American, had encouraged Townshend to adopt this method of taxation as unobjectionable in his letter of 9 April. 'Permit me to remark to you that it is certain by a regulation of the trade of America for the reciprocal interest of both mother and children, you may have a sufficient revenue to pay all Great Britain's expense for the colonies and in a manner perfectly agreeable to both under your conduct.'[62] There is no evidence of any opposition to or even criticism of the Townshend duties by colonial agents at the time of their enactment, a marked contrast to their efforts to avert the Stamp Act. Indeed, both Franklin and Johnson appear to have positively regretted the abandonment of the scheme for direct trade from Europe to America at the price of import duties for revenue on the commodities involved.[63]

Even though no resistance to the new taxes was anticipated, Townshend knew the difficulties of enforcing trade laws in America, and was determined to ensure that his duties came into effective operation. One method he adopted was a remedy long desired by customs officials there, the creation of a separate Board of Customs Commissioners based in America.[64] Townshend told MPs of the project when he announced his duties on 13 May. Charles Garth noted his claim that the new Board would not only oblige negligent or corrupt officials to do their duty but also give colonists a convenient and inexpensive way of making complaints about the working of the customs service.[65] America as well as Britain would benefit. By that date plans were well advanced. The Customs Board in London supported the idea, seeing the opportunity to protect customs officials from unfair prosecutions, and submitted proposals for a Board of seven members at Philadelphia. The Treasury decided on one of five Commissioners at Boston. The choice of that port proved a political blunder. Whereas New York would have welcomed the Board, Boston saw it as an

[62] Namier and Brooke, *Charles Townshend*, p. 187.
[63] *Franklin Papers*, XIV, 184; *Trumbull Papers*, p. 236.
[64] For more details on the creation of this Board see Barrow, *Trade and Empire*, pp. 218–24; Wickwire, *British Subministers and Colonial America*, pp. 124–30; and Chaffin, *WMQ*, 27 (1970), 109–11.
[65] *SCHGM*, 29 (1928), 228.

example of British oppression, especially as the conscientious and efficient behaviour of the officials did nothing for their popularity with the local mercantile community. On several occasions during the next few years mobs in that turbulent town were to oblige the Customs Commissioners to seek military protection in Castle William, an island fort conveniently located in Boston harbour. Final details were not settled until after the passage in June of an Act of Parliament to authorize the new institution.[66] On 29 July the Treasury approved the plan for the American Customs Board, and on 27 August Shelburne's office was formally notified.[67] The Board, all experienced customs officials, began work in November.[68]

Townshend's practical concern for enforcement of the customs laws was also shown by a provision in his Revenue Act authorizing American courts to issue writs of assistance to customs officers in all colonies. Hitherto valid only in New England, these writs were in effect search warrants, but Americans soon came to identify them, for purposes of political complaint, with the general warrants in Britain, authorizing the arrest of unnamed persons, which had been the central issue of the first controversy involving John Wilkes from 1763 until their condemnation in law courts in 1765. Writs of assistance became another colonial grievance against Britain during the next few years as sustained and often successful efforts were made to prevent their use.[69]

A third enforcement measure usually ascribed to Townshend, the establishment of additional Vice-Admiralty Courts in America, owed nothing to his initiative.[70] A new court established in 1764 at Halifax in Nova Scotia, in order to make possible more efficient and impartial prosecution of smugglers by customs officials, had proved a failure. Its remote location was both impractical and a ground of complaint; and ironically the repealed Stamp Act had contained a clause to rectify this mistake. Townshend was absent from the cabinet meeting of 19 August that decided there should also be courts at Boston and Charleston.[71] During the next session

[66] Simmons and Thomas, op. cit., II, 510, 512.
[67] T 29/38, ff. 443–4, 459–60.
[68] Gipson, British Empire, XI, 119–20.
[69] See Dickerson, 'Writs of Assistance as a cause of the Revolution', Era of the American Revolution, pp. 40–75.
[70] Chaffin, WMQ, 27 (1970), 111, corrects the error on this point of Ubbelohde, Vice-Admiralty Courts and the American Revolution, p. 130.
[71] Shelburne MSS, 161, ff. 7–9.

of Parliament, between 23 February and 8 March 1768, the ministry passed the appropriate legislation, a blanket measure making possible the prosecution in Vice-Admiralty Courts of all offences under trade and revenue laws. On 4 August four district courts were created, at Halifax, Boston, Philadelphia, and Charleston, to replace the existing Halifax court, which had overall jurisdiction in North America; and these courts eventually came into operation in 1769.[72]

[72] Gipson, *British Empire*, XI, 131–2, 135.

3

The Changing Face of British Politics.
July 1767–January 1768

DURING the first half of 1767 Charles Townshend had dominated the British political scene. His cabinet colleagues had informed and consulted Chatham about all political developments, and deferred to his every known whim, until it had become apparent that the great man did not intend to provide leadership, or indeed contribute anything, to the ministry he had created. But Townshend, the most junior member of the cabinet, had gone his own way. His flamboyant personality impressed itself on the contemporary political world by magnificent speeches and by outrageous and unpredictable behaviour. He was the man who had had his way in the policy decisions on India and America. By the summer of 1767 political speculation in the press, although not in more informed circles, forecast him as the next Prime Minister. Something of Townshend's public impact is captured by this newspaper comment on 4 July. 'He is now looked upon as a second Pitt, and may justly be called the Great Commoner, born to retrieve and advance the honour and dignity of his country.'[1]

Exactly two months later Townshend died, at the height of his reputation, 'of a putrid fever' on 4 September.[2] The shock of his sudden death stunned contemporaries, and overshadowed the choice of Lord North as his successor as Chancellor of the Exchequer. Yet this decision was to prove the political turning-point of the decade, and the chief reason for the sea change in British politics that began at this time. North also became Leader of the House of Commons at the beginning of 1768 and Prime Minister in January 1770, and was to hold all three positions until 1782. His evident talents in Parliament and government had already marked him out to his more percipient contemporaries as a politician of great promise. Even if few yet appreciated his political skills, especially in finance and Parliamentary management, everyone knew him to be sound and reliable, the antithesis of the dazzling Townshend. But North was no dullard. He

---

[1] *London Evening Post*, 4 July 1767.
[2] *London Evening Post*, 5 Sept. 1767.

possessed charm, wit, and intelligence, as well as industry and a conscientious concern to do his duty by his King and country. This combination of talent and character made him just the man for that time of political flux. North was soon the main prop of government, and around him during the next few years there developed the permanent administration George III had been seeking since his accession and that the country had lacked since the death of Henry Pelham in 1754.[3]

What form the ministry would take, and in particular whether or not it would be composed of self-styled 'friends of America', was also decided in the second half of 1767 by the outcome of two political negotiations. The failure of the July consultations meant that the Rockingham party was to remain in opposition throughout the next fifteen years, until America had been lost. The success of December discussions brought the Bedford group into administration and helped to set the tone of future American policy.

These negotiations arose out of the evident need to strengthen an administration in which Grafton had now replaced Chatham as effective head. The personal collapse of Chatham was only part of the explanation for Grafton's initiative. It was common practice for a ministry so hard-pressed in Parliament by opposition factions to bargain with one or more of them; and at the beginning of July Grafton was aware that his House of Commons Leader General Conway, under pressure from his former Rockinghamite colleagues, was on the point of resignation, a decision that would cripple the ministry.

The political manœuvres in the second half of 1767 not only settled the immediate future of British politics: they also revealed the confused state of British thinking on the American question, at a time when there was no specific colonial issue to concentrate minds and polarize opinion. It was on 3 July that Grafton persuaded George III to permit him to approach certain opposition leaders in order to strengthen the administration.[4] The King's consent was given merely to enable Grafton to do just that and was not permission for the creation of a new one, but this was a point of confusion for some three weeks. On 7 July Rockingham interpreted Grafton's personal offer of his own post at the Treasury as a royal invitation to form a new administration, and he acted thereafter under that misapprehension.

[3] Thomas, *Lord North*, pp. 20–53.
[4] For the definitive account of the July negotiations see Brooke, *Chatham Administration*, pp. 162–217.

Rockingham approached the Bedford group, who with his permission consulted Grenville; and he sent this reply through Richard Rigby. 'If the King thought fit to call Lord Rockingham into his government, upon a great and extended plan, carried on with vigour, and asserting the sovereignty of Great Britain over her colonies, he had no factious dispositions to disturb it, but that he could never alter his opinion on the subject of America.'[5] Rigby reported to Bedford and Rockingham on 12 July 'the good temper of mind in which he found Mr. Grenville, with regard to any administration . . . where measures should be pursued conformable to his sentiments about America'.[6] The Grenvillite stipulation was for an acceptable American policy, a point Rockingham apparently failed to grasp. But on 20 July, shortly before a conclave of the Rockinghamite and Bedfordite leadership that evening, he did see a letter of 16 July by Grenville with this proviso: 'that they adopted a plan of measures to our satisfaction, and particularly the capital measure of asserting and establishing the sovereignty of Great Britain over its colonies'.[7] At the meeting Rockingham soon launched into an indignant complaint that Grenville 'should create difficulties by starting questions on America for immediate discussion, the answer of which must depend on future and uncertain events'. Bedford tried to calm the discussion down, saying that Grenville's doubts might have arisen from the circumstance that, as Bedford put it, 'Lord Chatham, the Lord Chancellor and Lord Shelburne had all denied the sovereignty'.[8] This implication that Grenville believed Rockinghamite and Chathamite views on America to be similar merely rekindled the Marquess's fury. Rockingham declared that he was not responsible for what Chatham and his friends had said, and his own previous conduct gave no ground for any reason to doubt his intention to maintain the sovereignty of Britain over the colonies. Grenville's letter was produced and, so Rigby told him later, Dowdeswell proposed 'to put in the words *maintain* and *support*, instead of *assert* and *establish* . . . and we passed near four hours of our meeting upon this verbal dispute; which, however, was not finally resolved upon one way or the other'.[9] Consideration of the matter was eventually postponed, and the meeting began to consider the allocation of office. This soon put an end to the discussion. When

[5] *Grenville Papers*, IV, 230.   [6] *Bedford Journal*, pp. 604–5.
[7] *Bedford Papers*, III, 370.
[8] Wentworth Woodhouse Muniments, R1–838.
[9] *Grenville Papers*, IV, 83.

Rockingham named Conway as Leader of the Commons, Bedford refused to entertain the idea, and the conference broke up early on 21 July.

In an attempt to avert a breakdown of the negotiation Newcastle persuaded Bedford and Rockingham to meet again that evening at his house, Rigby and Dowdeswell being the only others present. In a postscript to his letter Rigby told Grenville that 'a more easy and acquiescing temper prevailed, touching the words concerning the future superintendence of this country over America, and that point was not dwelt upon'.[10] For the meeting soon adopted this compromise formula apparently devised by Bedford on the previous evening.[11]

That with regard to the American colonies, no new measures should be understood to be agreed upon at this meeting, unless new matter arises, but if new matter should arise the sovereignty of this country should be asserted and established with firmness and temper.

This astute wording retained Grenville's key phrase 'asserted and established', but robbed it of the alarming implication of immediate future action; while the inclusion of the words 'firmness' and 'temper', so contradictory in their tenor, satisfied conflicting shades of opinion. This was a verbal compromise, and the adoption of any actual policy based on the formula would present practical problems. That was not the concern of the meeting, which then resumed discussion of appointments in the proposed new ministry. Bedford now accepted Rockingham's point that as the First Lord of the Treasury he would need a Commons Leader in whom he had personal confidence, and suggested Dowdeswell. The Marquess refused, insisting on the nomination of Conway, and the meeting ended inconclusively. On the following day, 22 July, Rockingham at last had an audience with the King, to report the failure of the negotiation, and he learned that George III had not offered him the Treasury, let alone a commission to form a new ministry.

The opposition discussions had not broken down over America. Bedford had produced a formula that satisfied Rockingham, and such an intelligent and informed observer as Lord Mansfield commented to Whately that 'Lord Rockingham would, when the subject had come quietly into discussion, have been very easy, and

[10] Ibid., IV, 85.
[11] Brooke, *Chatham Administration*, p. 208, quoting Wentworth Woodhouse Muniments, R9–7.

have concurred in almost any measures short of re-enacting the Stamp Act.'[12] The crucial question had been whether or not Conway should be Leader of the House of Commons. It might be argued that Bedford's objection to Conway was based on his soft attitude to the colonies, and some contemporary observers certainly thought that a relevant consideration. Lord George Sackville commented to Whately on 23 July about Conway's 'American demerit',[13] and journalist John Almon subsequently put forward that interpretation in his account of the episode. But Almon's argument hinged on the contention that Bedford proposed his own man Rigby as Commons Leader.[14] No report of the meetings by anyone present supports this claim, and Bedford himself proposed another Rockinghamite. Dowdeswell was not as soft on America as Conway, but had actively participated in the policy of the Rockingham ministry. Bedford's objection to Conway was on the simple ground of his proven incompetence in two years as Commons Leader; and there is no good reason to dispute the opinion of Whately, who sent this verdict to Grenville on 22 July.[15]

I think our friends seem inclined to rest it principally on the nomination of Conway to be the Minister in the House of Commons, in the office of Secretary of State, because of that, they say, there can be but one opinion in the world, of the American measure there are two: his nomination was made absolutely *sine qua non*, whereas the other was never specified, and encouragement was given to expect that it might be settled by negotiation.

The failure of these political negotiations of July had an important long-term effect on the formulation of Britain's American policy. As John Brooke pointed out,[16] all the portents are that an administration based on the Chatham and Rockingham factions would have proved more conciliatory than the one based on members of the Bedford and Grenville groups that came into existence under Lord North. The July discussions contributed directly to that outcome. The next and successful attempt to strengthen the administration was not with Rockinghamite support.

It was some months before these consequences became apparent.

[12] *Grenville Papers*, IV, 143.   [13] Ibid., IV, 89.
[14] *Chatham Anecdotes*, II, 50–7.
[15] *Grenville Papers*, IV, 94. For similar opinions by Rockinghamites Newcastle and Richmond see Wentworth Woodhouse Muniments, R1–843, and *Rockingham Memoirs*, II, 61.
[16] Brooke, *Chatham Administration*, pp. 216, 232.

During the summer and autumn the Rockingham and Bedford groups remained in touch, with a view to vigorous opposition in the next Parliamentary session and the formation of a new ministry if the attack was successful. The Rockingham party decided to move a Commons amendment to the Address when Parliament met on 24 November, regretting the omission from the King's Speech of the conventional phrase promising measures to promote trade and industry. This was a move calculated to obtain the support of all opponents of government, and Bedford was given prior notice of the tactic.[17] The session therefore opened with good prospects of an effective opposition alliance, but Grenville wrecked any chance of co-operation. Already on 6 November he had written to Bedford of the overriding importance to him of the American question.[18]

The asserting and establishing the lawful authority of the King and Parliament of Great Britain over every part of our dominion in every part of the world. These, my dear Lord, I am sensible, are general expressions, which few gentlemen in words will venture directly to contradict; but I, as well as your Grace, mean the reality and not the words, and can therefore only give our assent to a system of measures conformable to them. I shall readily support these principles whoever shall propose them, and I never can support any ministry which acts in contradiction to them.

On 23 November, the eve of the session, Grenville was told that at the recent Newmarket race meeting Rockingham had announced 'that if ever he was to come into power he would never have anything to do either with Mr. Grenville or with any of his name'.[19] Incensed by this public proscription and also by news of further colonial defiance, Grenville went to Parliament the next day spoiling for a fight with the Rockinghamites over America. The colonies were not mentioned in the King's Speech. The ministry had no intention of introducing that subject for discussion, and the only matters of substance referred to were politically innocuous, the high price of corn and the National Debt. But the administration knew that America would be mentioned in the Commons. Nathaniel Ryder, who was to second the Address, noted in his diary that when Grafton showed him the draft on 14 November he had asked the Duke 'whether I might touch upon

[17] Wentworth Woodhouse Muniments, R1–885; BL Add. MSS 32987, ff. 75–7, 111.
[18] Bedford Papers, III, 397.
[19] Wentworth Woodhouse Muniments, R1–884.

America in my speech, and he seemed to have no objection to it'.[20]

America was discussed in both Houses of Parliament. In the Lords, according to Horace Walpole, 'the Duke of Bedford and Lord Lyttelton talked much against the ministers and the outrages of the Americans'; but no details of the debate are known.[21] In the Commons the Rockinghamite amendment, moved by William Dowdeswell, was rejected without a division after a debate in which no support had come from either the Bedfordites or Grenville. That was not the end of the story. Here is Rockingham's account to Lord Albemarle.[22]

Mr. Ryder, who seconded the motion for the Address had brought in North America by head and shoulders and talked much of coercion, etc. Dowdeswell in answer to him confined himself to the lines which the Duke of Bedford and his friends had held with us at Newcastle House, by saying that he was sorry to hear America brought up as a constant subject of debate. That when any fresh matter arose which might call for the assistance of Parliament, it would be the duty of the minister then to bring it before Parliament etc. etc.

As soon as Mr. Dowdeswell's motion was rejected, up rose George Grenville. Flames out upon the subject of North America. Complains that he had been traduced in print. Declares that he never had meant nor ever would *concur or assist* the formation of an administration, where he did not see that it was their full intention to reduce the colonies to obedience. That it was not men's *words* that he regarded, but their deeds (alluding to our Declaratory Bill of the right, and to the repeal of the Stamp Act) and attacking Dowdeswell for saying that he did not wish the subject of North America to be constant matter of debate, declaring that not to wish to have that matter under the deliberation of Parliament was unworthy of any man, much more so of one who was a member of that great council of the nation, etc. etc. That he, Mr. Grenville, always abided by the same sentiments which he had supported *over and over*, and that *measures* and not *men* would decide his conduct, and in short gave us and our conduct a very hearty dressing.

Rigby and the Duke of Bedford's friends who were in the House kept silent; though while he was speaking they told many of our friends that they were very sorry for what Grenville was doing, that they disapproved of it highly, but that he was wild and ungovernable.

[20] Harrowby MSS, 434, document 46.

[21] H. Walpole, *Memoirs*, III, 81. This may have been the occasion when Bedford mentioned an offending issue of the *Boston Gazette*, probably the one of 31 Aug. about which Grenville later complained in the Commons. See below, p. 43. *Franklin Papers*, XIV, 331. There was no formal motion on America: *LJ*, XXXII, 3–7.

[22] Wentworth Woodhouse Muniments, R1–885.

Rockingham complained about this Bedfordite silence that evening to Lord Weymouth, who replied with this disclaimer. 'That there was always much distinction to be made between what George Grenville, etc., did and what they (the Duke of Bedford's friends) did. That they were separate corps.'[23] Rockingham told Newcastle he thought that the Bedfordite position ought to be promptly clarified. 'It must produce either a thorough or fixed cordiality or will have the contrary effect. Indeed, we seem to have the advantage in this because upon the American matter Mr. Grenville does not appear to coincide with what the Duke of Bedford himself laid down as his own sentiments at our meeting.'[24] On the next day, 25 November, the Rockinghamite leadership decided that Newcastle should visit Bedford.[25] But before he did so the opposition crisis had been exacerbated by another Commons quarrel on America between Grenville and the Rockinghamites the same day.

In some sense this was a confrontation staged out of Rockinghamite resentment towards Grenville, for Edmund Burke sent this explanation to a friend. 'We went down to the House, and in our turn, in the strongest terms, renounced him and all his works.'[26] But Grenville himself twice raised the issue of America. It was almost certainly he who moved an amendment to the Address, about strengthening control over the colonies. After that had been negatived Grenville made formal complaint about the *Boston Gazette* of 31 August, 'as containing seditious and dangerous doctrines, and in breach of the privilege of the House'. That issue of the newspaper contained an attack on Parliament and suggestions for a ban on the import of British goods.[27] Consideration of this matter was adjourned for two days.[28]

On one of these motions Grenville had a hot argument over America with Dowdeswell and Burke; and Rigby, provoked by Grenville's behaviour, deplored the quarrel as being of assistance only to the ministry. Administration kept out of the debate, though one of their supporters, Colonel George Onslow, raised a laugh by suggesting that Grenville should be despatched to America, on the analogy of the old Roman practice of sending senators to inquire into the state of their provinces. When

[23] Wentworth Woodhouse Muniments, R1–883.
[24] BL Add. MSS 32987, ff. 87–8.
[25] BL Add. MSS 32987, ff. 111.   [26] *Burke Corr.* I, 336.
[27] The extracts were reprinted in the *Political Register*, 1768, pp. 26–9.
[28] *CJ*, XXXI, 426–7.

Grenville jocularly asked whether he would be safe there, Onslow replied that he could not guarantee his return but believed such a step would greatly improve Britain's relationship with the colonies: a rejoinder that increased the mirth.[29]

Grenville's complaint raised a procedural difficulty, for it was invariable Commons practice to come to a decision on any point of privilege. When consideration of it was resumed on 27 November other members tried to persuade him to withdraw it. He refused, and a long debate ended with an evasive adjournment for six months, as agent Johnson reported to Connecticut.[30]

Nobody attempted to justify, or even excuse those publications, but the ministry said it was below the dignity of Parliament to pay any regard to angry newspaper writers, who were as frequent and as impudent here as they could be in any country; that by the last accounts from thence it appeared that the sober, sensible, steady part of the people in America disapproved of these publications and were disposed to continue peaceable and easy, and enter into no new contests with this country; that they therefore hoped they would have no ill effect and be very soon forgot, or, if they must be prosecuted, it might be done by ministerial orders to the governor, without the interposition of Parliament.

During the first week of the new Parliamentary session America had been debated three times in the Commons and once in the Lords: but on each occasion those who advocated a harder line with the colonies had been rebuffed. 'These are favourable symptoms of the present disposition of Parliament towards America, which I hope no conduct of the Americans will give just cause of altering', Benjamin Franklin commented in a trans-Atlantic letter to Joseph Galloway on 1 December, and Franklin clearly thought that Grenville had overplayed the American issue. 'Our apprehensions of a change, and that Mr. Grenville would come in again, seem over for the present. He behaves as if a little out of his head on the article of America, which he brings into every debate without rhyme or reason, when the matter has not the least connection with it.'[31]

Franklin was a poor prophet for both Britain and America. The debates from which he had drawn comforting conclusions triggered off a series of events which led to the inclusion in the ministry of the hardline Bedford group, though not of the dreaded Grenville himself; and this had significant consequences for American

[29] H. Walpole, *Memoirs*, III, 84; *Letters*, VII, 147; *Franklin Papers*, XIV, 350.
[30] *Trumbull Papers*, pp. 247–8.   [31] *Franklin Papers*, XIV, 331.

policy at the very time when Franklin's other premiss for an improved relationship between Britain and her American colonies was rendered invalid. As in the Stamp Act Crisis he failed to anticipate the strength of the colonial reaction to British taxation.

The Parliamentary clashes of November confirmed the lesson of the political negotiations of the previous July. There was no genuine possibility of the opposition parties uniting to form a new ministry even if the administration could be defeated. In one sense the American question was a fatal barrier to opposition unity. At the beginning of December Lord Chancellor Camden was gleefully declaring, so James West reported to Newcastle, that 'the difference of the opposition was clear, as it was impossible for *Stamp Men* and *No Stamp Men* ever to agree'.[32] But too much should not be made of America as a divisive factor in the contemporary British political scene. The key factor was the mutual antipathy and rivalry between Rockingham and Grenville. Past differences over colonial policy did not inhibit the Bedford group from now approaching Grafton and his ministerial colleagues for office when realization came that there was no hope of a successful opposition. That was starkly obvious by the end of November. Newcastle's reconciliation mission to Bedford House came to nothing, and professions by Bedford on 26 and 27 November of a joint opposition with the Rockingham party looked hollow within a few days.[33] Before the end of the month the Bedford party had opened negotiations with the ministry.[34]

These discussions were protracted over several weeks, not through Grafton's unwillingness to meet Bedfordite demands for two cabinet posts and other offices, but because he took the opportunity of the ministerial reconstruction to create a new Secretaryship of State for America. The idea of such an office had been floated since at least 1751. Chatham had briefly toyed with the notion of taking such a post himself when forming the administration in July 1766, and in August 1767 the proposal had been put forward that Conway should take such an office instead of his Northern Secretaryship; but Attorney-General De Grey had then vetoed that plan on the ground that under the 1706 Place Act no holder of a new office could sit in the House of Commons.[35]

[32] BL Add. MSS 32987, f. 149.
[33] BL Add. MSS 32931, ff. 289–92, 303–4.
[34] For fuller detail see Brooke, *Chatham Administration*, pp. 324–33.
[35] H. Walpole, *Memoirs*, III, 71; *Chatham Papers*, III, 293. Yet Lord George Germain held the office when an MP from 1775 to 1782.

The idea was revived by the Bedfordite initiative, which included the suggestion that the office of Southern Secretary Shelburne should be divided, with an American Department forming a new Secretaryship. This scheme was welcomed by both Grafton and George III, but the King's real motive was to bring about Shelburne's resignation by an offer of the new American Department.[36]

The interview which Grafton had with Shelburne on 11 December was therefore difficult. He said that he had always thought that the Southern Department should be divided, and that Conway had held the same view when Southern Secretary. Grafton assured Shelburne that no criticism of him was implied. 'He thought the [American] business had been very sufficiently and ably managed' and for that reason he wanted Shelburne to remain responsible for the colonies. Shelburne modestly attributed to luck the circumstance that America 'had been reduced in the main to some degree of order and obedience to Parliamentary authority, from a very different state in which I found it', and asked for time to consider Grafton's proposal. On 13 December he agreed to the division of his office, but wished to remain Southern Secretary and not undertake the task of organizing the new American Department. Grafton still pressed him to do so, giving this new reason. 'If the Duke of Bedford's friends and not Lord Rockingham's, should be the party that is taken in, it would be impossible, in his idea or in the Chancellor's, he was sure, to place any of the Bedfords there, on account of the difference of principles.' But Shelburne refused to change his mind.[37]

This decision left Grafton with the double problem of accommodating the Bedford group and of filling the American Secretaryship. The first task was eased by the resignation of two colleagues. Gower could replace Lord Northington, who was anxious to retire as Lord President of the Council; and since Conway seized the chance to resign as Northern Secretary Weymouth could be given his post instead of Shelburne's Southern Department. It was now that Conway also gave way to Lord North as Leader of the House of Commons, but he remained in the cabinet, even though merely Lieutenant-General of the Ordnance. In retrospect the Bedfordite accession to office can be seen to have altered the political complexion of the ministry with respect to America, but at the

[36] *Corr. of George III*, I, 510.
[37] *Chatham Papers*, III, 292–8. This is Shelburne's account of the interviews to Lady Chatham.

time agent Johnson was sanguine about the event, since the Grenville party was weakened.[38] The Bedfordite and Grenvillite parties put quite a different interpretation on what had happened. Rigby assured Whately that the Bedfordites had had 'a precise explanation on the American measures, on which the Duke of Grafton gives way, so that there will be no difference of opinion between him and his new friends, for he acquiesces entirely in their system'.[39] On 1 January 1768 Whately commented to Grenville that Grafton 'enters with eagerness into the opinions of the Duke of Bedford concerning America. . . . Probably some of the Bedfords will, before they propose any [measures] respecting America, take an opportunity of speaking to you.'[40] This notion that Grenville would now be able to direct the administration's American policy by proxy was sheer fantasy; and the course of events during the next two years was to show that the belief that Grafton had fallen in with the American ideas of his new allies was deception or delusion.

The new office of Secretary of State for America, since the Bedford faction had been accommodated elsewhere by Grafton, was now filled from within the ranks of existing administration supporters.[41] Of the two men with appropriate experience Lord Halifax, President of the Board of Trade from 1748 to 1761 and Southern Secretary under Grenville, was probably deemed to be too old for such a demanding post: and the choice fell on Lord Hillsborough, President of the Board under Grenville and again from August to December 1766 at the beginning of the Chatham administration, when it was he who had insisted on the demotion of the Board to a mere office of report upon reference.[42] The Southern Department apparently could not cope with the sheer volume of business generated by the colonies after this administrative change, and so what had long been an obvious solution was now adopted. Hillsborough took up his appointment on 20 January 1768, but he did not also become President of the Board of Trade. Lord Clare retained that office, attending every meeting until 10 June, and it was not filled when he was appointed Vice-Treasurer of Ireland later that month. A new commission of the

[38] *Trumbull Papers*, pp. 251–2.
[39] *Grenville Papers*, IV, 198–9. For a similar assurance by Bedford to Lyttelton see ibid., IV, 249.
[40] Ibid., IV, 246.
[41] For this office see Spector, *American Department of the British Government*, pp. 11–24 being concerned with the origins.
[42] Thomas, *British Politics and the Stamp Act Crisis*, pp. 287–9.

Board on 12 July did not include Hillsborough, but he was named to attend as Secretary of State and did so regularly.[43]

Hillsborough tactfully awaited Lord Clare's departure before making any administrative changes, but there was evidence of a new broom in the circular of 23 January to American governors announcing his appointment. When stating formally that correspondence previously sent to the Southern Secretary should now go to his office, Hillsborough said that he expected 'a frequent and full communication of all occurrences' together with a punctual transmission of colonial legislation and relevant documents; and he added this reproof: 'His Majesty having observed with concern that this essential part of the duty of his officers in America has scarcely anywhere been duly attended to, and in several colonies particularly in the charter and proprietory governments almost entirely neglected.'[44] After Lord Clare's resignation Hillsborough took further steps. On 21 June he asked the governors to comment on the general instructions customarily issued to them on appointment.[45] On 4 July he informed them that since he had been directed by the King to attend the Board of Trade they need not in future send the Board copies of correspondence with him.[46] A week later, after news of colonial discontent and disorders, the governors were instructed to send dispatches by the first available private ship and not wait for the official packet, since private individuals were receiving public news before official intimation arrived.[47] Most important of all was the reversal of the 1766 demotion of the Board of Trade, Hillsborough informing the Board on 22 June that it was to return to the practice of before August 1766.[48] Hillsborough arranged that John Pownall, the long-serving Secretary to the Board of Trade, should both retain that post and become senior Under-Secretary in the American Department, together with a Richard Phelps transferred from the Northern Department. There had been rumours that Benjamin Franklin would become an under-secretary, so he told his son William on 9 January, 'but with little likelihood as it is a settled point here that I am too much an American'.[49] Lord Clare had put forward an American expert William Knox, whose qualifications included a

[43] JCTP 1768–75, pp. 1–312; London Chronicle, 18 June 1768.
[44] NYCD, VIII, 7.
[45] Ibid., VIII, 77–8.
[46] CO 5/241, ff. 81–2.
[47] Ibid., ff. 84–5; NYCD, VIII, 82.
[48] JCTP 1768–75, p. 33; NYCD, VIII, 78.
[49] Franklin Papers, XV, 16.

former agency for Georgia; he now successfully cultivated Hillsborough, and was appointed when Phelps left in 1770.[50]

The announcement of the creation of the American Department caused alarm in the colonies, and the idea was current in Britain that the decision was in some way part of a policy to curb American opposition.[51] This belief was given colour by the simultaneous accession to office of the Bedford group, and in retrospect strengthened by the later reputation of Hillsborough. But it is not a theory sustained by the course of events in December 1767, and the appointment of Hillsborough was certainly not at Bedfordite instigation, for that party bore him a grudge for not resigning with them in 1765.[52]

Immediate reactions to Hillsborough's appointment reflected the fact that he was something of an enigma. When Grenville's President of the Board of Trade he had taken an unsympathetic attitude towards the professed colonial need for paper currency; but he had also advised against the Stamp Act and had later voted for its repeal, or so he told the House of Lords on 15 December 1768.[53] Grenville himself professed to have no idea what line Hillsborough would take on America, making this comment on 31 December.[54]

I shall be curious to know what system is to be adopted for Ireland and America; whether the new Secretary of State for the Colonies will be reconciled to the idea of their *dependence* and obedience, agreeably to the letter and intention of the British Acts of Parliament, or whether their independence is to be openly avowed.

Massachusetts agent De Berdt was uneasy, sending back the comment that Hillsborough 'had never discovered any particular affection for America'.[55] But Connecticut agent Johnson entertained the hope that Hillsborough's Irish background might have led him to formulate 'reasonable notions' of the rights of the inhabitants of the empire outside Great Britain;[56] and Benjamin Franklin did not regard Hillsborough's appointment as the most disturbing aspect of the ministerial changes: here is his report home to Joseph Galloway.[57]

[50] *HMC Knox MSS*, pp. 95, 106; Bellot, *William Knox*, pp. 100–4.
[51] *Chatham Anecdotes*, II, 67 n.   [52] *HMC Knox MSS*, p. 264.
[53] See below p. 114. His name does not appear in the contemporary voting lists on either side. Simmons and Thomas, *Proceedings and Debates*, II, 343–6.
[54] *Grenville Papers*, IV, 206.   [55] *De Berdt Letters*, p. 330.
[56] *Trumbull Papers*, p. 252.   [57] *Franklin Papers*, XV, 16–17.

Some changes have taken place since my last, which have not the most promising aspect for America, several of the Bedford party being come into employment again; a party that has distinguished itself by exclaiming against us on all late occasions. Mr. Conway, one of our friends, has resigned, and Lord Weymouth takes his place. Lord Shelburne, another friend, is stripped of the American part of the business of his office which now makes a distinct department in which Lord Hillsborough is placed. I do not think this nobleman in general an enemy to America.

Hillsborough came to office at a time when another American crisis was building up. It was all very well for Shelburne to remark complacently that the period of eighteen months when he had been responsible for colonial affairs had seen both an improvement in imperial relationships and a tightening of British control. But it had been a lull between two storms, the Stamp Act Crisis and the Townshend Duties Crisis. Before this last came to a head, Hillsborough was faced with making some sort of decision on another issue, one that was to trouble him throughout his tenure of the American Secretaryship and to lead to his resignation from the office. This was the question of whether or how far to allow settlement in 'the western lands' acquired in 1763 between the Mississippi and the frontier of the thirteen old colonies. On this and other matters Hillsborough was soon to show himself less pliable than such predecessors as Conway and Shelburne. That there was a stronger hand at the helm of colonial policy was perceived by agent Johnson, who sent home this pen-portrait of the first Secretary of State for America.[58]

Lord Hillsborough is esteemed a nobleman of good nature, abilities and integrity, is a man of business, alert, lively, ready, but too fond of his own opinions and systems and too apt to be inflexibly attached to them; by no means so gentle and easy to be entreated as his predecessors in that branch of business, but much more to be depended upon if he once adopts your idea of any measure.

[58] *Trumbull Papers*, p. 252.

4

A Policy for the West. 1767–1773

CONSCIOUS of America's future 'manifest destiny' and aware of the 1763 Proclamation prohibiting colonial expansion over the mountain watershed of the Atlantic seaboard, historians have as a matter of course included Britain's policy for the west as a factor in the American decision to break with Britain. Mercantile thought, as reflected in the Proclamation and in important Board of Trade reports of 1768 and 1772, saw no useful purpose in distant inland settlements. At a more prosaic level British politicians and administrators soon became aware of the practical problems and unexpectedly enormous costs involved in the management, both military and civil, of the vast North American territories acquired as a result of the Seven Years War, in colonial parlance the French and Indian War.[1] Fear of provoking the Indian tribes scattered through this wilderness was also a prime motive behind British attempts to prevent westward settlement and to impose controls on Indian trade. At the beginning of the French and Indian War two Indian Superintendents had been appointed to manage relations with the northern and southern Indians on the borders of the British colonies. These offices were continued in peacetime, after sovereignty over the territories in which the Indians lived had been ceded by France to Britain, in the persons respectively of Sir William Johnson and John Stuart. The native tribes still retained ownership of their traditional hunting-grounds: any encroachments on them had to be by legal purchase, and individual acquisitions were prohibited by the 1763 Proclamation. The Superintendents had the unenviable task of protecting the Indian tribes from the activities of unauthorized settlers and unscrupulous traders; and they also had the immediate problem of establishing actual boundaries on the ground to accord with instructions from London to enforce the Proclamation Line drawn up on Whitehall maps.

In 1763 Britain also retained another wartime institution, the office of Commander-in-Chief for the comparatively large army

---

[1] I have omitted Quebec from this survey. A full study is being prepared by Philip Lawson.

retained in North America at the peace. In fact the projected army of 10,000 men in twenty-one battalions never amounted to more than 7,000 men in fifteen battalions. The post was held by General Thomas Gage, who had replaced Sir Jeffrey Amherst in that year. The chief motive for the maintenance of this army, so Parliament was informed at the time, was the potential danger from the French West Indies.[2] But the intention professed then to make the old British seaboard colonies pay for this defence had proved abortive, most conspicuously in the repeal of the 1765 Stamp Act designated for that very purpose. It was the heavy financial burden that in consequence fell unexpectedly on Britain that soon prompted reassessments of western policy.

The British politician most conscious of the difficulties and expenses involved in the possession of the new territories in North America was Secretary at War Lord Barrington, who had returned to that office under Rockingham in 1765 after having held it earlier during most of the French and Indian War, and retained it until 1778. Barrington could see no good reason why Britain need maintain a significant military force, or perhaps any at all, beyond the Proclamation Line of 1763; but his attitude was based on naïve ignorance of the true state of affairs in the wilderness between the seaboard colonies and the Mississippi, inhabited, in theory at least, only by Indian tribes. The French settlers in New Orleans and west of the Mississippi were both intriguing with and illegally trading with the Indian tribes in this area ceded to Britain; while prospective British settlers paid no heed to a line drawn on a map in London. Gage shared Barrington's attitudes, and was already beginning to reduce and withdraw garrisons in small forts from 1766 onwards; but his knowledge of the practical problems led him to make a cautious reply to Barrington's enquiries about general policy.[3]

Barrington nevertheless produced a report on 10 May 1766 advocating the withdrawal of most of the army garrisons in the wilderness south of the Great Lakes and east of the Mississippi. He based his argument on the huge expense of transporting army supplies over such vast distances, and on the contention that the presence of the army there served little useful purpose; since it did not fulfil any of the professed objectives of protecting the fur trade, affording defence against a possible French or Spanish attack, and providing control of the Indian tribes. With the recent Stamp Act

---

[2] Thomas, *WMQ*, 38 (1981), 111.   [3] *Gage Corr.*, II, 318–24.

riots in his mind Barrington could obviously think of a better use to which the soldiers might be put. But, whereas Gage wanted to place them in turbulent towns like Boston and New York,[4] Barrington thought that this would be provocative and suggested that they should be positioned in Nova Scotia and Florida, within a few days' sailing time of potential trouble-spots.[5] The Rockingham administration lacked the opportunity to consider Barrington's plan before its dismissal in July 1766, and the problem passed to the Chatham ministry.

Barrington was soon canvassing the new cabinet, and on 12 September informed Gage that Chatham and Shelburne agreed with him 'almost on every point', a claim that soon proved to be unfounded.[6] The Secretary at War also deliberately brought the financial problem to the attention of Parliament. It was his production of the colonial army estimate on 26 January 1767 that had spurred Charles Townshend to his public pledge for American taxes towards the cost, and his supplementary estimate on 18 February that caused Grenville to propose the reduction of such costs by maximum possible withdrawal of soldiers from the American interior. Townshend then promptly made it clear that the ministry already had this idea in mind, and on 12 March demanded in cabinet the implementation of such a policy. These demands for economy conflicted with the expansionist plans of Shelburne. The Southern Secretary was being subjected to heavy and sometimes conflicting lobbying. Canadian fur traders clamoured for a free Indian trade; but traders from Pennsylvania and other old colonies demanded protection against illegal French competition; and various land companies, new and old, pressed for the establishment of inland colonies. A cabinet meeting early in April agreed to postpone any decision on western policy until Shelburne was able to formulate proposals. Barrington told Gage on 10 April that both he and Sir Jeffrey Amherst had attended to give their opinions and had differed 'in every respect'.[7]

In June Shelburne submitted his draft proposal to the cabinet.[8]

---

[4] Ibid., II, 351.

[5] The report is printed in *Corr. of George III*, I, 432–41.   [6] *PCBG*, p. 25.

[7] *PCBG*, p. 27. For the above see Marshall, *JAS*, 5 (1971), 1–11; and Thomas, *British Politics and the Stamp Act Crisis*, pp. 338–40, 344–6.

[8] 'Minutes submitted to the cabinet in the beginning of summer 1767', Shelburne MSS 50/185–218; printed Alvord and Carter, *Trade and Politics*, pp. 12–21. For convincing arguments for June as the date rather than the previously accepted one of September see Marshall, *JAS*, 1 (1967), 156 n. The date is not a point of material significance.

He suggested the return of control of Indian affairs to the
individual colonies. This would involve the abolition of what has
been called the Indian Department. A 1764 Board of Trade report
had recommended the appointment under the Superintendents of
deputies, commissaries, interpreters, and smiths. This organization
had been established without formal sanction from Britain. The
costs had proved to be much higher than the estimate of £20,000,
and they fell on the army budget. On the wider issue of the west
Shelburne was inclined to follow Amherst rather than Barrington.
Stating that westward expansion could not be prevented, he
suggested two new colonies, in the Illinois area and at Detroit, to
be self-financing by land sales and quit rents. The development
would provide a safety-valve for colonial land hunger, give added
protection to the older colonies, and reduce army costs by making
possible both cheaper supply and the evacuation of some forts.
Among the various western land settlement proposals of the time
Shelburne was here giving preference to the Illinois Company over
the old Ohio Company and the newer Mississippi Company,
which proposed a colony at the confluence of the Mississippi and
Ohio.[9]

This was an important policy proposal, and Shelburne's colleagues
apparently took no action until after the summer break. On 11
September the cabinet decided to refer the matter to the Board of
Trade,[10] and Shelburne formally did so on 5 October in a letter
setting out his own ideas at length. He had by now accepted a
suggestion from Amherst for a third colony on the Mississippi,
and recommended letters from Amherst and Gage about the
various proposed colonies, and also some from private speculators.
Shelburne claimed that the project would curb the political
intrigues and the illegal fur trade of the French and Spanish, and
increase the market for British manufactures. He also repeated his
arguments about reduced army costs, with the new colonies
providing a line of defence for the old.[11]

Land speculators evidently expected the Board of Trade merely
to fill in the details, and their hopes were high.[12] The Board got
down to work immediately, with five meetings on the subject

    [9] Sosin, *Whitehall and the Wilderness*, pp. 136–45.
    [10] Cabinet minute, printed Alvord and Carter, *Trade and Politics*, p. 21.
Sosin, op. cit., pp. 157, 161, is mistaken when he assumes that such a reference
was equivalent to cabinet approval.
    [11] Alvord and Carter, op. cit., pp. 77–81.
    [12] *Franklin Papers*, XIV, 324–6.

before interviewing London merchants on 27 October.[13] Two days later there was a gathering of merchants and agents to consider their response to the proposal, attended among others by Benjamin Franklin and Richard Jackson.[14] This meeting unanimously endorsed the opinions reported to the Board next day by Barlow Trecothick: that the Indian trade would be best served by returning control to the individual old colonies, and that the creation of new western colonies would help to increase the consumption of British manufactures.[15] Further evidence received from Amherst in November was also in favour of new colonies.[16] But the Board of Trade, sceptical and well-informed on America, resisted this high-pressure campaign. After all, it still contained some members, Soame Jenyns, Edward Eliot, and George Rice, who had been there at the time of the 1763 Proclamation. The Board's President Lord Clare, in an interview with Franklin at this time, stated that he favoured an Ohio colony but not the one at Detroit.[17] The proposal to hand over control of Indian affairs met with as much resistance from the Board as the demand for new colonies, and in November Shelburne had a private discussion with Board member Jeremiah Dyson to work out a compromise: the colonies would control trade, and the Superintendents would be retained to deal with other matters relating to Indian relations.[18] Despite four more Board of Trade meetings on the subject before the end of the year,[19] no report was forthcoming, much to the exasperation of Lord Barrington, who wanted prompt implementation at least of Gage's ideas of reducing the size and number of the expensive garrisons in the interior of America. He wrote in disgust to Gage on 12 December.[20]

They are making references from time to time, get reports, and do nothing. I am so provoked at this unmanly conduct, that the day when the army was voted, I advised them publicly in the House of Commons to bring the matter thither for advice to the Crown, if they could not determine on any advice themselves.[21] Every hour shows the fatal effects of Lord Chatham's indisposition which still continues. One finds twenty men of parts before one finds one who has decision in him, and yet no man

---

[13] *JCTP 1763–1767*, pp. 420–1, 423–4, 427, 429.
[14] *Franklin Papers*, XIV, 303.
[15] Alvord and Carter, op. cit., p. 102.   [16] Ibid., pp. 103–4.
[17] *Franklin Papers*, XIV, 325–6.
[18] Humphreys, *EHR*, 50 (1935), pp. 257–64.
[19] *JCTP 1763–1767*, pp. 429–30, 440–1.   [20] *PCBG*, p. 33.
[21] There is no record of any debate on 1 December, when the army estimates were presented to the House of Commons.

should be a minister who cannot decide on the most intricate subjects after reasonable consideration.

In this thinly veiled attack on Shelburne Barrington was being unreasonable and obtuse. The problems were complicated, and matters of genuine conflicts of opinion. The implementation of an expansionist scheme would prevent any significant troop reductions, for soldiers would be needed at first to defend any new settlements. The delay in any policy decision was obviously explained also by the ministerial reshuffle in progress at that very time, and which would remove Shelburne himself from the control of American affairs. Despite the evidence received by the Board in 1767, its report would now be tailored to suit the opinion of the new American Secretary, and Hillsborough was a known anti-expansionist, who had been President of the Board of Trade at the time of the 1763 Proclamation. The Board began to draft its report on 26 January 1768, and after two further discussions signed it on 7 March.[22]

The lengthy and important document began with the attempt of the 1763 Proclamation to remove the two chief causes of Indian discontent: the encroachment on their lands had been checked by prohibiting settlement beyond the boundary of their hunting-grounds, and the abuses of white traders curbed by a system of licences. These arrangements had been temporary, and it was time to reassess the situation. The two Superintendents, Johnson and Stuart, should be retained to deal with Indian complaints, and the desirability of their continuing to negotiate boundary lines with the tribes was reaffirmed. They would also be needed to handle matters affecting more than one colony. A maximum annual budget of £8,000 was proposed for these purposes.

Neither the Superintendents nor the army were to control or regulate the trade with the Indians, for no general plan was applicable to all the different Indian nations: confining trade to certain specified places was unsuitable for the nomadic northern tribes and impracticable for the western Indians. The expense of the existing arrangements was moreover quite disproportionate to the value of the trade. Control of this was to be returned to the individual colonies, a situation admittedly unsatisfactory in the past and one that might need future attention: but the Board hoped that the colonies now perceived that Indian goodwill was

[22] *JCTP 1768–1775*, pp. 6, 11, 14; Alvord and Carter, op. cit., pp. 182–3. For the report see ibid., pp. 183–204.

the key to profits and peace. Those changes would reduce to three the forts needed for trade, Detroit, Niagara, and Michillimachinac, at the north-east corner of Lake Michigan. The army should judge how many other forts would be required for military purposes.

These suggestions constituted one significant policy decision, and on the most important proposal, for the establishment of new colonies, the Board had ventured into a consideration wider than the Shelburne guide-lines pointing to an affirmative answer. Beginning with the warning that if new colonies were envisaged the Board could not recommend any reduction of military expenditure, the report considered the proposals for the three new colonies, one at Detroit, one at the mouth of the Ohio, and one in the Illinois region. This idea of inland colonies was an entirely new concept, for British policy hitherto had always been to confine settlements to coastal areas. The traditional and accepted motives for colonization were the fishing industry, the provision of naval stores and of potential naval bases, and, of course, commerce. Having thus examined 'the proposition of colonising in the interior country . . . as a general principle of policy', the Board then considered the detailed case in question. Geography would prevent such inland colonies, 1,500 miles from the sea, being a valuable market for British trade, and the Board favoured instead continuance of the existing policy of encouraging settlement of Nova Scotia, Georgia, and the Floridas. Other claims made for new colonies received short shrift. Such colonies would not be able to compete with New Orleans in the fur trade, and that trade might in fact suffer unless the Indians were left 'undisturbed in the possession of their hunting-grounds'. Nor did the Board think they would afford any protection to the old colonies. Even the long-term reduction of military costs could not be assessed. The army could supply the government needed by the few French settlers south of the Great Lakes. No recommendation about the desirability or otherwise of the proposed new colonies was made, but these observations clearly pointed to a negative response.

In this instance doing nothing positive was itself a policy decision, and that was what happened. A cabinet meeting, with Lord Barrington present by invitation, met to consider the Board of Trade report on 11 March, but postponed any decisions for a week.[23] Benjamin Franklin read the omens correctly, writing to his son the next day that 'the purpose of settling the new colonies

[23] *PCBG*, p. 34.

seems at present to be dropped, the change of administration not appearing favourable to it'.[24] The cabinet on 18 March took no formal decision about the new colonies, but approved most of the suggestions in the report. Detroit, Niagara, and Michillimachinac were to be maintained and garrisoned. So were three other forts: either Crown Point or Ticonderoga on the route between New York and Quebec; Fort Chartres or some other post in the Illinois country; and, for the present, Fort Pitt. Gage was to be instructed accordingly, and it was left to his discretion whether to keep any or all other forts, with a recommendation to abandon as many as possible. The cabinet approved both the continuation of the Indian Superintendents in the manner proposed by the Board, and the appropriate instructions to them and the colonial governors concerning the boundary.[25]

Barrington had not been able to attend, but told Gage privately on 4 April that the military recommendations had been based on the minute of a consultation between Hillsborough, Adjutant-General Edward Harvey, and himself. Unfortunately their recommendations for a more or less complete evacuation of the wilderness had been watered down as a result of two dissentient opinions in the cabinet, 'though not the most weighty of the meeting'. One was presumably Shelburne, since the implication of such troop withdrawals was contrary to westward expansion. Barrington, therefore, confidently and confidentially advised Gage that he could proceed with military evacuation as far and as fast as he wished, and that he might even recommend the abandonment of Forts Chartres and Pitt, and Crown Point, if he so desired.[26]

This advice was unnecessary, for Hillsborough had already taken steps towards the same end. On 27 March the American Secretary sent to George III draft copies of the documents that would formally execute these cabinet decisions, a dispatch to Gage and a circular letter to the colonial governors. In the former, Hillsborough, in the words of the King's approving comment, had 'restored the original opinion of the majority at the meeting without greatly deviating from the words of the [cabinet] minute'. George III suggested that he should circulate to everyone who had been present copies of the drafts so as to obtain 'the concurrence of the majority in the mode you have digested this most weighty

---

[24] *Franklin Papers*, XV, 74.
[25] Cabinet minute (misdated 19 Mar.), PRO 30/29/3/2, f. 103. Another copy is printed in Alvord and Carter, op. cit., pp. 219–20.
[26] *PCBG*, pp. 35–6.

business'.[27] This evidently led to altercation and consequent delay, for on 10 April Hillsborough told George III that he would see Grafton and endeavour 'to get this dispatch put into such a shape as may answer your Majesty's intentions and at the same time satisfy His Grace. I can clearly perceive whence this trouble comes.'[28] Grafton was probably acting as mediator between cabinet colleagues rather than as a dissentient voice. Not until 15 April did Hillsborough send the circular to the governors[29] and a lengthy dispatch to Gage. This informed him, concerning the project for new colonies, that 'His Majesty has doubts concerning the utility of establishments in such remote situations'; and it strongly urged the evacuation of all forts except those named unless 'absolutely necessary for public safety in general'.[30] This would have been the alteration of emphasis from the cabinet minute commended by George III.

If Hillsborough and the Board of Trade had blocked one path to western expansion, they were unable to close another. On 23 December 1767 the Board had urged upon Shelburne the desirability of a final settlement of the northern boundary line provisionally agreed between the Iroquois Indians and Sir William Johnson in May 1765 at the end of the Pontiac Rising, but never ratified. The Indians had then also agreed to compensate the losses of traders by land grants around Fort Pitt.[31] John Stuart was already negotiating a boundary with the southern Indians from Florida up to the Cherokees west of Virginia, authorized to terminate his line where the Kanhawa River met the Ohio, Johnson being instructed to end his line at the same place when on 5 January 1768 Shelburne gave him authority to proceed.[32] Hillsborough on 15 April informed Johnson of the cabinet decisions of 18 March and specifically ordered 'that the line described in the report of the Board of Trade shall be notified and confirmed in every part, and the colonies required to enact the most effectual laws for preventing all settlement beyond such line'.[33] When Johnson pointed out, through his deputy, that the northern part of his line needed to be extended to continue across New York, Hillsborough gave him the authority to do so on which he had by then already presumed.[34] A careful reading of Johnson's acknowledgement of

[27] *Corr. of George III*, II, 13–14.
[28] Ibid., II, 18–19.
[29] *NYCD*, VIII, 55–6.
[30] *Gage Corr.* II, 61–6.
[31] *JCTP 1763–1767*, p. 441.
[32] *NYCD*, VIII, 2, 160–1.
[33] Ibid., VIII, 57–8.
[34] Ibid., VIII, 76–7, 102.

his instructions on 17 August should have rung alarm-bells in Whitehall.[35]

My duty is solely to treat with, and obtain a cession for and on behalf of the Crown of a tract of country along the frontiers, the rear of which is to be the boundary line between the English in general and the several Indian nations, agreeable to which I mean to act, according to my best judgement, and as correspondent as possible with the line described on the map transmitted by your Lordship.

Johnson was reserving considerable discretion for himself, and with ulterior motives. He was heavily involved in land speculation, and had arrangements of mutual benefit with such other interested parties as Proprietor Thomas Penn of Pennsylvania. Many friends and acquaintances saw this boundary negotiation as the opportunity to realize old and new hopes, and Johnson did not let them down.[36] After weeks of difficult negotiation and after £10,460 in local currency and presents had been given to the Indians, the final treaty line agreed at Fort Stanwix on 5 November was west of the 1765 line for much of the way. The Ohio boundary was taken from north of Fort Pitt right down to the Cherokee (now Tennessee) River, some 400 miles beyond the Kanhawa boundary authorized by the Board of Trade. Johnson's excuse was that this extra land between the Kanhawa and Cherokee Rivers, which the Board of Trade understood belonged to the Cherokees, was claimed by the Iroquois and that to refuse what he said was their voluntary offer of it would have cast insulting doubt on their right. The treaty also included private cessions to compensate traders for wartime losses. When on 18 November Johnson sent Hillsborough an account of the negotiation, he claimed that the treaty had to be accepted without alteration, for he had staked his reputation with the Indians on it. Otherwise the cost and effort would have been wasted.[37]

The acquisition of all this new territory between the Kanhawa and Cherokee Rivers was contrary to official policy on inland settlements and threatened the financial economies anticipated from military evacuation of the Mississippi and Ohio valleys. Without waiting for a cabinet meeting Hillsborough wrote to reprimand Johnson on 4 January 1769 for departing from the

[35] Ibid., VIII, 94–5.
[36] For the detailed story see Marshall, *JAS* 1 (1967), 149–79.
[37] *NYCD*, VIII, pp. 110–11. For his account of the negotiation see ibid., VIII, 111–34. There is a map of the new boundary at p. 136.

boundary line 'which . . . had been determined upon political and commercial principles to be the most desirable one' and that he had been ordered to obtain. The ministry, he wrote, considered 'the obtaining so large an additional tract of land in that part of the continent . . . as productive only of disadvantage and embarrassment'. Worse still, 'it will not only probably produce jealousy and dissatisfaction among the Cherokees, but will also tend to undo and throw into confusion those settlements and agreements for the other part of the Boundary Line, which the Superintendent for the Southern Department has concluded so ably and so precisely according to his instructions'. Stuart had negotiated his boundary line with the southern Indians up to the junction of the Kanhawa and Ohio Rivers, by treaties of 14 October and 12 November. The matter would be referred to the Board of Trade, but Hillsborough instructed Johnson that he should if possible 'settle the line according to your instructions' and explain to the Iroquois that the King declined to accept 'the large additional cession . . . out of his paternal tenderness and affection . . . and not from any doubts he entertained of their right to the lands'.[38]

Hillsborough's cabinet colleagues read 'this foolish letter', as Lord Camden designated it, 'in amazement'. They thought the American Secretary 'mad' in his objections to the treaty, and it was the 'unanimous opinion of them to confirm it in all its parts [if] the Six Nations [of the Iroquois] would not depart from its terms'.[39] The rest of the cabinet evidently thought that Johnson had concluded a very successful negotiation, and were less concerned than Hillsborough about the implications of such westward expansion. In retrospect this reaction in 1769 can be seen to anticipate the ministerial behaviour in 1772 on the same western policy that led to the American Secretary's resignation.

Hillsborough was isolated in the cabinet on this issue, and rumour had it that there was also a split between the American Secretary and the Board of Trade, which apparently feared that rejection of the Stanwix Treaty might precipitate an Indian war.[40] Hillsborough was therefore unable to secure any forthright condemnation of Johnson's behaviour when the Board made its

[38] Ibid., VIII, 144–5.
[39] *Johnson Papers*, VII, 17–18. The quotations are from a letter of 14 June from land speculator Samuel Wharton to Johnson, reporting comments by Lord Camden when at dinner with his fellow speculator and Chathamite MP Thomas Walpole the previous day. The leak was deliberate. See below, p. 63.
[40] Marshall, Thesis, p. 229.

report on the boundary arrangements on 25 April. Since Johnson's line afforded more scope to Virginia's claims than that negotiated by Stuart, the Governor and Council of that colony had now asked for Stuart's line to be altered, claiming that there already were settlements between the Kanhawa and Cherokee Rivers. Stuart in a letter of 12 February had therefore proposed a modification of his line to take in the actual settlements but not extending anywhere near the Cherokee River. This would have to be done by purchase, at an estimated cost of £2,000, which should fall on Virginia. The Board recommended this change, but only in this indirect manner a rejection of Johnson's line. The report did however propose nullification of the compensatory land grants made to traders, for Johnson had improperly permitted private negotiations to be introduced into the treaty. The claim that this had been according to the 1765 treaty was invalid, for that treaty made such grants conditional on royal approval.[41]

Hillsborough's objections to the Stanwix Treaty were public knowledge by May, and, ignorant of the situation within the cabinet, Johnson's friends in London feared that it would not be ratified.[42] The ministerial impasse was resolved when Hillsborough wrote to Johnson this face-saving letter of 13 May.

If you have not been able, in consequence of my letter of the 4th January last, to induce the Six Nations and their allies, to except out of the cession to his Majesty the lands lying south of the Ohio, below the Kanhawa, upon the ground and argument suggested in that letter, or if you shall be of opinion that insisting upon such an alteration will have the effect to excite jealousy and discontent, in that case his Majesty, rather than risk the defeating the important object of establishing a final boundary line, will, upon your report of this matter, give the necessary directions for the confirmation of it as agreed upon at Fort Stanwix.

Hillsborough, after this climb-down, had been allowed to have his way on less important matters. He informed Johnson that settlement was not to be permitted in the Kanhawa area beyond the borders of Virginia, and that the private grants to the traders would not at present be confirmed.[43] Decisions would be made when applications came for title to the land, as was to happen in the Vandalia scheme.

Camden, perhaps remembering Hillsborough's practice of wording colonial correspondence to suit his own purposes, as he had done

---

[41] *NYCD*, VIII, 158–63.   [42] *Johnson Papers*, VII, 16–17.
[43] *NYCD*, VIII, 165–6.

on 15 April 1768 and 13 May 1769,[44] was concerned that Johnson might not be able to interpret his letter correctly and understand 'the true meaning and design of the cabinet'. On 13 June he deliberately leaked the true position within the cabinet to MP Thomas Walpole, a man heavily involved in land speculation, rightly confident that he would at once pass on this information to Johnson's friends, and they to him.[45]

Johnson, on receiving Hillsborough's letter of 4 January, had replied on 26 June that he would be able to persuade the Indians to accept refusal of the cession between the Kanhawa and Cherokee Rivers, although he expressed uneasiness about the potential problems of Virginia settlers in that area. He believed that the Cherokees had given up the region twenty years earlier, and therefore pointed out that the Board of Trade instruction to use the Kanhawa River as the boundary had been based on a misapprehension in London.[46] Johnson changed his tune after receiving Hillsborough's letter of 13 May. Whether or not he had received the inside information leaked by Lord Camden, he read the situation correctly. A long justification on 21 August of his behaviour during the Stanwix negotiations ended with the blunt statement 'that since my late tour into the Indian country I find my former opinion so much strengthened, that I think it highly prudent to decline the mention of the affair unless I receive your Lordship's orders to the contrary'.[47] Hillsborough had to accept the *fait accompli* of the Treaty of Fort Stanwix.

The western policy of 1768 had been early undermined. Nor did the attempt to make each colony responsible for its trade and frontier prove much more than a pious hope. Gage had already warned Hillsborough on 3 February 1769 that the colonists did not believe that they either should or had to bear this burden. 'The trade has for some time been supported at the expense of Great Britain, and they seem to choose that it should be continued in the same hands. Without considering how many people here gain their livelihood by the Indian trade, its said the profits thereof centre in Great Britain.'[48] This selfish assumption was reinforced by the valid argument that the trade did not correspond with provincial frontiers; men from different colonies traded with the same Indian areas.

[44] See above, p. 58–9; below, p. 139–40.
[45] *Johnson Papers*, VII, 17–19.   [46] *NYCD*, VIII, 172–3.
[47] Ibid., VIII, 179–82.   [48] *Gage Corr.*, I, 216.

The colonies lacked not only the incentive to take effective action, but also the opportunity to work together. The British government deterred any attempt at co-operation, viewing inter-colonial meetings with suspicion. On 14 April 1770 Hillsborough criticized an initiative in this direction by Lieutenant-Governor Colden of New York, stating that such meetings had been 'of little utility', and 'of dangerous use' when delegates represented conflicting interests.[49] Since the colonies made virtually no effort to regulate Indian trade or control their frontier settlers, the Indians were soon complaining of a chaotic state of affairs, as Johnson reported to Hillsborough on 14 August 1770.[50] On 15 November the American Secretary therefore circularized seven colonial governors, from Quebec to North Carolina, enclosing part of Johnson's letter and ordering them to recommend to their councils and assemblies 'in the strongest manner' the need for regulations to prevent trade abuses and frontier violence.[51] But when this command was interpreted as a call for a conference, and Governor Dunmore of New York summoned one for December 1771, Hillsborough acted to prevent the meeting. On 14 June 1771 the Privy Council, on a Board of Trade recommendation, disallowed an act of Virginia for appointing delegates.[52] News of this decision deterred other colonies from taking similar action, and no delegates at all went to New York.[53] Before his resignation Hillsborough had accepted the failure of the attempt to transfer the responsibility and cost of the Indian problem to the colonies: for he made this comment to Gage on 18 April 1772.[54]

I cannot but think that any meeting of commissioners for the purpose of settling arrangements for the Indian trade would be altogether as fruitless as the measure itself is improper and impolitic, and altogether it appears to me to be highly unreasonable that the Crown should bear the expense of smiths, interpreters, etc., yet I see no effectual remedy to this inconvenience . . . until men's minds shall be better reconciled to that which I think the only sensible proposition upon this head, viz. the regulation of Indian affairs upon some general plan by Act of Parliament that shall at the same time create a fund of duties upon the trade for defraying the expense of it.

With the situation deteriorating all the time Johnson made one last effort to prod the British government into action after news reached America late in 1772 that Dartmouth had replaced

[49] *DAR*, II, 76-7.   [50] Ibid., II, 163-7.
[51] Ibid., II, 256-7.   [52] *JCTP 1768-1775*, pp. 257-8.
[53] *NYCD*, VIII, 288.   [54] *Gage Corr.*, II, 143-4.

Hillsborough as American Secretary.[55] But Dartmouth, in his reply on 3 February 1773, was as unwilling as Hillsborough to risk Parliamentary legislation.[56]

The advantages of a regular plan for Indian trade are apparent and the want of it in the present situation is very much to be lamented. But as I apprehend there is not sufficient authority in the Crown for the execution of such a plan; and as the colonies do not seem disposed to concur in any general regulations for that purpose, I am at a loss to suggest any mode by which this important service can be otherwise provided for than by the interposition of the authority of the supreme legislature, the exertion of which would be in such a case unadviseable until truth and conviction have removed the unhappy prejudices which have so long prevailed in the colonies on this subject.

The consequences of the failure to place responsibility for Indian affairs on to colonial shoulders were worsened by the successful implementation of the other finance-saving expedient of the new western policy, the military evacuation of as much of the wilderness as possible. This took some time to initiate. Hillsborough continually had to inform Gage that nothing had been decided, as on 17 February 1770 when he admitted the need for prompt action, at least with respect to the remote and consequently expensive Illinois area on the north Mississippi.[57] Misunderstanding may have caused Gage and Hillsborough to be at cross purposes, for Barrington sent this private comment to Gage on 1 July 1770. 'I continually press Lord Hillsborough to remove the troops from the Mississippi and the Ohio, but he says you do not approve the abandoning Forts Chartres and Pitt.'[58] Gage's confidential reply on 8 September made his position clear. 'I wish most sincerely that there was neither settler or soldier in any part of the Indian country, and that England was free of both the trouble and expense of Indian affairs.'[59] Barrington returned this comment on 1 November. 'I think the sentiments of the ministers are not different, though hitherto they have not acted with the decision which their stations require.'[60] The Illinois country presented a dilemma, and since it was the most distant area nothing else could be decided until this was resolved. Hillsborough, as he commented to Gage on 31 July 1770, believed settlement of so remote a region to be contrary to the mercantilist principles of empire, but there was no other way of

[55] *DAR*, V, 211–14.
[56] *NYCD*, VIII, 348–9.
[57] *Gage Corr.*, II, 88, 94, 98.
[58] *PCBG*, p. 78.
[59] Ibid., p. 84.
[60] Ibid., p. 85.

depriving New Orleans of its illegal fur trade.[61] Gage's reply on 10 November proposed abandonment of the Illinois area.[62] This was a clear response, and any misunderstanding had been clarified, but the Falkland Islands crisis of 1770–1 postponed any decision, for it raised the possibility of war on the Mississippi.[63] Gage was left to bemoan to Barrington the military expenditure about which he was more concerned than anybody.[64]

What I grudge the most, is paying the money of Great Britain for forts, posts, vessels and Indian presents, towards which America does not contribute one farthing. And I believe if we took less trouble about the savages, we should be full as friendly with them, as we are now. In short, my Lord, if the Americans will not pay to save their own scalps, they deserve to lose them.

The cabinet at last came to a decision on 1 December 1771, authorizing the evacuation, if Gage thought fit, of Fort Chartres, which was anyway in danger of falling into the Mississippi, and of Fort Pitt on the Ohio, since its sole military value was to maintain communications with the Illinois area: but such Lakes posts as Detroit and Michillimachinac were to be retained.[65] Hillsborough's letter of the same date reached Gage on 22 February 1772, and he acted promptly.[66] In August the Chartres garrison arrived at Fort Pitt, and orders were at once issued for the evacuation of that post in turn. By the beginning of 1773 Gage had abandoned twenty-four forts in the Mississippi and Ohio valleys.[67] Only one remained in the interior, at Kaskaskia in the Illinois, where Dartmouth instructed Gage to retain the small garrison since there had been Indian trouble.[68]

The failure to establish any successful solution for the Indian problem and the withdrawal of the army from the interior constituted an unpromising background for the most famous settlement project of the period, the plan for a colony in the Ohio Valley, to be named Vandalia. The evacuation of Fort Pitt in late 1772 was thought by supporters of this scheme to be an event that would 'greatly impede the settlement of the new colony, and which has already alarmed and discouraged many people from

---

[61] *Gage Corr.*, II, 107–10.
[62] Ibid., I, 274–81.   [63] Ibid., II, 124–5.   [64] Ibid., II, 580.
[65] *HMC Dartmouth MSS*, II, 81.
[66] *Gage Corr.*, I, 318–19; II, 137–8.
[67] *PCBG*, p. 108; Marshall, Thesis, pp. 220–1.
[68] *Gage Corr.*, II, 511–12.

settling to the westward'.[69] But Sir William Johnson was to reverse the argument by urging on Hillsborough's successor Dartmouth that the lawless chaos of the Ohio area was an additional reason to establish a proper government there.[70]

Vandalia was to be in the area east of the Ohio whose cession had been negotiated by Johnson at the Treaty of Fort Stanwix.[71] Many of the speculators who had been concerned in the abortive Illinois Company were involved in the scheme, notably Philadelphia businessman Samuel Wharton, who both before and after the Stanwix treaty was buying up the claims of the traders who were to be compensated by Indian land grants. In 1769 Wharton went to London to put together a project that became ever more ambitious. Among those involved in America was Benjamin Franklin's son William, then governor of New Jersey, and Johnson's deputy George Croghan, soon to be joined by Johnson himself. In Britain Wharton built up a formidable lobby drawn from across almost the entire spectrum of British politics. His early London contacts were Benjamin Franklin and Thomas Pownall, though the latter was to drop out. The banker MP Thomas Walpole, a Chathamite, soon became so prominent that the project was often known as the Walpole Company, and negotiations were usually conducted in the names of Walpole, Franklin, Wharton, and former MP John Sargent. Among other influential men early drawn in were three more MPs Richard Jackson, who was Solicitor to the Board of Trade from 1770, Grenvillite Thomas Pitt, and Sir George Colebrooke, the banker and merchant prominent in the East India Company. Later useful contacts, all with shares, included the two Treasury Secretaries John Robinson and Grey Cooper, Anthony Todd of the Post Office, Lords Hertford and Temple, and, after he left office, Lord Camden. The tentacles of Vandalia were subsequently to reach even into the cabinet.

On 14 July 1769 Wharton formally submitted a petition to the Treasury, offering to pay the £10,460 costs of the Stanwix Treaty in return for a land grant of 2,400,000 acres in the Ohio valley, and his associates soon constituted themselves into the Grand Ohio Company. The proposal was referred to the Privy Council on 4

[69] *Franklin Papers*, XIX, 363–4.
[70] *NYCD*, VIII, 315–16.
[71] For full surveys of this episode see Marshall, Thesis, pp. 226–50, and *EHR*, 80 (1965), 717–39; Sosin, *Whitehall and the Wilderness*, pp. 181–210; Rees, Thesis, pp. 277–302; and Hamer, Thesis, pp. 300–29.

August and to the Board of Trade on 20 November.[72] Hillsborough as an anti-expansionist was opposed in principle to any such scheme, but at first preferred a deceptive snare to overt hostility. When the Company's representatives met the Board of Trade on 20 December the American Secretary unofficially suggested that the application should be for 20,000,000 acres, sufficient for a separate new colony, believing that this would prove to be too expensive a purchase. The Company accepted the idea at face value, and Hillsborough's trap failed when Grafton's Treasury Board on 4 January 1770 accepted this bid without raising the price.[73] The next hurdle to surmount came in the form of protests from older land companies, made by George Mercer and Arthur Lee on behalf of the Ohio and Mississippi Companies respectively: but the Mississippi Company dropped out, and in May the Ohio Company withdrew its objections on being given shares in the new enterprise.[74]

With the way now apparently clear Wharton wasted no time. On 8 May 1770 the Grand Ohio Company petitioned the Privy Council for a grant, describing the location of the proposed new colony as extending some sixty miles down the Ohio beyond the Kanhawa River, thus including much of the extra land negotiated by Johnson at Fort Stanwix. The claim also covered most of the area between the Ohio and the three old colonies of Virginia, Maryland, and Pennsylvania.[75] The Council's Committee on Plantation Affairs referred the matter to the Board of Trade on 25 May;[76] but counter-claims came from the colony of Virginia, pitting the case of small settlers against the Company's speculators, and this situation gave Hillsborough the opportunity of causing further delay. On 15 June 1770 the Board of Trade, reviving a procedural practice that had lapsed twenty years before, resolved 'that it was a matter of too great importance for them to give an opinion upon without the advice and assistance of the great officers [of state] who are members of the Board', but whose membership had long ago been deemed nominal; and their attendance could not be arranged until at least October.[77]

No progress was made during the next year. Hillsborough was in

[72] *Acts PC Col.*, V, 202.
[73] *HMC Knox MSS*, p. 253. *JCTP 1768–1775*, pp. 152, 154–5, 163.
[74] *JCTP 1768–1775*, pp. 159, 163, 188.
[75] *DAR*, V, 166. Sosin, *Whitehall and the Wilderness*, p. 188, reproduces a sketch-map.
[76] *Acts PC Col.*, V, 202–3.   [77] *JCTP 1768–1775*, p. 194.

no hurry, and between November 1770 and May 1771 political attention in Britain was engrossed by the Falkland Islands Crisis and then by the spectacular clash in 1771 between Parliament and the City of London over the reporting of debates.[78] By this time Wharton had perceived the need for direct personal contacts within the administration, and at leat two cabinet ministers, the impecunious Southern Secretary Lord Rochford and Lord President of the Council Lord Gower were persuaded to accept shares.[79] On 11 July 1771 Rochford convened a cabinet of those members still in London to discuss the subject. Lord Chancellor Apsley, Lord North, and Rochford spoke in favour of the grant, with only Hillsborough opposing it. The meeting agreed that a full cabinet was to decide the matter by a majority vote, but Gower, First Lord of the Admiralty Lord Sandwich, and Northern Secretary Lord Suffolk all failed to return to London. Their absence may have been deliberate, for Wharton understood that Hillsborough's colleagues were reluctant to override a fellow minister in his own department.[80] The campaign meanwhile took on a new momentum within the government, with that expert political organizer John Robinson busy on the project. The return of Grafton to office as Lord Privy Seal was a further encouragement, and his political man of business Thomas Bradshaw sounded Hillsborough himself in November, reporting back that the American Secretary had declared 'that his own opinion was immovably fixed, as to the policy of not suffering settlements over the mountains, but at the same time he mentioned, that he would be governed by a majority of the cabinet, *and he wished his opinion might be overruled*, as so many of his friends were concerned, in what he called a very advantageous business'.[81]

On 12 December Rochford summoned another cabinet, which ordered an immediate report from the Board of Trade. This was finally drafted on 15 April 1772 and signed a fortnight later.[82] It reaffirmed the 1763 and 1768 policy of prohibiting inland colonies: 'the confining the western extent of settlements to such a distance from the sea coast as that those settlements should lie within the reach of the trade and commerce of this kingdom upon which the strength and riches of it depend, and also of the exercise

[78] For these events see respectively Goebel, *Struggle for the Falkland Islands*, pp. 271–410; and Thomas, *BIHR*, 33 (1960), 86–98.

[79] Sosin, op. cit., pp. 200–1.   [80] Marshall, *EHR*, 80 (1965), p. 727.

[81] Ibid., pp. 728–9, quoting a letter of Samuel Wharton.

[82] *JCTP 1768–1775*, pp. 293, 297, 299.

of that authority and jurisdiction which was conceived to be necessary for the preservation of the colonies in a clear subordination to and dependence upon the mother country'. That was why every project for inland colonies had hitherto been rejected. The report stated the necessity of avoiding conflict with the Indians, in view of earlier assurances about their hunting-grounds, and then systematically disposed of all the arguments for the new colony, as by the statements that 'the pretence of forming barriers will have no end . . . and there is room enough for the colonists to spread within the present limits for a century to come'. The conclusion was unequivocal. 'Upon the whole, therefore, we cannot recommend to your Lordships to advise His Majesty to comply with the prayer of this memorial, either as to the erection of any parts of the lands into a separate government or the making a grant of them to the memorialists; but on the contrary, we are of opinion that settlements in that distant part of the country should be as much discouraged as possible.'[83]

This report was to prove waste paper. Gower used his position as Lord President of the Council to rule that the Committee on Plantation Affairs on 5 June should ignore it and proceed on evidence submitted by the Grand Ohio Company. Hillsborough and Barrington, as well as Lord North, were among those present to hear testimony so perfunctory and unconvincing as to suggest that the decision had in reality already been made. Barrington was scathing in his later comment to Gage about these proceedings. 'It is amazing that so material a point of government should have been determined on a cursory examination of witnesses whose names had been never heard, and whose faces had been never seen before, brought by parties interested in the event, and examined *ex parte* only.'[84]

The Committee was scheduled to make a decision on 1 July. On the previous day North asked Gower for a postponement, since Hillsborough felt 'obliged in honour to resign' if the grant to the Grand Ohio Company was approved. One ground for delay, North suggested, lay in the circumstance that since the evidence given before the Council's Committee had not been submitted to the Board of Trade there was sufficient cause for a new reference to that Board.[85] This plea failed. Neither Hillsborough nor North

---

[83] *DAR*, V, 79–89.

[84] *PCBG*, p. 109. For summaries of the proceedings seem Hamer, Thesis, pp. 312–13; and Sosin, op. cit., pp. 203–4.

[85] PRO 30/29/1/14, ff. 635–8.

attended the Committee meeting of 1 July, when only Lord Barrington opposed the grant, Gower, Rochford, and Suffolk being among those in favour.[86] Partiality was the hallmark of the Committee's decision. One pretext for ignoring the Board of Trade report was that 'the most material part' of the evidence had not been produced at that Board, and yet on 28 March the Grand Ohio Company had declined the Board's invitation to submit further evidence.[87] The Committee disregarded the Board's contention that there was abundant land for settlement in the seaboard colonies and accepted instead the pragmatic argument that settlement in the Ohio valley was already in progress and would require a form of government. And by the claim 'that the lands in question do not lie beyond the reach of advantageous intercourse with this kingdom' the Committee professed to be acting in accordance with the mercantilist view of empire. The Committee's report therefore recommended acceptance of the petition and the creation of the settlement into 'a separate government'.[88]

This decision precipitated the ministerial crisis North had sought to avoid. The episode has sometimes been portrayed as a political conspiracy, a view based on the opinions of three famous contemporaries. Horace Walpole thought that North feared a plot of Bedfordites Gower, Sandwich, and Weymouth to oust him, though Walpole himself believed the aim was merely to replace Hillsborough by Weymouth.[89] Edmund Burke also suspected a scheme to obtain an office for Weymouth.[90] Benjamin Franklin thought that Hillsborough's colleagues eagerly seized the opportunity to get rid of him.[91] But none of those three men, so often cited as sources, possessed inside information as to what was going on within the administration. The correspondence of Lord Gower concerning this matter reveals no Bedfordite desire to get rid of Hillsborough.[92] It was Rochford, not himself a Bedfordite, who for motives of his own was the driving force in the cabinet behind the Vandalia project. Hillsborough's colleagues may indeed have been astonished at the American Secretary's behaviour,

---

[86] Rees, Thesis, p. 291.

[87] *JCTP 1768–1775*, p. 294.

[88] *DAR*, V, 166–8.

[89] H. Walpole, *Last Journals*, I, 126–7.

[90] *Burke Corr.*, II, 327.

[91] 'His brother ministers disliked him extremely . . . so seeing that he made a point of defeating our scheme, they made another of supporting it, on purpose to mortify him, which they knew his pride could not bear.' *Franklin Papers*, XIX, 243.

[92] PRO 30/29/1/14, ff. 635–64.

in view of his professed desire the previous November to be overruled by a cabinet majority.

North's sustained effort to keep Hillsborough in the ministry prolonged the crisis throughout July and involved George III himself. On 4 July North asked Gower for delay of the Committee's report to the Privy Council, or its recommittal because of the need to consult Gage and Johnson, so that he could 'preserve the administration as it is'.[93] Rochford, pressing Gower for final settlement of the grant, was willing to meet North half-way. 'If it is wished, by any of the cabinet, though I believe Lord North is alone, that this should be postponed for six weeks or two months, to a certain day, in order to give Lord North time to endeavour to hit on some scheme that would reconcile all parties, there would be less objection to it, but sending to Virginia or the Indians is absurd.'[94] The hitherto absent Suffolk offered his services as a mediator on 21 July, but by then it was too late. The King told him next day that Hillsborough was intent on resignation.

I find Lord North takes the thing much to heart, and has certainly been actuated upon by Lord Hillsborough. . . . Lord North's natural good nature and love of indecision, added to too much precipitation in Lord Rochford, and suspicion in Lord Hillsborough, with want of confidence in all the parties have brought this to the present strange situation.

The King had made it clear that he did not want to retain Hillsborough at the expense of Gower, who had threatened to resign;[95] and this gives some credence to Benjamin Franklin's surmise about George III's attitude. 'The King too was tired of him, and of his administration, which had weakened the affection and respect of the colonies for a royal government.'[96] North reported the outcome to the absent Lord Chancellor early in August. 'This unpleasant business has not ended as I wished. Notwithstanding all my endeavours Lord Hillsborough is bent upon resigning.'[97] Lord Weymouth was offered the American Secretaryship by 1 August, and refused because he did not consider it equivalent in rank to the other Secretaryships. North then offered it on 3 August to his own step-brother Lord Dartmouth, who had accepted by 8 August.[98]

[93] Ibid., ff. 639–40.
[94] Ibid., f. 641. He agreed to a postponement of the report on 22 July: Ibid., f. 650.   [95] Corr. of George III, II, 369–70.
[96] Franklin Papers, XIX, 243.   [97] HMC Bathurst MSS, pp. 12–13.
[98] HMC Dartmouth MSS, II, pp. 86–7, HMC Knox MSS, p. 107. Corr. of George III, II, 376.

The other ministers, like George III and most contemporaries, saw Hillsborough's behaviour not as a stand upon principle but as foolish obstinacy. Rochford commented to Gower on 15 August: 'Hillsborough has in my opinion acted a very silly part, and has at last got the shitten end of the stick.'[99] But those closely associated with Hillsborough understood and supported his decision. 'He has resigned in perfectly good humour, because he did not choose to carry into execution a measure tending to settle the interior parts of America which he thoroughly disapproved', so Lord Barrington explained to Gage on 2 September. 'Nothing can be more incomprehensible to my understanding than this project, which I hope, after all, will not be executed; if it is, the public and the army will be again burdened by stations in the interior parts of America.'[100] Barrington therefore continued the campaign against the proposed colony, and the next month sent to North, Dartmouth, and Gower extracts from a letter by Gage on 5 August criticizing inland settlements.[101] Gage himself had written to Hillsborough on news of his resignation.[102]

Be assured that your loss is regretted, by all connected with the employment your Lordship filled with such distinguished abilities. . . . The firmness with which your Lordship opposed a project you judged pernicious to your country, and the noble part you acted afterwards, rather than be an instrument towards the carrying it into execution, has raised your Lordship in the esteem of the world, and you have retired with a mind conscious of an upright conduct, and with the applause of every honest man.

There was an ironic sequel to this episode. Hillsborough retired with an English Earldom, and with peace of mind, writing to Knox on 29 August: 'I did not, you know, wish to resign, but am not now at all sorry it was necessary that I should.'[103] But the Grand Ohio Company never got its colony. This outcome was the more remarkable in that Dartmouth was a man positively in favour of westward expansion, and himself a land speculator, though not in the Ohio valley. He naïvely accepted the argument that the new colony would control the white settlers and protect the Indians after Sir William Johnson on 4 November described the settlers as

[99] PRO 30/29/1/14, ff. 163–4.   [100] PCBG, pp. 105–6.
[101] PCBG, p. 107. For the letter see Gage Corr., II, 615–16. Gage approved Barrington's move: ibid., II, 631. He had on 10 Nov. 1770 written fully to Hillsborough on the subject: ibid., I, 274–81.
[102] Gage Corr., I, 339.
[103] HMC Knox MSS, p. 108.

'a lawless set of people' and claimed that the Indians were hoping that a formal colony would impose restraints on them.[104]

At first things went smoothly. The Privy Council adopted its Committee's report on 14 August, and directed the Board of Trade to report on the terms of settlement and prepare a plan of government.[105] The Board received this order on 2 November, but did not complete its report until 6 May 1773, a delay attributed to Bamber Gascoyne, a Hillsborough appointment to the Board.[106] The report suggested the usual constitution of a royal colony, with a nominated governor and council and an elected assembly. It was to be given the name of Vandalia, as a compliment to the Queen, said to be descended from the Vandals.[107] The Privy Council on 19 May referred the report to its Committee of Plantations, which on 3 July requested the opinion of Attorney-General Thurlow and Solicitor-General Wedderburn.[108] But Thurlow thought the proposed colony 'an infamous job',[109] and Wedderburn was by now an inveterate foe of Benjamin Franklin. Their report of 16 July raised legal objections on three grounds: the proposed method of land grants by joint tenancy would present intractable problems and prevent rapid settlement; nor would there be the other benefit of revenue, for the device of quit-rents was unsatisfactory; while the description of the boundaries was 'loose and uncertain'.[110] Supporters of the scheme remained confident that these difficulties would be overcome, but the project was a casualty of the final American crisis sparked off by the Boston Tea Party. The last official record was of a Company petition to the Privy Council in August 1774 asking for an end to the delay: it was buried in Committee.[111]

An examination of British policy for the west raises qualifications about, and perhaps even a question mark against, the assumption that it formed a significant contribution towards the break between Britain and her American colonies. That has often rested on the facile citation of such well-known decisions as the Proclamation Line of 1763 and the Quebec Act of 1774, with such

[104] Johnson, not a disinterested party, was replying to an enquiry of 2 September. For a general survey of Dartmouth's attitude to the west see Bargar, *Dartmouth*, pp. 68–73.
[105] *Acts PC Col.*, V, 208.
[106] *JCTP 1768–1775*, pp. 316, 351–4, 356; Bargar, op. cit., p. 71.
[107] *DAR*, VI, 134–42; Sosin, op. cit., p. 207.
[108] *Acts PC Col.*, V, 210.   [109] Bargar, op. cit., p. 73.
[110] PRO 30/29/2/3, ff. 256–7.   [111] *Acts PC Col.*, V, 210.

additional evidence as the leadership of land speculator George Washington in the War of Independence. But although Britain began with a formal policy of prohibiting westward expansion, American Secretary Hillsborough was evidently fighting a lone battle in the cabinet to maintain it almost from the time of his appointment in 1768, and it was effectively ended by the Privy Council decision of 1 July 1772. As a practical grievance it had never had much substance, since individual settlements over the mountains had proved impossible to check. Nor were the men in America who were actively leading the break with Britain, men like Sam Adams, much concerned with events on the remote frontier. And Benjamin Franklin himself, at the very time he was becoming alienated from Britain, had no reason to believe that Vandalia would not actually come into existence.

In so far as the question of the west worsened relations between Britain and the colonies it might even be argued that the boot was on the other foot. British politicians in London, and opinion-forming officials like Gage in America, developed a strong and growing resentment at colonial attitudes. Americans were refusing to pay for the cost of the military arrangements on the frontier and beyond, and they also declined to shoulder the financial and administrative burden of Indian relations. The British government was so far from applying pressure on them to do so that both Hillsborough and Dartmouth refused to resort to Parliamentary legislation in the matter. Yet the colonists, without incurring any of the burden, wanted to enjoy all the benefits of trade and settlement that derived from British possession of the wilderness. The men formulating British policy were fully apprised of the whole western situation, and knowledge of it would have contributed to the hardening of attitudes in Whitehall and Westminster.

5

A New American Crisis.
December 1767–November 1768

THE Stamp Act Crisis had erupted promptly and universally throughout the colonies, and had been resolved within a few months by a united ministry in Britain. The course of events during the second crisis over American taxation was to be very different. Colonial resentment at the Townshend duties was a plant of slow growth, in deed if not in word. No general meeting of colonial delegates ever took place. Not for nearly two years did there develop any effective boycott of British goods. Nor did this embargo have any significant impact on the formulation of ministerial policy. In Britain the administration was undecided as to what it should do; a state of mind induced both by uncertainty and doubt as to the gravity of the colonial situation and by a difference of opinion among ministers as to whether to adopt coercive or conciliatory measures. Nor did the opposition factions, intent though they were on criticism of whatever proved to be official policy, agree upon or even produce any positive view on the American crisis. In sharp contrast to the clarity of issues in the first clash of 1765–6, there was a general sense of confusion in Britain over the American question.

News of the Townshend duties reached the colonies when the assemblies were in recess during the summer of 1767. Initial responses therefore took the form of unofficial complaints made privately in correspondence and publicly in the colonial press. British newspapers reprinted many American press items, as Massachusetts agent De Berdt reported in December to his Assembly Speaker Thomas Cushing. 'I am sorry there has been such a parade in the newspapers, which the enemies of America will construe an insult on their mother country, and several things in your papers have lately given offence, and it was with concern I saw them copied from paper to paper here.'[1] By the end of 1767 it was known in London that there was widespread discontent in America, and that a Boston town meeting of 28

[1] *De Berdt Letters*, pp. 328–9.

October had passed resolutions against the importation of fifty-four specified articles after 31 December.[2] This was not yet an overt challenge to Britain, for the ostensible reason adduced was economic necessity, the professed fear of a collapse of the Massachusetts economy; and this transparent excuse sufficed to allay immediate indignation in Britain, or so agent Johnson thought.[3] Other agents were less sanguine, Benjamin Franklin informing his son William on 29 December that 'the resolutions of the Boston people concerning trade make a great noise here. . . . The newspapers are in full cry against America.'[4] Indicative of the incipient gap between America and Britain is this private comment by Rockingham on 13 December. 'I can hardly think that the *act* of combination or association against the use of European commodities on the pretence of patriotism or economy, *is* or should be deemed *criminal*.Though I would say, that the *intention*, in those who set it on foot in Boston, is deserving of the *private* censure of every man, who means well either *here* or *there*.'[5] During the next few months British political attention and public opinion was engrossed by the forthcoming general election, due by March 1768, a circumstance that encouraged Franklin to think that 'nothing will be done against America this session'.[6]

Franklin was correct in this surmise, but American resistance spread rapidly in the same period. By February 1768 many towns in Massachusetts, Rhode Island, and Connecticut had followed the lead of Boston. More significant than this New England reaction was the publication in Philadelphia newspapers between 2 December 1767 and 18 February 1868 of the 'Letters of a Pennsylvania Farmer', written by wealthy landowner and lawyer John Dickinson. He explicitly challenged the right of Parliament to levy any taxes whatsoever, internal or external, on the colonies; but he conceded Parliament's right to regulate colonial trade and industry. The *Farmer's Letters* were widely reprinted throughout the colonies, and endorsed by many town meetings from Massachusetts to Georgia. This unequivocal denial of any Parliamentary right of taxation was a clear escalation of the conflict of opinion between Britain and her American colonies, and raised a controversial issue that it would not be easy to avoid or evade.

---

[2] The Boston resolutions were printed in the *London Chronicle* for 12 Dec. 1767. See also H. Walpole, *Memoirs*, III, 98.

[3] *Trumbull Papers*, pp. 248–9.   [4] *Franklin Papers*, XIV, 349.

[5] Wentworth Woodhouse Muniments, R1–912.

[6] *Franklin Papers*, XV, 15.

Dickinson looked for support to Massachusetts rather than to his own colony, where the conservative Assembly on 20 February merely instructed its agent to act with other agents in seeking repeal of the Townshend Duties Act. In Massachusetts the Assembly had already on 20 January voted a petition for repeal to the King.[7] It then began consideration of the idea of circularizing other assemblies to secure united colonial action, a suggestion put forward by Sam Adams and James Otis. This was opposed by some members as the first step to a meeting of delegates like the Stamp Act Congress of 1765, while others shrank from an open challenge to Britain when the attitude of other colonies was unclear. Before the end of the month the proposal had been rejected by 'a majority of two to one', so Governor Francis Bernard reported back to Britain. His joy was to be short-lived. As the Assembly's session drew to an end country delegates left for home. This circumstance and a fortnight's campaigning by Adams and Otis produced a majority for the circular letter on 11 February, when the earlier vote was erased from the record.[8] The Massachusetts Circular Letter began by stating that Parliament was 'the supreme legislative power over the whole empire'. But the Townshend Duties Act, as a tax, was an infringement of the 'natural and constitutional rights' of 'American subjects . . . because they are not represented in the British Parliament'. It was also inequitable that they should be taxed on British manufactures by duties in both Britain and America. Nor could 'any people . . . be said to enjoy any degree of freedom' if the Crown both appointed governors and judges and paid their salaries. The circular letter also complained of the financial burden of the 1765 Mutiny Act and of the patronage placed in the American Customs Board. Implicitly, by reference to 'the advantages arising to Great Britain from the acts of trade', the letter adopted the same position as John Dickinson concerning Parliamentary control over the colonial economy.[9]

This new constitutional stance of the colonies was not known in Britain until after the end of the expiring Parliament on 10 March, and no important debate on America took place in early

---

[7] Almon, *Prior Documents*, pp. 175–7.
[8] *Barrington–Bernard Corr.*, pp. 145–6; Gipson, *British Empire*, XI, 121–3.
[9] Almon, op. cit., pp. 191–3. The assembly, between 15 Jan. and 17 Feb., also sent letters to Shelburne, Rockingham, Camden, Chatham, Conway, and the Treasury Board: ibid., pp. 177–91.

1768. But the indefatigable Grenville, whose behaviour in November had revealed an obsession with the American question, saw in the Boston resolutions of 28 October an opportunity to embarrass the administration. In the House of Commons on 15 February he suddenly attacked the Chatham ministry for never having laid before the Commons papers requested by the House on 27 March 1766 concerning the state of manufacturing in America. The Boston resolutions provided a convenient launching pad for the charge that the colonies were a potential threat to Britain's own manufacturing industries, and agent Johnson noted that Grenville had seemingly found a dangerous line of attack.[10]

Upon this occasion, some severe things were said against the colonies, and it seemed to be the sense of several gentlemen, that they had good right to restrain the manufactures of America, especially if they were carried to such a pitch as to prejudice those of this country; that they ought even to do it very soon, and declare such meetings and associations as those held at Boston illegal and punishable, and especially that some method should be taken to prevent the manufacturers of this country from going in such numbers to America. These were, however, only the sentiments of particular members, upon which the House came to no resolutions.

On 17 February American Secretary Hillsborough therefore ordered the Board of Trade to prepare and lay before the Commons the accounts of manufactures in the colonies, and the Board's President Lord Clare next day presented to the House reports from a dozen governors.[11] They proved to be little to Grenville's purpose, as Benjamin Franklin told his son. 'They are all much in the same strain, that there are no manufactures of any consequence . . . These accounts are very satisfactory here, and induce the Parliament to despise and take no notice of the Boston resolutions.'[12] Grenville implied that the reports must be incomplete and withdrew from the field of battle with honour, declaring that if the administration promised to keep a close watch on the situation and to reprimand those governors who had been negligent or tardy in their replies he would not trouble the House with a motion. Appropriate noises were made from the ministerial bench, and the subject was dropped.[13]

Even George Grenville did not bring before Parliament the question of whether the behaviour of the New York Assembly, in

---

[10] *Trumbull Papers,* p. 265; *CJ,* XXXI, 609.
[11] *JCTP 1768–1775,* pp. 11–12; *CJ,* XXXI, 616–7.
[12] *Franklin Papers,* XV, 77.   [13] *Trumbull Papers,* pp. 265–6.

voting an adequate sum of money for the army units within the colony but omitting any reference to the 1765 Mutiny Act, could be construed as obedience to that act. Such an interpretation would give validity to any measures of that assembly since 1 October 1767, the date the New York Restraining Act had been due to come into operation in the event of the colony's non-compliance. On this point the administration was disposed to turn a blind eye to the equivocal nature of the colonial response. Grenville held a characteristically forthright view, making this comment to Thomas Whately on 13 April 1768. 'I do not see how the conduct of the assembly of New York, in giving a sum of money to the Crown, but refusing to take the least notice of the Mutiny Act, can be called a submission to that law, or represented as a discouragement to the popular opinions of America not being bound by our laws.'[14] But Grenville did not raise the matter for public discussion, and during 1768 the ministry buried the question with due constitutional propriety, after the law officers of the Crown, Attorney-General William De Grey and Solicitor-General John Dunning, gave this opinion to the Privy Council on 24 July: 'the only object of the Act of Parliament appears to us to have been fully accomplished by the supply of the money which is admitted to be competent to the service'.[15]

News of events in America caused the ministry to act during the interval between the end of the old Parliament on 10 March and the meeting of the new one on 10 May, but after the general election was over. America had nowhere been an issue except when Barlow Trecothick's opponents in London sought to exploit his colonial connections.[16] But among the MPs returned was outlawed radical John Wilkes, home from his French exile and chosen for the metropolitan county of Middlesex. There had been no attempt to arrest Wilkes by an administration determined to adopt a low profile. Wilkes then surrendered to justice, and on 10 May the so-called St George's Fields Massacre occurred when soldiers fired on a crowd outside the King's Bench prison where he was being detained, and several fatalities occurred.[17] The repercussions of that incident and, more importantly, of the subsequent

[14] *Grenville Papers*, IV, 266.
[15] PRO 30/29/3/2, ff. 106–7. For the formal procedures see *JCTP 1764–1767*, pp. 416–20; *JCTP 1768–1765*, pp. 9, 27; *Acts PC Col.*, V, 137–9.
[16] *Trumbull Papers*, p. 267. For the election see Namier and Brooke, *House of Commons 1754–1790*, I, 67–73.
[17] For a contemporary account of this event see Thomas, *London Journal*, 4 (1978), 221–6.

ministerial decision to expel Wilkes from Parliament were to dominate the British political scene for the next two years, both at Westminster and in the country at large; and America received only intermittent attention from November 1768 to March 1770.

During April 1768, preliminary consideration was being given in government circles to the question of Wilkes's expulsion from the Commons, but this fateful decision was postponed. American news required more urgent measures. From early March the administration knew of the constitutional doctrines being promulgated by Dickinson in the *Farmer's Letters*,[18] but it was news on 15 April of the Massachusetts Circular Letter that spurred ministers into action. Hillsborough at once brought it before the cabinet, and despite Shelburne's opposition received authority for the action he took.[19] This initial ministerial response took the form of two letters. On 21 April, Hillsborough sent a circular letter to all governors in North America, denouncing the Massachusetts Circular for encouraging 'an open opposition to and denial of the authority of Parliament'. The governors were instructed to use their 'utmost influence' to prevail upon their respective assemblies to ignore that letter, and this was intended to be and was interpreted as an order for, if necessary, prorogation or dissolution of assemblies to prevent any response.[20] The next day Hillsborough wrote to Governor Bernard. This letter stated that 'after the declared sense of so large a majority when the house was full' the Massachusetts Circular Letter had been voted in 'a thin house at the end of the session'. It was deemed to be 'contrary to the real sense of the assembly', which Bernard was to call upon to rescind the resolution. In the improbable event of a refusal to do so he was to dissolve the assembly and report the circumstances so that the matter could be laid before Parliament.[21]

In a conversation with William Knox a month later Hillsborough claimed full personal responsibility for this policy, and said that both Bernard and the other governors were under instructions to prevent recalcitrant assemblies from sitting. Any expenses of civil government left unprovided for because of such action were to be defrayed 'out of the American revenue', that is from the Townshend

[18] *Franklin Papers*, XV, 75.
[19] Fitzmaurice, *Shelburne*, I, 366–7.
[20] CO 5/241, f. 28. There are printed copies in *NYCD*, VIII, 58–9, and Almon, op. cit., pp. 220–1. This last was the one sent to the Governor of Rhode Island, who in effect published it by laying it before his assembly on 18 June.
[21] CO 5/765, pp. 6–8.

duties. This was a harder policy line than had been expected in Britain or America, and Knox, reporting the news to Grenville, made this comment. 'I think this measure will bring matters to a crisis very speedily, and if the colonies see this country is in earnest, they will probably make their option and take the part of peaceable subjects in future.'[22] If men like Knox approved this tough attitude, disbelief and dismay was the reaction of Connecticut agent Johnson when, after for long failing to obtain accurate information, he sent the news to his colony on 23 July.[23]

I hope, indeed, that I am misinformed and that so despotic a measure has not been in fact adopted; but it is certain they are enough offended at every measure taken there to prejudice the trade, and prevent the consumption of the manufactures of this country. The approbation, also, which the Farmer's Letters have so generally met with in America, gives much umbrage.

Johnson did not then know that the cabinet had already decided to send soldiers to Boston even before news came of violence there. The move was in response to two letters from that town. On 4 March Bernard told Secretary at War Lord Barrington that he did not even dare to ask his Council for permission to apply for soldiers;[24] and on 12 February the American Customs Board informed the Treasury that enforcement of the revenue laws would be impossible 'until the hand of government is strengthened'.[25] This plea, criticized then and later as groundless panic, was to be justified within a couple of months. Hillsborough enclosed copies of these letters with his 'secret and confidential' dispatch of 8 June to General Gage at New York. The army Commander-in-Chief was instructed 'that you do forthwith order one regiment, or such force as you shall think necessary, to Boston, to be quartered in that town, and to give every legal assistance to the civil magistrate in the preservation of the public peace; and to the officers of the revenue in the execution of the laws of trade and revenue'. That the ministry was not blindly risking confrontation can be seen in Hillsborough's request for a prudent officer to command this operation, 'a service of delicate nature and possibly leading to consequences not easily foreseen'.[26] Simultaneous orders were given to the Admiralty that one frigate, two sloops, and two cutters were to be sent to patrol Boston harbour. Three days later

[22] *Grenville Papers*, IV, 297–8.   [23] *Trumbull Papers*, p. 291.
[24] *Barrington–Bernard Corr.*, p. 148.   [25] CO 5/757, ff. 60–2.
[26] *Gage Corr.*, II, 68–9.

Hillsborough wrote a firm letter to Governor Bernard, informing him that his commission did not require him to consult the Massachusetts Council before acting. 'It is you to whom the Crown has delegated its authority and you alone are responsible for the due exercise of it.' He was being sent military assistance because it had been obvious 'for some time past, that the authority of civil power is too weak to enforce obedience to the law'.[27] This was the British government's riposte to defiance and incipient disorder in the colonies. It intensified the new crisis, but did not initiate it. Massachusetts was already in an uproar, and violence erupted there before news of any of these ministerial decisions reached Boston. Nor can the counter-circular to the governors be blamed for creating a colonial unity that would not otherwise have existed. The various assemblies had already begun to respond to the Massachusetts initiative before the arrival of Hillsborough's circular letter.

The political temperature in Massachusetts had been rising since February, with a feud between the governor and the assembly, and open defiance of the trade laws.[28] This exploded on 10 June when Boston custom officials impounded for smuggling the ship *Liberty*, owned by that prominent patriot John Hancock. Mob violence ensued, with attacks on the officials, resulting in personal injury and property damage; and, without as yet any military protection, four of the five Customs Board members took refuge in Castle William.[29] By an unlucky coincidence Hillsborough's letter to Governor Bernard arrived at this moment of confrontation. On 21 June Bernard informed the assembly of the British government's demand for repudiation of their circular letter, and within a few days the assembly knew of the threat of dissolution in the event of non-compliance.[30] Hillsborough's high-handed assumption and encouraging news from other colonies stiffened the assembly's attitude. When on 30 June it rejected by 92 votes to 17 a motion to rescind the resolution for a circular, the majority included some of Bernard's customary supporters. The governor then dissolved the assembly as it began to prepare a petition for his own removal.[31]

---

[27] CO 5/765, pp. 9–14.
[28] *Barrington–Bernard Corr.*, pp. 146–50, 157.
[29] For graphic details see Watson, *WMQ*, 20 (1963), 585–95.
[30] For the part of the letter communicated to the assembly see Almon, op. cit., pp. 203–4; for the part that was not, see ibid., p. 205.
[31] Ibid., pp. 206–13; Gipson, *British Empire*, XI, 152–7.

It is apparent that the Massachusetts Assembly would not have backed down even without the provocation of Hillsborough's arrogant demand. It is as obvious that the other colonial assemblies would have rallied round Massachusetts even if the American Secretary had never penned his counter-circular. The pattern of colonial defiance was patchy and prolonged only because some governors prevented their assemblies from meeting until late in the year: General Gage told Hillsborough on 19 August that several assemblies had been 'prorogued with design, it is supposed, to keep them out of the combinations though it is generally believed they will act with the rest as soon as they meet'.[32] The response of the different colonies varied in form as well as date, from official petitions to mere instructions to agents; but beneath the differences in timing and procedure there was a basic unanimity of objections to the Townshend duties clearly based on a denial of Parliament's right of taxation.

Some colonies had already responded to the Massachusetts initiative before the arrival of Hillsborough's circular letter. Petitions to the King had been voted by the assemblies of four colonies, New Jersey on 6 May, Connecticut on 10 June, and Maryland on 24 June having followed the lead in this respect of Virginia, which made the earliest and most direct response on 16 April. The council of the colony endorsed the assembly's claim not to be taxed without consent. The assembly then sent a memorial to the Lords and a remonstrance to the Commons as well as a petition to George III, and also authorized its Speaker to write to the Speakers of all the other American assemblies publicizing its decisions and exhorting them to similar action. He did so on 9 May. The British government was to view with particular concern and alarm not only this call to other colonies but also the council's behaviour, for in British eyes the constitutional function of that body was to give support to the governor.

Four other colonies, although not petitioning, had also given early indications of their intention to oppose the taxation. Pennsylvania on 20 February instructed its agent to press for repeal, and Georgia and South Carolina did so in April, while New Hampshire had sent a favourable reply to Massachusetts in March. There had therefore been some sort of positive response to the Massachusetts Circular from eight colonies before news came of the British attempt to prevent any such reaction. Later in the

[32] *Gage Corr.*, I, 190.

year three of these colonies strengthened their protest, while the other four that had hitherto been unable to act did so. Petitions were voted by the assemblies of New Hampshire on 27 August, Pennsylvania on 22 September, Delaware on 24 October, New York on 18 December, and Georgia on 24 December. That of Rhode Island voted an Address to George III on 12 December, and North Carolina did so on 5 December. By the end of 1768 a universal reaction of protest against the Townshend duties had surfaced in the thirteen colonies.[33] A significant aspect of the colonial response was that all the petitions and addresses were directed to the King. Parliament's role in the empire was deliberately ignored, although some colonies like Pennsylvania and Virginia had also sent protests to the Lords and Commons. The invariable riposte of governors had been a prompt prorogation or dissolution of the assemblies.

Colonial deeds did not as yet match words. Another boycott of British goods was the obvious way to bring Britain to heel, after the apparent success of such a tactic in the Stamp Act Crisis. But in 1768 a Boston initiative for a ban on imports from Britain failed to obtain significant support. On 4 March a meeting of Boston merchants voted to introduce such a prohibition, conditional on its adoption by other colonies. A meeting of New York merchants in April adopted a similar resolution to come into effect on 1 October. But the plan was killed by the refusal of the Philadelphia merchants, at meetings on 26 March and 25 April, to follow suit.[34] General Gage had always been sceptical of this tactic, writing privately to Lord Barrington on 10 March. 'Surely, my good lord, the people in England can never be such dupes as to believe that the Americans have traded with them so long out of pure love and brotherly affection. If they do not smuggle manufactures from other countries, they must take them from Britain, or go naked.'[35] Later in the year Gage feared that political opinion in Britain might be misled by colonial propaganda about the efficiency of a boycott. On 26 September he wrote to tell Hillsborough that New York and Boston were believed to be importing and ordering more manufactured goods from Britain 'than for many years past', and he warned the American Secretary not to be bluffed by the colonial tactics.[36]

[33] Gipson, op. cit., XI, 167–81.
[34] *Gage Corr.*, II, 468; Gipson, op. cit., XI, 181–2; Schlesinger, *Colonial Merchants*, pp. 114–19.
[35] *Gage Corr.*, II, 450.   [36] Ibid., I, 197.

The chief dependence of the Americans, is upon those in Great Britain, who either through an opposition to all measures of government, or for their private interests, they flatter themselves will betray the interests of Great Britain, to serve the purposes and designs of America. They rely greatly upon the influence of the merchants trading to America, and very much upon the manufacturers, whom they even hope will commit riots and tumults in their favour. These views gave birth to the project not to import goods, and they have their emissaries in England, who put various paragraphs in the newspapers concerning the people of Birmingham and other manufacturing towns, that they are starving for want of employment, through the resolutions taken in America not to import their manufactures.

The reason for Gage's concern was that both Boston and New York had by then made their own boycott agreements. Boston merchants on 1 August decided to send no further orders, to suspend all imports from Britain for one year from 1 January 1769, and to stop all imports of the duted goods until the taxes on them were removed. New York merchants followed on 27 August with a decision to cease imports from 1 November until the Townshend duties were repealed. Despite the pressure of these examples Philadelphia merchants refused to do the same until all other means of redress had been explored. The Pennsylvania petition of 22 September was followed on 1 November by a memorial from Philadelphia's merchants to British merchants and manufacturers.[37] By the middle of October it was known in London that other American ports had failed to follow the lead of Boston and New York.[38] The British ministry was not confronted by any serious trade embargo when it took cognizance of the colonial situation at the end of 1768.

The cabinet had already taken executive action to deal with the problems presented by events in Massachusetts and Virginia. On 19 July Hillsborough received three dispatches from Governor Bernard concerning the *Liberty* riots in Boston. He sent them to the King, and proposed an immediate cabinet.[39] But with ministers scattered in the country this proved difficult to arrange, and further details and more disturbing news arrived from the colonies. On 23 July the American Secretary obtained an eyewitness report of the Boston riots from that port's Controller of Customs, Benjamin Hallowell.[40] The day before Hillsborough received news

[37] Schlesinger, op. cit., pp. 120, 124–8.
[38] *Grenville Papers*, IV, 369–73.
[39] PRO 30/29/3/2, ff. 104–5; *Corr. of George III*, II, 35–6.
[40] *Grenville Papers*, IV, 319–20; *Barrington–Bernard Corr.*, p. 160.

of what had happened in Virginia, and suggested to George III that to save time 'four or five ships of war and a body of mariners' should be put in a state of readiness.[41] 'Everything wears the face of war', agent Johnson wrote, as military and naval preparations were being reported in the newspapers.[42] They were certainly proposed also by Treasury Secretary Thomas Bradshaw when he reported Hillsborough's news and views to Grafton on 22 July.[43]

He has received dispatches from Virginia of the most alarming nature, and thinks that colony in a much worse state, than even the colony of Massachusetts Bay. . . . He is of opinion, that Parliament should meet as soon as its forms will allow it. His Lordship seems really alarmed, and he is not apt to start at trifles. General Gage cannot send a great force to any part of America, and if that force should meet with a check, it is but too likely that the whole continent would join in actual opposition to government. The *Council*, as well as the Assembly of Virginia, have joined in the most indecent remonstrances against the late Act of Parliament, and they have called on the other colonies, to make it a common cause.

It is impossible to reconstruct the ministerial consultations before the policy decisions taken at a cabinet of 27 July, the first meeting attended by Grafton himself. During the preceding week contradictory rumours of ministerial discussions, decisions, and dissensions were rife.[44] So many meetings were being reported that agent Johnson hoped that indignation would cool. Stories of military coercion were balanced by one that Chathamite Lord Granby would be sent 'to visit the colonies and make report before any force is made use of'.[45] Ministers still believed the Massachusetts Circular Letter to be the work of a small unrepresentative minority, though some thought it 'little better than an incentive to rebellion', and De Berdt, after an interview with Hillsborough, warned Massachusetts that the administration was determined to uphold the authority of Parliament.[46] Popular rumour predictably focused on an alleged rift between Chathamite and Bedfordite ministers.[47] It is apparent that the reports of ministerial discord were much exaggerated, and there is no evidence that the cabinet was divided over the two important decisions formally taken on 27 July, the replacement of Sir Jeffrey Amherst as governor of Virginia by Lord Botetourt, and the dispatch of two more

[41] *Corr. of George III*, I, 36.
[42] *Trumbull Papers*, p. 293.
[43] Grafton MSS, no. 305.
[44] *Grenville Papers*, IV, 321–2.
[45] *Trumbull Papers*, pp. 293–4.
[46] *De Berdt Letters*, p. 336.
[47] Fitzmaurice, op. cit., I, 386; *Grenville Papers*, IV, 321.

regiments to Boston, this time from Ireland; and it is known that Shelburne did not oppose the latter decision.[48] The failure of the cabinet to devise any long-term policy was less the consequence of disagreement than of the need for fuller information and of Parliamentary sanction, since it was not within the power of the executive to alter or make laws, merely to enforce them.[49]

Both the decisions taken on 27 July had been canvassed and considered for some time before that cabinet meeting. The governorship of Virginia had long been a cause of colonial complaint and ministerial concern. Amherst had been appointed governor after his return to Britain in 1763, in recognition of his role as army Commander-in-Chief in North America during the Seven Years War. The post was a reward for past services, given on a clear understanding that Amherst would not have to perform the duties of the office. He had never since returned to America, and for nearly five years the colony had been governed by his deputy, Lieutenant-Governor Francis Fauquieur. It so happened that Virginia was the only American colony to have made permanent and full provision out of its own funds for the governor's salary. Other colonies, when requested to do the same by the British government, cited the fate of Virginia, which had found itself ruled by a deputy while its money was being spent in England. The appointment of a resident governor for Virginia could therefore be expected to be a popular move in America. It would also be a politic step. The colony had been foremost among those leading the opposition to Parliamentary taxation both in 1765 and now again in 1768. A resident governor should prove a curb on the spirits of the recalcitrant Virginians. The death of Fauquieur on 3 March provided an opportune occasion to make the change, and the Virginian news in July precipitated a prompt decision. The cabinet, without consulting Amherst beforehand, assumed that he would be unwilling to take up residence in the colony and sought a replacement.[50]

The choice of Lord Botetourt was Hillsborough's personal decision,[51] and the appointment was settled on 23 July,[52] four days

[48] *Grenville Papers*, IV, 332.

[49] *De Berdt Letters*, pp. 337–8. Hillsborough's colleagues must have soon disabused him of the notion that Parliament could be summoned in the depth of the summer recess.

[50] BL Add. MSS 42086, ff. 82–5, 106–9; printed in *Grenville Papers*, IV, 326–42, 344–7.

[51] Lord Albemarle told Rockingham on 14 Aug. that 'all the ministers deny having any share in it, and lay the blame on Hillsborough': Wentworth Woodhouse Muniments, R1-1089.   [52] *Grenville Papers*, IV, 350.

before its ratification by the cabinet. It led to a minor political storm. There were two apparent grounds for criticism, Botetourt's nomination for the post and the shabby treatment of Amherst. Some contemporaries suspected sinister political undertones, for Botetourt was widely regarded as a protégé of Lord Bute, still thought by many to have the private ear of the King; and in 1768 he had recently been impoverished by business failures. Hillsborough was therefore believed to be courting royal favour.[53] But what looked like a 'job' was not one. Neither Botetourt nor any patron of his had solicited the post, and he had no idea of going to America until the offer was made.[54] The initiative came from the American Secretary, who knew the problem of finding capable administrators for colonial governorships, and had identified Botetourt as one in need of such an office. Americans, and their friends in Britain, might well look askance at his political record on the colonial question. A Lord of the Bedchamber since George III's accession in 1760, he had been one of the court party who had opposed repeal of the Stamp Act in 1766; but under the Chatham administration he had supported ministers over America in 1767, even attacking the Stamp Act on 10 April.[55] Despite this volte-face, Connecticut agent Johnson, while describing him as 'of great affability, a soft address, attentive to business, and in a high estimation here' warned that 'from some things I have heard fall from him in the House of Lords, I fancy the Virginians will not find him so great a friend to American liberty as they could wish'.[56]

The issue of Botetourt's appointment paled into political insignificance by comparison with the controversy over the administration's treatment of Amherst.[57] Hillsborough's inept handling of this matter exposed him to criticism and gave offence not only to Amherst but also to the man who had been his patron and was still nominal head of the ministry, Lord Chatham. On 27 July, after cabinet endorsement that day of the decision to have a resident governor in Virginia, Hillsborough sent a letter to Amherst. The American Secretary stated that if Amherst would go to Virginia the King would be very pleased, and that if he declined to do so he would be given an official income equivalent

[53] H. Walpole, *Memoirs*, III, 161.   [54] *Barrington–Bernard Corr.*, p. 175.
[55] Simmons and Thomas, *Proceedings and Debates*, II, 95, 336, 449, 451, 452, 459, 499.
[56] *Trumbull Papers*, p. 295.
[57] For a fuller account of this episode see Rees, Thesis, pp. 172–90.

to the one he would forfeit as governor. Amherst heard that an official letter had been dispatched to him and called at the American Department the next day, the colonial crisis apparently having led him to expect a request for military advice or even reappointment as head of the American army. Instead Hillsborough handed him a copy of the letter. Amherst was, as expected, unwilling to go to America, and disposed to accept the loss of his governorship if he obtained some mark of favour as well as financial recompense. But he then found out from Botetourt and others that the effective decision about the Virginia governorship had been taken before this ostensible offer to him from Hillsborough of a choice between a resident governorship and pecuniary compensation. Amherst therfore demanded ample compensation for the treatment he had received. On 30 July he asked for a British peerage, a grant of the coal-mines on Cape Breton Island, and an income equivalent to the £1,500 he was forfeiting as Virginia's governor.[58] Despite warnings from Grafton that George III would find these terms unacceptable Amherst insisted on the Duke presenting them to the King on 10 August. George III agreed to an equivalent income being granted for life, but rejected the other two requests. Grafton explained to Amherst that the King had set his mind against any new peerage creations, and that there was a Privy Council prohibition on commercial working of the Cape Breton mines.[59] Amherst nevertheless spurned the pension and threatened resignation of his remaining military commands, the colonelcies of regiments in Britain and America. He carried out this threat at a personal interview with his sovereign on 17 August.[60] This loss of all his official sources of income left Amherst dependent on limited private means, and he was soon making obvious financial economies.[61] The ministry was left in the embarrassing situation of having made a political martyr out of a famous war hero.

General Conway, as a military man himself, was the obvious member of the cabinet to mollify Amherst, and by the end of August had virtually succeeded in doing so by the promise of a British peerage at the next creation.[62] Before Parliament met on 8 November the opposition had been deprived of the Amherst affair

---

[58] Grafton MSS, no. 695. [59] Ibid., nos. 689, 691–4, 696.
[60] Ibid., nos. 123, 690; *Corr. of George III*, II, 38–40; *Barrington–Bernard Corr.*, p. 166; *Grenville Papers*, IV, 351.
[61] *Grenville Papers*, IV, 354; *Burke Corr.*, II, 14.
[62] Grafton MSS, nos. 688, 690; H. Walpole, *Memoirs*, III, 162.

as a political weapon. For the administration, under royal pressure, added to the promise of a future peerage the restoration of Amherst's regiments and the bestowal of a pension;[63] and although the whole episode had attracted a great deal of attention in the press, public opinion was by no means altogether hostile to the ministry: here is Benjamin Franklin's judicious appraisal to his son.[64]

The sending a new chief governor to Virginia in the place of Sir Jeffrey Amherst made a noise for a while, but the public seems generally satisfied that the measure in itself was a right one, and that Sir Jeffrey's friends are in the wrong to make such a clamour about it, if indeed they are his friends that made the clamour. Something affronting in the circumstances is however supposed by some but denied by others, and perhaps the chief thing he has to complain of is, that the change was made a little hastily, and before any equivalent was given to him.

Such was the personalized nature of politics at the time that the Amherst affair engendered more immediate public interest than the other and much more significant decision taken by the cabinet on 27 July, the deployment of military force to subdue Boston. Gage had already been instructed by Hillsborough's letter of 8 June to send at least one regiment to that town. He had received and acted upon this order by the end of August, authorizing the dispatch there from Halifax in Nova Scotia of as many soldiers as Governor Bernard deemed necessary, under the command of Lieutenant-Colonel Dalrymple.[65] The actual force requested was to comprise two regiments. By late July the ministry knew that the situation in Boston had deteriorated into one of mob rule, with Governor Bernard helpless to maintain order, and the Customs Board having taken refuge in Castle William. The cabinet, ignorant of how many soldiers Gage would be sending to Boston, decided to order two more regiments there at once, from Ireland, and Hillsborough notified Gage of this intention on 30 July.[66] Gage received this letter on 26 September, and promptly cancelled preparations he was himself already making to send to Boston two more regiments from Florida.[67]

A sense of crisis prevailed in the political world of London during the autumn of 1768. Because armed conflict with the colonies did not commence until 1775, it is easy to overlook the

---

[63] *Trumbull Papers*, pp. 303–4.   [64] *Franklin Papers*, XV, 224.
[65] *Gage Corr.*, I, 191.   [66] Ibid., II, 72–4.   [67] Ibid., I, 195–8.

circumstance that as far as people in Britain knew it had already begun seven years earlier. During the summer many Bostonians had been professing their intention of resisting any military coercion, Sam Adams claiming that the British government could not even suppress riots in London and that unemployment created by the colonial boycott would soon cause further disturbances in Britain's manufacturing towns. On 3 September Governor Bernard released news of the imminent arrival of soldiers. Adams resorted to his power base, the Boston town meeting, filled by the mob and shunned by men of property. A meeting of 12 September demanded that Bernard should summon the assembly, a request already rejected on 13 June and 11 September. Correctly anticipating another refusal the meeting decided to circularize all Massachusetts towns for a meeting of delegates at Boston on 22 September. Other resolutions implied an intention of armed resistance, military preparations being advocated on the transparent pretext of a French invasion threat.[68]

Towards the end of October reports of these events reached Britain, where the purpose of the proposed Convention was widely believed to be the organization of resistance to the British soldiers. When on 27 October Hillsborough was informed that delegates from sixty-six towns had met in the Convention on 22 September the American Secretary panicked and unsuccessfully pressed George III for still more soldiers to be sent to Boston.[69] Alarmist feelings in Britain were reflected in two Grenvillite comments. Augustus Harvey wrote on 31 October that 'everything in America is as bad as it can be'; and William Knox the next day that 'the revolt of New England is now unquestionable. Private advices since the 22nd of September say the Convention had met and agreed to all the resolves of the town of Boston, and appointed inspectors to see that all the militia of the country were properly armed.'[70] Since the soldiers had already been ordered to Boston and there was no possibility of their recall, a clash of arms was deemed inevitable. British opinion did not flinch in this apparent moment of military confrontation. The prospect of war with the colonies was viewed with horror, but seen as a regrettable necessity; and in London there was every confidence that the army and navy would succeed in restoring Britain's authority in America.[71]

The two sides never came to blows. On 19 September the sobering news reached Boston of the approach of some 1,000

[68] Miller, *Sam Adams*, pp. 144–53.   [69] Grafton MSS, no. 529.
[70] *Grenville Papers*, IV, 394–5.   [71] *Trumbull Papers*, p. 300.

soldiers, and this caused even the most militant townsmen to have second thoughts about armed resistance. The Massachusetts Convention, far from organizing opposition to the arrival of the army, sought to prevent it. Some towns had refused to respond, others sent delegates pledged to adopt only constitutional means, and Sam Adams found himself outvoted by a moderate majority. The Convention, eventually comprising some 125 delegates from ninety-six towns and eight districts, petitioned Governor Bernard to call the assembly; but he stated that the Convention was illegal and refused to have any discussions with the delegates. The Convention otherwise merely sent to the King another copy of the petition of 20 January 1768, and deliberately prolonged its sitting until the British troop-ships were actually in sight, in order to prevent any rash action by Boston hotheads.[72] The two regiments from Halifax sailed into Boston harbour on 28 September, and quietly disembarked three days later under the guns of a naval escort.[73] The military presence was reinforced to a total of over 1,000 soldiers by the arrival of the two regiments from Ireland in mid-November.[74]

It was on 4 November that news reached Britain of this blood-less coup. Writing that day to Rockingham Barlow Trecothick said that he agreed in 'fearing that some unhappy incident may still arise in Boston' despite the moderation displayed by the Convention.[75] But a few hours later he sent this good news. 'By the ships arrived today I find the two regiments from Halifax were quietly landed in the town and quartered in the public buildings.'[76] And in a third letter of the same date he supplied further details. The Convention had decided to give quarters to the first two regiments at Castle William and to supply the provision specified by the 1765 Mutiny Act.[77] The immediate reaction in Britain was one of joy and relief. It was soon replaced by one of contempt for the Bostonians as vain blusterers whose bluff had been called.[78] But the pacific outcome refuted the contention of hardliners in Britain that the colonists were determined to resist by force the authority of Britain, and ripe for rebellion. The apparent collapse of colonial defiance would make it politically possible for Grafton to propose conciliation with Britain seemingly in a position of strength.

[72] Brown, *WMQ*, 26 (1969), 94–104; Miller, *Sam Adams*, pp. 154–62.
[73] *Gage Corr.*, I, 201; Gipson, op. cit., XI, 161–4.
[74] *Gage Corr.*, I, 208.
[75] Wentworth Woodhouse Muniments, R1-1112.
[76] Ibid., R1-1113 (a).   [77] Ibid., R1-1113 (b).
[78] *Trumbull Papers*, pp. 300–1.

6

The British Response: Negative.
July 1768–February 1769

THE decision to send the army to Massachusetts appeared a master-stroke, with the colonial bluff of violent resistance called, and Boston cowed. No policy of military rule was intended, Hillsborough assuring Massachusetts agent De Berdt on 25 August that the army had 'strict orders to preserve the peace and act under the civil magistrate, and that no unconstitutional methods shall be taken'.[1] The measure provided a breathing-space, an opportunity for long-term policy decisions to be formulated, and the general expectation was that this would be done when Parliament met towards the end of the year.

America was in the public eye throughout 1768, and news of colonial defiance had from the first produced a reaction that was generally hostile. As early as March the American background of Barlow Trecothick proved a liability when he was a candidate for London in the general election;[2] and in June, before the Boston riots of that month were known, De Berdt was reporting that 'very unreasonable prejudices prevail against America, both in the ministry and public'.[3] And this is agent Johnson's account of the reception of that news in late July.[4]

The impressions it at first made were surprising: the merchants were in fear for their property and their trade: the stocks fell greatly and there seemed to be a general consternation: but indignation soon took place of every other sentiment, and all parties united in denouncing vengeance (as they expressed it) against that insolent town.

Such colonial behaviour lessened the already poor prospects of an effective lobby in Britain to work for repeal of the Townshend taxes. Merchants trading with America were prospering, as Rockingham in Yorkshire told Dowdeswell on 11 August. 'The demand for goods to go to America from the manufacturing parts of this country have been I am told the greatest ever known. We

[1] *De Berdt Letters*, p. 340.   [2] *Trumbull Papers*, p. 267.
[3] *De Berdt Letters*, p. 332.   [4] *Trumbull Papers*, p. 293.

trade here through the London merchants to North America.'[5] Whether this was a natural boom or stockpiling by colonists before a boycott was not a matter of immediate concern, and there still lingered the resentment Franklin had noted in 1767, Johnson reporting home on 20 October that 'the merchants say they had no thanks for what they did upon a former occasion, and do not seem yet to interest themselves much in our favour'.[6] Even the colonial agents themselves were a long time making any positive moves: by mid-September they had had a meeting, but without any decision on what tactic to pursue.[7] During the next few weeks some received instructions from America, and on 20 October Johnson expected that 'we shall very soon have a meeting to consider the subject, and lay down a plan to be pursued by each individual in their several applications'.[8]

A campaign by agents and merchants for repeal of Townshend's taxes would be of no avail without the prospect of a favourable response from the administration, and the American news had produced a hostile reaction in that quarter. In February Johnson had picked up a rumour that some ministers were so angry at the Boston town meeting resolutions that they were contemplating action too severe even for Grenvillites.[9] Any assessment of whether the news of American defiance and violence did genuinely prevent ministerial repeal of Townshend's taxes in 1768 depends in the end on the credence to be attached to retrospective claims by Hillsborough: there is no contemporary evidence of such an intention until it had already been avowedly abandoned. What is clear is that the argument that Townshend's duties were contrary to the economic interest of Britain had certainly been grasped by Hillsborough and some of his colleagues, for Johnson sent home this report on 23 July.[10]

Some of the ministry, I am told, had said they wish they may be fairly able to repeal the act, not because the Americans are uneasy with it, nor for the reasons they urge, but as being in its principle prejudicial to Great Britain, and to be considered in no other light than as giving premiums to encourage American manufactures, for which reason, say they, we were equally fools to make, and the Americans to find fault with it.

Hillsborough told Johnson in October that one of his first proposals on taking office had been to suggest to Lord North the

---

[5] Wentworth Woodhouse Muniments, R1-1083.
[6] *Trumbull Papers*, p. 298.   [7] *De Berdt Letters*, p. 341.
[8] *Trumbull Papers*, p. 298.   [9] Ibid., pp. 266–7.   [10] Ibid., p. 292.

repeal of the Townshend duties as 'extremely anti-commercial';[11] and in July he informed De Berdt that he had settled the repeal with North before the 'spirited opposition' in America made it 'absolutely necessary to support the authority of Parliament'.[12] The American Secretary was then attributing the ministerial change of mind to the violence in Boston: 'that it had been agreed upon by himself and others in administration, to repeal the late act and that it would undoubtedly have been done had not these disturbances happened'.[13] But by October, Hillsborough was blaming the colonial challenge to Parliament's right of taxation.[14]

Professions of good will towards the colonies were part of the American Secretary's stock in trade, even to the point of improbability. 'Lord Hillsborough highly approves of all your schemes of economy and thinks you exceeding right to pursue them', De Berdt reported to Massachusetts in June. The occasion was the presentation of the colony's petition of 20 January, and the agent was then persuaded not to deliver it by the argument that the challenge to Parliament's right of taxation would do more harm than good.[15] Johnson was more cynical about the American Secretary, suspecting that, in the light of his character and political principles, 'his declarations, which are extremely warm and friendly to the colonies', should be taken as 'rather the language of the courtier than of the minister'.[16] In October Johnson had two meetings with Hillsborough, when the American Secretary conveyed the impression of a man in a predicament. 'We wish by every reasonable means to avoid any severities towards you, but if you refuse obedience to our laws, the whole fleet and army of England shall enforce it.' The American argument, based on non-representation in Parliament, would logically mean, he said, an exemption from all British laws. On the eve of the Parliamentary session Johnson reported that though many still thought repeal would be the policy adopted he himself was doubtful, but not entirely pessimistic. 'There is room to hope that some expedient may be hit upon to save the honour of Parliament,

---

[11] Ibid., p. 298.   [12] De Berdt Letters, p. 336.

[13] Trumbull Papers, p. 294. This passage is given by agent Johnson as a quotation from Hillsborough.

[14] Ibid., p. 296.

[15] De Berdt Letters, p. 332. Public opinion in Britain later accused Hillsborough of suppressing the petition. De Berdt put a denial in the Gazetteer for 26 Aug., and this was widely reprinted in the colonial press: De Berdt Letters, pp. 338–9.

[16] Trumbull Papers, p. 290.

about which they are so exceedingly concerned, and at the same time to get rid of the act, which is agreeable to none on either side of the question.'[17]

That was the nub of the problem. Simple and complete repeal would be unacceptable to Parliament, and to wider British political opinion, as an apparent admission of the American argument; and a face-saving formula would be difficult to devise. The behaviour of Massachusetts, too, in many eyes called for retribution, and there was widespread speculation as to what in that case would be the attitude of such Chathamites as Shelburne and Camden. America was expected to be the pretext for the resignation or dismissal of Shelburne, now as personally obnoxious to Grafton as he was politically so to the Bedfordites. But Camden's opinion on America remained a mystery, and with good reason: he did not yet have one![18] An enquiry from Grafton produced a long and inconclusive reply on 4 October.

We are shifted, by I know not what fatality, upon Mr. Grenville's ground; and being pressed on the one hand by the Declaratory Law, and on the other by the colony's resolute denial of Parliamentary authority, that the issue is now joined upon the right, which in my apprehension, is the most untoward ground of dispute that could have been started, fatal to Great Britain, if she miscarries; unprofitable if she succeeds. For it is (as I believe your Grace thinks with me, it is) inexpedient to tax the colonies, as we maintained, when the Stamp Act was repealed. After both sides are half ruined in the contest, we shall at last establish a right, which ought never to have existed.

After analysing the problem to the point of despair, Camden confessed, 'I do not know what is best to advise'. He did put forward one suggestion that he said no one else would accept, repeal of the taxes except for Massachusetts, where they should be enforced 'with proper rigour'; and feared 'that upon the American question the Bedfords and myself will be too far asunder to meet'.[19] Before he could relate this unhelpful answer to the formulation of policy Grafton became involved in a cabinet crisis. Public rumour was correct in that he and George III had decided on the removal of Shelburne; but on 29 September Camden warned Grafton that this might cause Chatham's resignation, which would in turn place Camden himself 'under the greatest

[17] Ibid., p. 297.
[18] For two contradictory views on Camden see *Grenville Papers*, IV, 364, and BL Add. MSS 32919A, ff. 101, 111.
[19] Grafton MSS, no. 32; printed, *Grafton Autobiography*, pp. 215–17.

difficulty'.[20] On the King's suggestion Grafton therefore saw Lady Chatham on 9 October to explain the reasons for the decision.[21] This precaution precipitated the very event it had been intended to avert. The message was misunderstood, for on 12 October Grafton received a letter from Chatham resigning his post of Lord Privy Seal. Chatham gave his poor state of health as the ostensible explanation, but added this remark. 'I cannot enough lament the removal of Sir Jeffrey Amherst and that of Lord Shelburne.'[22] Grafton knew that this comment might trigger off a series of resignations by Camden and other Chathamites, and at once wrote to correct Chatham's misapprehensions. Shelburne had not been dismissed, and Amherst had misunderstood ministerial intentions. Chatham persisted in resigning, but now gave ill health as the sole reason, and the crisis was averted.[23] Chathamites could stay in office without embarrassment. The only cabinet resignation was that of Shelburne, followed by his Commons henchman Barré; and the cabinet reshuffle was as devoid of political significance as possible. A Chathamite, Lord Bristol, succeeded Chatham as Lord Privy Seal, but without a cabinet seat. Lord Rochford, a diplomat unconnected with any faction, became Northern Secretary, Weymouth moving to replace Shelburne as Southern Secretary.

Grafton was now indisputably Prime Minister.[24] Most contemporaries anticipated an era of political stability, but Grafton himself was to go before that ensued. His ministry was to be destroyed in little over a year, not by the American question but by the political storm over the elections of John Wilkes for Middlesex, an issue that exposed the fissures within the administration. The cabinet still contained five appointed by Chatham in 1766; Grafton himself and three other Chathamites in Lord Chancellor Camden, Sir Edward Hawke at the Admiralty, and Lord Granby, head of the army; and former Rockinghamite Conway, now without an office. But it also included two

---

[20] Ibid., p. 214.   [21] Corr. of George III, II, 49–52.
[22] Grafton Autobiography, p. 221.
[23] Corr. of George III, II, 53–8; Grafton Autobiography, pp. 221–5; Chatham Papers, II, 338–42. For fuller accounts of the episode see Brooke, Chatham Administration, pp. 375–84; and Hamer, Thesis, pp. 14–24. Grenville, on hearing the news, suggested there should be an Address to Chatham from both Houses of Parliament 'for having delivered the King and Parliament from the incumbrance of two or three millions of subjects in America'. Grenville Letter-Books, Vol. 2: Grenville to Harvey, 1 Nov. 1768.
[24] Grenville Papers, IV, 394.

Bedfordites, Weymouth and Lord President Gower; and three members not linked with any of the old political factions, Rochford, Hillsborough, and Lord North. On America opinion was finely balanced between coercion and conciliation.

Opposition reactions over America in 1768 were twofold, concerned with the colonial news and then with the measures and anticipated policies of the administration. The parties of Rockingham and Grenville, despite their differences in stance over America arising from their clash in the Stamp Act Crisis, could unite in criticizing whatever the ministry had done or was thought to be planning. This co-operation had the basis of genuine suspicion that the administration, or at least the Chathamite part of it, might be insufficiently concerned to maintain Parliament's supremacy over the colonies; and apparent blunders and tactical mistakes by ministers were of course fair game.

The comments of the Rockinghamite leadership reflected full and prompt awareness of the gravity of the colonial situation. Newcastle, drawing on even more than his own lifetime of experience, lamented on 23 July that 'these New England people always were a refractory people, ever since, and indeed even in King William's time'.[25] Eight days later Yorkshire MP Sir George Savile sent Rockingham this percipient comment.[26]

I am afraid these same colonists are above our hands and I am almost ready to think that G.G's. Act only brought on a crisis twenty or possibly fifty years sooner than was necessary. . . . In my opinion (which may be in this a little singular) it is in the nature of things that, some time or other, colonies so situated, must assume to themselves the rights of nature, and resist those of law, which is rebellion.

Rockingham himself was so perplexed by the colonial news that on 11 August he wrote to Dowdeswell that 'affairs in North America tend more and more to confusion'.[27] His Commons leader responded three days later to this plea for guidance with a full analysis of the colonial problem.[28] The American opposition was to 'the general principle of raising *any* revenue in America', but underneath was the question of Parliamentary sovereignty over the colonies.

[25] BL Add. MSS 32990, ff. 340–1.
[26] *Rockingham Memoirs*, II, 76.
[27] Wentworth Woodhouse Muniments, R1-1083.
[28] Dowdeswell MSS: partly printed in Brooke, *Chatham Administration*, pp. 369–73, and Thomas, *British Politics and the Stamp Act Crisis*, pp. 367–9.

The distinction between external and internal taxes has been found frivolous, as indeed I always thought it. And your Lordship knows that I have never been able to distinguish between the right of passing one law and the right of passing another. Their claim of rights admitted will give them in my opinion a charter against being bound to any laws passed without their consent.

Dowdeswell was against the easy solution of repeal on the pretext that the Townshend duties prejudiced the colonial market of the taxed goods; but he would be willing to support a colonial petition based on a claim of economic distress, if it did not deny Parliament's right of taxation. Later his determination to emphasize the contrast with the Stamp Act Crisis led him into an implicit contradiction. The Stamp Act, he claimed, had been 'a real grievance, a very heavy tax from which we meant to relieve the colonists. The tax now in question is no heavy burden upon them, and the objections to it should rather come from this side of the water than from them.' Dowdeswell's distinction between the two colonial crises in terms of the respective tax burdens was specious, or self-deceptive. But his analysis ended with the perception that in a struggle with America Britain had 'everything to lose and nothing to gain'.

Incredulity and consternation was the response of Rockinghamite peers to the ministerial measures of July. The choice of the warm-tempered Botetourt for Virginia was seen, in Rockingham's words, as 'a most unwise, absurd and dangerous measure'.[29] Newcastle commented on the dispatch of soldiers, 'we are making war upon our colonies', and looked to a Parliamentary reckoning with 'these wild young hot-headed Ministers'.[30] Dowdeswell held a different opinion, observing to Rockingham in his letter of 14 August that he did not regard the use of the army and navy to be 'a reprehensible measure in a ministry which at present at least does not intend to come to a repeal'. If order was restored, repeal could 'add good humour to submission'.[31] Newcastle on reflection read a policy decision into the use of the army, so he told Rockingham on 13 September: 'By great mismanagement, the measure of conquering the colonies, and obliging them to submit, is become

[29] Wentworth Woodhouse Muniments, R1-1083. He ascribed the appointment to Bute. Ibid., R1-1080. For similar comments by other peers see BL Add. MSS 32990, ff. 384–5, 405–7.

[30] Ibid., ff. 372–5, 389–90, 399–400. Note however that Newcastle died on 17 Nov.

[31] Dowdeswell MSS.

more popular than it was. It is certainly the measure of the administration.'[32]

If Newcastle was mistaken in seeing the administration's action as anything more than an attempt to restore order in America, Grenville was equally wrong in suspecting that the ministry had the ulterior constitutional motive of advancing the authority of the Crown at the expense of that of Parliament. In Grenville's eyes the earlier behaviour of the men who were now ministers provided ground for such an interpretation. On 21 August, when writing to Whately, he recalled the denials in 1766 by Chatham and Camden of Parliament's right of internal taxation;[33] and he no doubt also remembered that among the first measures of the Chatham administration had been the issue of a royal proclamation for an embargo on corn exports, a decision illegal under the Bill of Rights of 1689 and for which Parliamentary indemnity had subsequently been sought. Now, so Grenville understood, the use of the army and navy in America was being accompanied by talk in ministerial circles 'that the Crown and not the Parliament is the proper authority to reduce the colonies to obedience'.[34] Even before he heard this political gossip Grenville had made this comment on the behaviour of the colonists. 'We shall see whether they shall submit to put themselves entirely under the authority of the Crown after having openly resisted and declared that they would resist the authority of the legislature of Great Britain'.[35] Some such constitutional solution of equality with Britain under the Crown might well have satisfied America at this time; but it was not the policy of the ministry or an idea acceptable to Parliamentary opinion: Grenville's fears in this respect were without foundation.

The distinctive keynote of Grenville's stance on America continued to be his insistence on the right of taxation. Britain should not give up this principle even in return for a promise of revenue. As the Townshend Duties Crisis broke, Grenville saw the issue as identical to that of the Stamp Act Crisis. 'The question as to the right and expediency of enforcing any *revenue* or other laws by virtue of an Act of Parliament upon the colonies without the consent of their assemblies stands exactly upon the

[32] BL Add. MSS 32991A, ff. 94–6.
[33] Grenville-Letter Books, Vol. 2: Grenville to Whately, 21 Aug. 1768.
[34] *Grenville Papers*, IV, 364–6. For the gossip see BL Add. MSS 42086, ff. 127–8.
[35] Grenville Letter-Books, Vol. 2: Grenville to Whately, 21 Aug. 1768.

same ground as the arguments for and against the repeal of the Stamp Act.[36] The correspondence of Grenville and his political associates contains significantly little discussion about policy. There was no doubt in Grenvillite minds over what ought to be done, but great concern about whether the ministry would do it. As early as 18 May 1768 Thomas Lyttelton had raised the American question in the Commons during the brief and formal Parliamentary session of that month.[37] The subsequent news of the American challenge to British authority rekindled Grenvillite uneasiness as to whether the administration possessed the requisite qualities to handle the crisis. 'Force alone will not do', Grenville observed to Whately on 7 August: 'there must be system, firmness and moderation, positive and intelligible instructions, and certainty of support to those who obey them.'[38] Grenville was never one of those who believed that the ministry had devised any policy or intended to do so before Parliament met.[39] But he did hope that the flow of news about American defiance would 'serve to open the eyes of all both here and in the colonies as to the real state of the question and probably make the decision of it immediate and unavoidable'. On 30 October he sent this opinion to Captain Hood, Commodore of the naval squadron in American waters and one of his chief sources of information on the colonies.[40]

If Great Britain, by which I mean the legislature of Great Britain not the King only, is to give up its sovereignty in all cases over the colonies and they are to be considered as independent communities in alliance with us and only governed by the same Prince as Hanover is, the sooner that is known and settled for us the better, that we may take our measures accordingly. If on the other hand they are bound by our Acts of Parliament and in all cases subordinate to the authority of our legislature (which till this unhappy time was never doubted and cannot well now I believe admit of a question), surely it is necessary for the sake of the colonies as well as of Great Britain that this great point should be established without delay, and that sovereign authority forthwith acknowledged and confirmed.

Even the previous clash of the Rockingham and Grenville factions over the issue of colonial taxation during the Stamp Act Crisis was not to prevent their co-operation in the new American

---

[36] Ibid., Vol. 2: Grenville to Whately, 7 Aug. 1768.
[37] BL Egerton MSS 215, f. 81.
[38] Grenville Letter-Books, Vol. 2: Grenville to Whately, 7 Aug. 1768.
[39] *Grenville Papers*, IV, 365–6; *HMC Knox MSS*, p. 99.
[40] Grenville Letter-Books, Vol. 2: Grenville to Hood, 30 Oct. 1768.

crisis. Rockingham at first thought that Grenville might return to office in an administration determined upon coercion. But by early August he had revised this opinion after Grenville's brother Lord Temple had approached Rockinghamite lawyer Charles Yorke with a suggestion of joint action to defeat the ministry.[41] Before the Parliamentary session began, such soundings had blossomed into a genuine prospect of opposition unity. On 28 October Whately reported to Grenville a recent discussion in Yorkshire between Wedderburn and Rockingham himself. 'His Lordship's language was that it was impossible the several parts of the Opposition could differ now on American measures.' Whately himself had spoken with Edmund Burke the previous day. 'I find they are very hostile to the Administration, condemn their whole conduct with respect to America, and seem inclined to attack Lord Hillsborough's letter for rescinding.'[42]

It has been conventional wisdom that the Grafton ministry, divided in opinion on America and overwhelmed by the political crisis at home arising from the Middlesex Elections case, took no decision on colonial policy until after the end of the Parliamentary session of 1768–9. Such an interpretation is erroneous. Grafton and his cabinet colleagues did devise an agreed colonial policy before the John Wilkes affair blew up in their faces in December 1768, albeit one of a negative character. But when positive action was being urged and expected, on the one hand for strong action against defiant colonists and on the other to repeal the Townshend duties, the cabinet decision to do neither represented a deliberate choice; and what the ministry had in mind for the long run was more constructive. All this was widely known in the political world of London by the end of 1768.

This policy was phased into two parts, the application of the big stick before the offer of the olive branch. First of all retributive action would be taken or rather, as soon became apparent, merely threatened against those inhabitants of Massachusetts who had violently and, in many British eyes, illegally defied the authority of Crown and Parliament. Only after this had been approved by Parliament and colonial submission could be claimed or assumed would redress of American grievances be considered. The overall policy aim was a compromise intended, as in the Stamp Act Crisis, to solve the double problem of British indignation and

[41] Wentworth Woodhouse Muniments, R1-1083.
[42] BL Add. MSS 42086, ff. 157–8; printed in *Grenville Papers*, IV, 391–3.

colonial defiance. But this time government policy was less clear-cut than in 1766 and its enactment far more prolonged. These circumstances have made it appear not to have been a coherent policy at all. Here an analogy may be found with the tactics in early 1775 of the North ministry during the final American crisis. Coercive measures were then also first announced without any mention of conciliation, even though they formed part of the same policy, and for a long time the concessions offered were believed to have been a belated afterthought.[43] Historians have taken a similarly mistaken view of the American policy of the Grafton ministry in 1768-9.

At the end of 1768 circumstances in America and Britain combined to make possible the formulation of a colonial policy. The American problem suddenly appeared less intractable, with the news both of the colonial failure to organize an effective boycott and that there had after all been no armed confrontation in Boston. The resignation of Chatham gave the cabinet a free hand to act: no longer would it have to take account of the opinions of that unpredictable and formidable character. The opening of the new Parliamentary session on 8 November provided evidence of British political opinion on the subject of the colonies, and at the same time doubtless helped to concentrate the minds of ministers: it would soon become incumbent on them to produce an American policy.

Any such policy would require the sanction of Parliament, and the state of Parliamentary opinion on recent events in the colonies was an unknown factor. The King's Speech on 8 November mentioned the American situation at length. The Address of the House of Lords in reply was moderate and uncontroversial, and was approved without a debate. But the Commons' Address proposed to thank the sovereign for the actions taken to support the constitution and suppress disobedience.[44] The ministry, by requesting approval of its measures, had set the stage for a full debate on America. The discussion lasted until midnight, embracing the international scene in Europe, notably the French seizure of Corsica, as well as the American crisis. It was the first opportunity for eighteen months for MPs to voice their opinions on what had been happening in America.[45]

[43] Donoughue, *British Politics and the American Revolution*, pp. 219-65.
[44] Simmons and Thomas, *Proceedings and Debates*, III, 1-3.
[45] In this account of the debate the quotations are from the Cavendish Diary, BL Egerton MSS 215, ff. 96-134, partly printed in Simmons and Thomas, op.

Hans Stanley, holder of a court office, threw down the gauntlet when seconding the Address. 'I don't at all regret we have put the obedience of the Americans to the test.' Governor Bernard's problems, he said, arose from two features of the Massachusetts constitution; the choice of council members by the assembly, for this deprived the governor of the support he should receive from that body; and the elective nature of the Massachusetts juries, which made it impossible to secure redress against malefactors. 'The head of the mob is at the head of the Grand Jury.' The arrival of soldiers in Boston had only ensured a temporary pacification, and riots would begin again when they were withdrawn. Whether or not Stanley was flying a kite on behalf of the ministry, no subsequent speaker took up his hint about the need for a permanent change in the Massachusetts constitution.

The pattern of the debate, in so far as it concerned America, was set by the next speaker, Rockinghamite William Dowdeswell. He moved an amendment to omit the laudatory part of the Address and substitute an assurance that the House would inquire into what measures had been taken to secure peace, order, and obedience in America. Dowdeswell queried the prudence of Hillsborough's order for the withdrawal of the Massachusetts Circular Letter, for it had not been illegal, and he said that the ministry should have come to Parliament before threatening the dissolution of colonial assemblies. He was supported by two Rockinghamite colleagues, Sir George Savile and Edmund Burke, who attacked Chatham and Camden for their change of attitude. 'These two persons pleaded the cause of the Americans, but they have changed their minds. . . . Nothing can tend to estrange America more from us than an opinion, that there is no person in Great Britain steady.' Charles Townshend, said Burke, 'never gave as the reason that these duties were intended as a test of America. . . . It was to strengthen and fortify the governments of America. With regard to when this was laid before the House, I expressed the little opinion I had. I shall prove a true prophet, that you will never see a single shilling from America.'[46] Burke concluded with the warning that 'it is not votes and resolutions, it is not arms that govern a people'.

Administration yielded no ground. Lord Clare, President of the

cit., III, 3–12. For a list of other reports see Thomas, 'Sources for Debates . . . 1768–1774', *BIHR* Supp. no. 4, 2.

[46] No record has been found of any speech by Burke during the enactment of the Townshend taxation of 1767.

Board of Trade until June, said that Dowdeswell's amendment might be interpreted by the colonists as approval of their behaviour. Secretary at War Lord Barrington called the Americans 'traitors' to Crown and Parliament, and defended the use of soldiers to bring rioters to justice. Bedfordite Rigby got in a hit at Hillsborough: 'I do not approve of any minister taking upon himself to dictate.' But he would not support any tax concessions while disorder and defiance prevailed in America. Leader of the House Lord North put this point more strongly, declaring that he would be against repeal of the taxes 'until he saw America prostrate at his feet'.[47] He then stated this uncompromising view. 'There has been no proof of any real return of friendship. In America they will give you no credit for affection, no credit for commercial interest. Taxation and regulation: if America is to be the judge, you may tax in no instance, you may regulate in no instance.'

The Rockinghamite attack created difficulty for other factions. Chathamites now in opposition faced the consequences of decisions taken when their leaders had been in office. One who still was, Solicitor-General John Dunning, spoke in support of the Address, but William Beckford, for long Chatham's link with the City of London, deplored the deliberate creation of a new colonial crisis. 'Why would you stir these waters? Let the nation return to its old good-nature and its old good-humour.' Shelburne's spokes-man Barré made a similar plea and acted very much as his master's voice when he declared: 'You have no right to tax the Americans. You wish to have their money, if not by one way, by another. Why not get their money by requisitions? If they refuse that, every body must turn out under those circumstances.'

Both Beckford and Barré supported Dowdeswell's amendment, but Grenvillites were in a predicament. Wedderburn declared that 'part of America's conduct was right, and part wrong'. He disapproved of Hillsborough's circular letter, but accepted 'the duty of government to quell force by force'. Grenville admitted his dilemma. He did not wish to encourage the Americans to riot, but disapproved of the dissolution of colonial assemblies. 'Would to God that they were no greater enemies to themselves, than we are to them. I think they have a right to every privilege of British subjects.' Agent Johnson sent home this impression to Connecticut. 'Mr. Grenville himself upon this occasion became the advocate of

[47] This phrase, missed by diarist Cavendish, was noted by agent Johnson, *Trumbull Papers*, p. 303.

the colonies, and declared it to be an illegal and unconstitutional step, an arbitrary attack upon the rights of a corporation, and an exercise of power which belonged only to the supreme legislature of Great Britain.'[48] Grenville's speech was so convoluted that Charles Garth reported back to South Carolina that he had favoured Dowdeswell's amendment.[49] He in fact supported the Address, whereupon Dowdeswell tactfully observed that he and Grenville must respect each other's point of view.

The general tone of the debate was more important than the predictable clash of factions or the negativing of Dowdeswell's amendment without a vote. Friends of America could gain some consolation from the discussion. It was to have been expected that MPs would condemn the disturbances in Massachusetts; and Charles Garth was merely stating the obvious when he informed South Carolina that 'no applications founded upon the sole right in the assemblies to lay taxes upon the people of the colonies can meet with admittance or reception'.[50] But speakers on both sides had deplored the crisis and advocated moderation: it was Rigby who had urged, 'we ought to act in the most temperate manner'. While no immediate repeal of the Townshend Duties would be possible, that issue remained an open question, and agent Johnson made this overall assessment of the debate. 'Upon the whole, the temper of the House seemed to be enough against us, though not so violent as many feared. I do not, therefore, yet quite despair of our obtaining some relief, though I think we must expect that Boston will meet with some chastisement.'[51]

Grafton was now able to formulate an American policy that would be acceptable to both Parliament and his cabinet colleagues. Within a month he had devised one that virtually reconciled the differing opinions within the administration. The two broad principles were that retributive action would be taken against Massachusetts, but only that colony, even though the King's Speech had made reference to 'a spirit of faction' in 'some' colonies. After colonial submission had been achieved, relief would be afforded to America. That some such general programme had been agreed upon within a week is suggested by events in Parliament on 15 November. Lord North informed the Commons that an unacceptable communication had been received from Virginia, but was being withheld to prevent resentment: this was that colony's Remonstrance addressed to the House. North then

[48] Ibid., p. 302.   [49] SCHGM, 30 (1929), p. 230.
[50] Ibid., 30 (1929), pp. 231–2.   [51] Trumbull Papers, p. 303.

informed MPs that all papers relating to Massachusetts would be laid before the House. They would provide information for judgement on that colony, and this would precede any action that might be taken to redress colonial grievances. A brief discussion arose after Beckford announced his intention of moving for a Committee on America. 'Truth is not come out. America has been misrepresented. . . . America complains that we will not hear their grievances.' North rejoined that such a step would be a cause of fresh dispute, not a move towards conciliation. His moderate stance in this debate may have reflected his awareness of policy-making within the cabinet. Beckford retorted that only one side of the American question was known, and then advocated the Chathamite view of an empire to be exploited through trade, not taxation. 'The Americans contribute more by living in America, and taking our manufactures, than if they lived here. You ought to be the monopolists of America.' Barlow Trecothick urged MPs to keep matters in proportion. There might be a few factious individuals in America, as in Britain; but Boston did not have one-thirtieth of the population of Massachusetts.[52]

A fortnight later, on 29 November, Grafton informed George III that he had devised a colonial policy: 'an idea of his on the subject of the American parturbators [sic] of the peace, and, indeed, if it is practicable, the only one measure of any efficacy, on which the Duke of Grafton has any hopes of bringing his Majesty's servants to one mind upon'.[53] By 6 December the cabinet had held three meetings on America, with Conway apparently the only objector to the final proposals concerning Massachusetts.[54] These comprised a series of Parliamentary resolutions concerning events in that colony, and a Parliamentary Address to the King. The resolutions condemned the Massachusetts Assembly votes of January and February; the Massachusetts Circular Letter; the resolutions of the Boston town meetings of 14 June and 12 September; and the summoning and meeting of the Convention of delegates on 22 September. Other resolutions declared Boston to have been in a state of riot, and asserted that neither the Council nor the magistrates had exerted their authority.[55] None of this, however

[52] Cavendish Diary, BL Egerton MSS 215, ff. 152–3 (from which the quotations are taken). SCHGM, 30 (1929), pp. 233–4. Trumbull Papers, p. 306. Lord Hillsborough made a similar announcement to the Lords on 28 Nov. about the Memorial from Virginia addressed to that House: LJ, XXXII, 185.

[53] Corr. of George III, II, 59.

[54] The Gazetteer, 7 Dec. 1768; H. Walpole, Memoirs, III, 189–90.

[55] LJ, XXXII, 209–10.

satisfying to enunciate, represented a plan of action. Grafton may well have left such matters to Hillsborough, whose departmental responsibility it was. Certainly an early idea of the American Secretary was to be the basis of the Address. On 30 July he had ordered Governor Bernard to inquire into the *Liberty* riots for evidence of treason, so that any persons accused could be brought to England for trial under a treason statute of 35 Henry VIII.[56] The Address adopted by the cabinet proposed to use this Henrican treason law. It asked George III to order Governor Bernard to submit names and evidence concerning any treason committed in Massachusetts during 1768, so that the King could issue a Special Commission to try such offences 'within this realm' if there appeared sufficient ground for such proceedings.[57]

The resolutions and Address constituted the only formal policy decision presented to Parliament during this session. Behind them lay a story of dissension in the cabinet. Although only Conway had objected to this emasculated outcome of the deliberations, other ministers had vainly pressed for practical measures of retribution and redress. Hillsborough had asked Attorney-General William De Grey and Solicitor-General John Dunning whether the events in Massachusetts provided sufficient evidence for the forfeiture of the colony's charter, only to receive a negative reply on 25 November.[58] The alteration of the charter uppermost in Hillsborough's mind was probably that urged upon him by Governor Bernard, the transfer of the nomination of the council members from the assembly to the Crown.[59] Two resolutions relating to the council were at first approved by the cabinet, and then dropped;[60] and Hillsborough certainly did put forward this idea within three months. According to William Knox, by now his close confidant, the American Secretary had been outvoted in cabinet over his demand for action rather than words; and, thinking the resolutions and Address a meaningless gesture, he declined to move the latter, even though it had presumably developed from his own initiative about the treason law.[61] Lord Barrington, not in the cabinet but well placed to hear what had happened, gave Governor Bernard a similar version of events.

[56] CO 5/765, ff. 24–33.   [57] LJ, XXXII, 210.
[58] CO 5/757, ff. 464–5.   [59] Barrington–Bernard Corr., p. 179.
[60] Trumbull Papers, p. 309.
[61] BL Add. MSS 42087, ff. 1–2. On 1 Nov. 1769 Hillsborough told Massachusetts agent De Berdt that the Address had not been his idea and that he had refused to move it: De Berdt Letters, p. 382.

I wish there were a better prospect of such measures at home, as will tend to preserve the obedience of the colonies, and such have been proposed. I can moreover assure you that they have been relished by the majority of the cabinet; but by some fatal catastrophe, two or three men there, with less ability, less credit, less authority and less responsibility than the rest, have carried their point and produced that flimsy unavailing Address.

The only redeeming feature Barrington could report was a unanimous cabinet decision not to repeal the Townshend taxes 'till the colonies have submitted thoroughly to them'.[62] But the administration's failure to take any effective measures either to punish the defiance of 1768 or to remedy the evident defects of the Massachusetts constitution was to astonish friend and foe alike in America. The political leadership in Boston had expected retribution, and was delighted to escape scot-free. General Gage, to whom Barrington had privately expressed the view that James Otis and others like him should have been arrested and tried, in reply asked rhetorically what better evidence could the ministry have required than the writings and behaviour of such men, and then summarized what in his opinion should have been done.[63]

The impeachment of those who signed the letters of Convention, the appointment of the Council by the King, and the abolition of the town meetings of Boston . . . are three points which I sincerely hoped would have been carried into execution.

The colonial agents were promptly informed of the cabinet decisions, at a meeting on 6 December attended by six of them.[64] This was in accordance with a promise by Lord Hillsborough, who, to counter the tactic agents had adopted of canvassing him one at a time, had announced that he would inform them at a general meeting what had been agreed upon by the cabinet. Here is agent Johnson's report of what the American Secretary said.[65]

Administration had taken the matter into consideration, and concluded to enforce the authority of the legislature of Great Britain over the colonies in the most effectual manner, but to proceed therein with all the moderation and lenity that the nature of the thing would admit of; that all the petitions they had received were very offensive, as containing a denial of the authority of Parliament to bind the colonies by their laws, though some of them were expressed in more decent terms than others; that as to the Acts complained of, they had no particular fondness for them, and

---

[62] Barrington–Bernard Corr., p. 182.
[63] PCBG, pp. 52, 56; Gage Corr., II, 509–10.
[64] De Berdt Letters, p. 349.   [65] Trumbull Papers, p. 305.

particularly the late Duty Act was so anti-commercial that he wished it
had never existed, and it would certainly have been repealed had the
colonies said nothing about it, or petitioned only upon the ground of its
inexpediency, but that the principle they went upon equally extended to
all laws whatsoever, and they could not therefore think of repealing it, at
least this session of Parliament, or until the colonies had properly
submitted to the authority of Parliament and dropped the point of right;
that the conduct of the people of Boston, in particular, had been such as
rendered it impossible for government to recede in the least degree, or
even let their proceedings pass without a severe censure, and that the
matter would in a few days come before Parliament.

William Knox was not at the meeting, but he was later informed
that the agents assured Hillsborough that they would tell their
colonies that the American insistence on 'the point of right' was
the obstacle to repeal as far as the ministry was concerned. Knox
told Grenville on 15 December that he therefore understood 'the
riddle' of the resolutions condemning Massachusetts. 'The people
of England are to be made believe that the right is admitted by the
colonies . . . and the colonies' petitions saying nothing of it, will be
interpreted into their tacit submission, and an express one will
not be required.' This Knox regarded as a cynical scheme, by
which the rights of Parliament were to be sacrificed for the sake of
peace and quiet.[66] The cabinet had in mind a more positive long-
term policy than Knox then knew, and had unofficially disclosed
it by the end of the month, as Johnson reported to his colony on 3
January 1769. 'It is given out that if the colonies are quiet, and
show a proper submission, that probably, next session, the Duty
Act will be repealed, and no others be in future proposed; that the
right, being once established, shall not however be exercised, and
the controversy suffered to sleep.'[67] By December 1768 the Grafton
ministry had devised and effectively publicized a complete policy
for the American crisis; but during the next few months it was to
be postponed and modified.

Before the administration could introduce its policy in Parliament,
two debates on America took place in the House of Commons on
7 December. The colonial agents had for some time been
concerned about how to put the American viewpoint before
Parliament. All the colonies except Virginia and Pennsylvania had
sent protests only to the King, for a complaint to Parliament

[66] BL Add. MSS 42086, f. 167; printed in *Grenville Papers*, IV, 400–1.
[67] *Trumbull Papers*, p. 311.

might be interpreted as a tacit acknowledgement of Parliament's right of taxation. No member of either House would submit Virginia's Memorial to the Lords or Remonstrance to the Commons, for these documents claimed repeal of the Townshend taxes as a right, not as a favour. The Pennsylvania protests were more respectful in wording and couched in the form of petitions to the two Houses, but both claimed the right of taxation for the colony's own assembly. Agent Benjamin Franklin was unable to persuade any peer to present the one to the Lords, but after some difficulty prevailed on John Huske to put forward that addressed to the Commons.[68]

The implicit denial of Parliamentary right was enough to condemn the petition in the eyes of the House. Lord North admitted 'the decent words' and said that such petitions put Parliament into a dilemma, since rejection conveyed the impression that the Commons would neither hear nor redress grievances. Huske reminded MPs that Pennsylvania had not joined the trade boycott, and Lord Barrington that the colony had accepted the 1765 Mutiny Act in its entirety. Beckford and Conway spoke in favour of receiving the petition, but this was opposed by George Grenville, who put the issue in unequivocal terms.

I do declare, if you have not a power to tax this people, I think you have no right to bind them in other things. You have put them under a military power. Every act you have made is *ipso facto* null, being convinced you have no right. It is all or none. If you are not the representatives, you have no right to bind. The Americans have Parliaments of their own. . . . If you mean to give way, give way universally, give way at once. Why will you keep them up? Put an end to them one way or another.

The ministry accepted the contention of Huske that if the House rejected the only petition received, it would be the last one from any colony. Lord North therefore suggested that the petition should be withdrawn, and Huske did so, saying he would offer it again on a future occasion.[69] But Franklin was told by every MP he consulted that if the petition was again offered the House would send for the Pennsylvania charter, which reserved the right of taxation to Parliament, and he realized such a step would serve no useful purpose.[70]

The second debate of 7 December was over Beckford's motion

[68] *Franklin Papers*, XVI, 14–17.
[69] For this debate see BL Egerton MSS 215, ff. 281–6.
[70] *Franklin Papers*, XVI, 15–16.

for a full inquiry into the ministry's American decisions, with the avowed purpose of amending Townshend's taxation. Merchant Barlow Trecothick seconded on the ground that the trade laws were 'a tax above all taxes'. North blamed the crisis on the Americans, 'the false apprehension of their rights'. A second surrender would destroy Britain's authority. In answer to a taunt from Barré, North rendered his offending phrase of 8 November as 'till America is under foot', not 'America lying prostrate', and said this simply meant until the colonies obeyed the law. Both Grenville and Dowdeswell supported the call for a general inquiry, but that the opposition factions had found common ground on America availed them nothing. Beckford's motion was defeated in a half-empty House by 127 votes to 72.[71]

By this time the Grafton administration was poised to introduce its Parliamentary proposals. The strategy had been revealed by the laying before both Houses of many papers on Massachusetts and none at all on any other colony.[72] In the Commons a Committee of the Whole House was appointed to consider them, but this met only twice before the Christmas recess, and then merely to read the papers.[73] The ministry had decided to begin its Parliamentary campaign in the Lords only, and not simultaneously in both Houses, as had been done in the Stamp Act Crisis. But before the administration could do so, the Middlesex Elections case had exploded into a political crisis of the first magnitude.

Until December Grafton had steadfastly resisted pressure for the expulsion of Wilkes from the Commons, pressure from George III and from such colleagues as North and the Bedfords. Even after Wilkes had been sentenced to twenty-two months' imprisonment in June, for offences arising out of the 1763 *North Briton* case, Grafton had still hoped to defuse the controversy. It was Wilkes, fearful of penurious obscurity, who forced the issue, the final straw for Grafton being a newspaper libel. In the *St. James' Chronicle* for 10 December Wilkes accused the ministry of having planned the St George's Fields 'Massacre' of 10 May. This provocation alienated even Grafton, who himself moved in the Lords on 16 December a resolution condemning Wilkes' statement as 'an insolent, scandalous and seditious libel'.[74] The administration

[71] BL Egerton MSS, 215, ff. 287–327.
[72] *CJ*, XXXII, 74–6, 91–2; *LJ*, XXXII, 182–5, 192–3.
[73] *CJ*, XXXII, 105, 107.
[74] *LJ*, XXXII, 212. For the above sequence of events see Hamer, Thesis, pp. 48–59.

now decided on the expulsion of Wilkes, and the consequent Middlesex Elections case was to dominate the remainder of the Parliamentary session and push America into the political background. Grafton's early forbearance concerning Wilkes may have been dictated in part by his desire to concentrate on resolving the American crisis without any political distraction at home. The contribution of John Wilkes to the loss of the American colonies can be held to embrace the sabotage of Grafton's colonial policy as well as the apparent example of the British government's threat to liberty that his cause represented in many American eyes. There was a twofold link between John Wilkes and the coming of the American Revolution.

The administration had already launched its Parliamentary programme on America. The Lords read the American papers on 9, 12, 13, and 14 December. On 15 December Lord Hillsborough introduced the ministry's eight resolutions condemning the year's happenings in Massachusetts; and Bedford then moved the Address asking the King to obtain information from Governor Bernard concerning any possible evidence of treason.[75] The administration was evidently resolved to portray itself as less hardline than Grenville. Hillsborough criticized the Stamp Act, even though he had been President of the Board of Trade at the time of its passage: here is agent Johnson's summary. 'He thought the Stamp At was inexpedient, had advised against it when first proposed, and voted for its repeal upon that principle, as he believed almost everybody else had done.' After condemning the defiance and violence in Massachusetts, he declared that 'the matter was now brought to a point; that Parliament must now give up its authority over the colonies, or they be brought to effectual submission to its laws'. He hoped that nobody would suggest repeal of the Townshend taxation. 'It was not the amount of the duties (which he believed would not be more than £8,000 or £10,000 per annum in all North America) that was complained of, but the principle upon which the laws were founded.' Hillsborough nevertheless urged the House to 'proceed with moderation and temper, that he considered the North Americans in general as a very good set of people, and only misled by their leaders'. He

[75] LJ, XXXII, 208–10. The ensuing debate took place on the Address, after the passage of the resolutions. For it see Trumbull Papers, pp. 306–9 (agent Johnson's report, from which all quotations are taken); De Berdt Letters, pp. 349–50; Franklin Papers, XVI, 12; H. Walpole, Memoirs, III, 194–5; and Cobbett, Parl. Hist., XVI, 475 n (a minute from the Hardwicke Papers).

hoped the resolutions would persuade the colonists to 'see their error and quietly submit, in which case it would be right to give them every relief and encouragement that they could reasonably desire; that this he hoped would be sufficient, but if it was not, that the hand of power must be so lifted up, and the whole force of this country exerted to enforce its laws, and bring the colonies into due subjection'.

The Rockinghamite party had prepared for the debate in expectation of a different policy. On 12 December Rockingham, when particularly urging Dartmouth to attend, as having been President of the Board of Trade in his own ministry, wrote that 'what the resolutions are, does not transpire, and yet there are expectations that they will be much too hot for our politics'.[76] Richmond observed to Rockingham that since Hillsborough's attitude was 'the reverse of ours, I do hope we shall assert our old opinions and divide upon it'. He hoped for support elsewhere. 'Lord Shelburne will certainly be with us, and be a great help in debate.' Even the Grenvillites like Lyttelton, Richmond thought, would 'join us upon the ground of the papers being partial and our not having the whole of the information'.[77]

The ministry's moderate stance caused an opposition débâcle. Hopes of Grenvillite support were promptly shattered by Lord Temple, who rose immediately after Bedford. 'He was weary of a paper war', he said, and declaring that the House had been presented with 'insignificant and futile' resolutions instead of 'some large, wise, and well-concerted plan' he stalked out of the House. Grafton countered this attack by emphasizing that acceptance of the resolutions and Address would preclude any change in the Townshend taxes that session. In view of the American Secretary's known hostility to the duties on commercial grounds, Grafton was anxious to correct any misapprehensions arising from Hillsborough's mention of 'relief'.

The administration was attacked on the other flank by Richmond and Shelburne, both in a predicament: for how could such a policy be construed as anti-American? Shelburne, though in the cabinet himself two months earlier, complained of ministerial negligence in not acting more promptly to secure any evidence of treason. Richmond could find no particular objection to what the ministry

<hr />

[76] Dartmouth MSS D (W) 1778/II/294. Dartmouth, trapped in the country by bad weather, was not able to attend. Wentworth Woodhouse Muniments, R1-1132.

[77] Wentworth Woodhouse Muniments, R1-1129.

proposed, and asked what revenue had been collected from the new duties. Grafton was apparently happy to answer that none at all had been received when interrupted by a colleague, probably Weymouth, who declared that Richmond's question was irrelevant. The resolutions and Address were agreed without a division and sent to the Commons; but that House, busy with Wilkes, adjourned consideration of America until 23 January 1769.[78]

By the Christmas recess the Grafton ministry's policy on America had been made clear to Parliament. Public condemnation of events in Massachusetts was to be followed if possible by punitive action against individual culprits: that at least was the threat implicit in the Address. If the colonial response was favourable, and by that was envisaged acceptance of British authority, some redress of grievances would be offered to America; and that had been unofficially leaked as repeal of the taxes next session. At the end of 1768 such an outcome did not appear unrealistic. News of the quiet landing of the soldiers in Boston had been accompanied by reports of the refusal of Pennsylvania and of the southern colonies to join the trade boycott advocated by Boston. This time, it seemed, the colonies were not united.

When Parliament reassembled in the New Year it was the turn of the House of Commons to discuss American policy, but the American Committee was put off to 25 January because of a debate on Wilkes. William Beckford then began the proceedings by attempting to present a petition purporting to be from the majority of the Massachusetts Council and signed by Samuel Danforth as President. North put forward two formal objections, that the council had not met as a body for this purpose and that the governor was ex officio its President. But after Trecothick accused the ministry of rejecting all petitions the administration relented, with its procedural expert Jeremiah Dyson suggesting that the petition could simply be accepted as one from Danforth. The concession extended only to allowing the petition to lie on the Table of the House, to permit possible future consideration, and administration carried this point by 133 votes to 70.[79]

This discussion caused a postponement of the main American debate, and the next day it was delayed by another petition, from William Bollan as agent for the Massachusetts Council: this asked the House not to concur with the Lords and asserted that the

---

[78] *LJ*, XXXII, 209–11; *CJ*, XXXII, 107–9, 113; *Trumbull Papers*, p. 309.
[79] BL Egerton MSS 216, ff. 94–104; BL Add. MSS 35375, f. 3; *CJ*, XXXII, 130, 136–7.

Treason Act of 35 Henry VIII did not extend to America. Grenville
spoke in favour of the right of petitioning, and Dowdeswell in the
support of this petition, while Edmund Burke mocked the poverty
of the ministerial case. 'Though they have a minority of speakers,
they have a majority of votes. There is an economy of argument on
the other side, which I thought was prudence, I now find to be
beggary.' The ministry rejected the petition only by a majority of
thirty-one, 136 votes to 105, and the House resolved itself into the
Committee on America.[80]

'The grand debate then commenced on the North American
affairs', reporter John Almon began: 'the debate was very fine
indeed: not one bad speaker in it.' It lasted until nearly 4 o'clock
the next morning.[81] North stated that MPs were now being asked
to give their opinion on what the ministry had done.[82] Dowdeswell
objected to any blanket approval, and particularly attacked
Hillsborough's circular letter as a threat to freedom of debate in
the assemblies. He ended with the two obvious criticisms of the
Address: that Britain had no colonies when the Treason Act was
passed; and that it would deprive the colonists of the right of being
tried where the crime was committed, a principle of English law.

George Rice of the Board of Trade replied that Hillsborough had
given the Massachusetts Assembly the opportunity to change
their mind, and he reminded MPs that the economic advantages of
empire, the very argument against colonial taxation urged by
some opposition politicians, depended on the ability of customs
officers to enforce the trade laws. Attorney-General De Grey cited
precedents concerning application of the Treason Act in Ireland,
and also in Antigua in 1711. 'I hope we shall not act upon it. But I
hope we shall inquire.' Two Chathamite lawyers still in office
spoke for the ministry. Richard Hussey said that America
disputed Britain's supremacy, and Solicitor-General John Dunning
expounded the current Chathamite doctrine that Parliament's
right of taxation had been decided by the Declaratory Act. 'That
opinion which was innocent then becomes criminal now.'

Edmund Burke encountered derision and noise when blaming
the folly of ministers for having led America into confusion,
but Grenville met with more respect. Any dissolution of the

---

[80] BL Egerton MSS 216, ff. 106–13; *CJ*, XXXII, 151.
[81] Almon, *Debates*, VIII, 43.
[82] For this debate see BL Egerton MSS 216, ff. 113–79 (the Cavendish Diary,
from which all quotations are taken unless otherwise stated); *Trumbull
Papers*, pp. 312–15 (Johnson); and Almon, op. cit., VIII, 43–7.

assemblies, he said, should have been executed by Parliament, as with the New York Restraining Act of 1767, and not by the Secretary of State. But his main thrust was scorn at the lack of any ministerial policy.

In truth you don't mean to send for anybody. This is waste paper. . . . If I saw anything like establishing a plan, no man would set his foot firmer to support it than myself. . . . This way we hold out angry words on the one hand, and give no remedy on the other. It is a sort of wisdom which fools put on, and think they are wondrous wise. It is not only odious and contemptible, but destructive. Make your words like your actions, and your actions like your words.

Grenville's attack brought North to his feet. The ministry could not have waited until Parliament met before enforcing the law in Massachusetts. Hillsborough's instructions had been in a private letter to Governor Bernard, and not a direct command to the assembly. Order had been restored: all that remained was Parliamentary approval. North depicted the cabinet's policy as a middle course of action. 'Maintain your ground there. At the same time do not unnecessarily irritate the people. Do not let us have fresh grounds of dispute.' The resolutions did not preclude future policy decisions, and since repeal of the Townshend Duties was widely expected in America the refusal to carry it out was in effect a policy. North ended on a note of moderation, portraying the potential use of the Treason Act as a warning to the colonists. 'It is proper to give them notice, that they are not to depend upon impunity from an American jury, but to depend upon an English jury.'

The most notable speech of the day, according to agent Johnson, was made by Colonel Isaac Barré, whom he drily described as 'now out of administration and unembarrassed with former opinions'. Whereas Grenville had insisted that the issue was the authority of Parliament, Barré made taxation his main theme. Every MP in the House admitted the Townshend duties to be 'contrary to all commercial principles'. He himself did not believe that America ought to be taxed, but if the majority thought otherwise, requisitions were the method most acceptable to the colonists. Parliament must make up its mind whether or not to tax, and if so how. 'Let us enforce the Stamp Act, or let us take the other system. This is neither the one nor the other.' He ended with this warning. 'I say without repealing this law, you run the risk of losing America.'

A significant number of MPs with personal knowledge of colonial life joined in the attack on administration. Rose Fuller, William Beckford, and Liverpool MP Richard Pennant had West Indies connections. Thomas Pownall and George Johnstone were former governors respectively of Massachusetts and West Florida, and Barlow Trecothick a long-time resident of Boston. The ministry won the votes easily, by 213 to 80 on the resolutions and 155 to 89 on the Address: Grenville, and presumably his followers, voted for the resolutions but against the Address.[83] The weight of the argument was heavily on the side of opposition, so agents thought, and Benjamin Franklin even claimed that 'the ministry had been so staggered' that the report from the Committee was postponed longer than administration had intended.[84] A more obvious explanation was the series of proceedings and debates on Wilkes that culminated in his expulsion on 3 February.

Not until 8 February was the report made from the Committee on America to the House proper. Another debate began when Rose Fuller moved a fortnight's postponement and asked what exactly was the ultimate aim of the ministry. 'Do they expect that before it is ended the Americans should in their assemblies declare the power of taxing them to be in this country?' The opposition attack focused on the Townshend duties and on the Address, but Dowdeswell's speech contained a Rockinghamite objection to the resolutions: this was that one colony should not be censured without information on any of the others. The ministry did not challenge the contention that Townshend's taxes were unenforceable and harmful to British exports; the rejoinder, voiced by Treasury Secretary Grey Cooper, was that the American denial of the right of taxation made repeal impossible. The Address Grenville described as 'a delusion to the people of England, an offence to the people of America'. Altogether twelve MPs spoke in opposition and only six for administration, who carried the Address by 169 votes to 65.[85]

The Grafton ministry had known it would face criticism of whatever American policy was devised, from advocates of coercion or conciliation. Their adoption of a posture of standing fast

---

[83] BL Add. MSS 35609, f. 326.
[84] De Berdt Letters, p. 355; Franklin Papers, XVI, 29–30.
[85] BL Egerton MSS 217, ff. 248–309 (all quotations are from this source); Trumbull Papers, pp. 315–17; Almon, op. cit., VIII, 93–117; CJ, XXXII, 185–6. The resolutions and Address were returned to the House of Lords next day, and the Address presented to the King on 13 Feb.: LJ, XXXII, 248, 249.

without actually doing anything increased the wrath of both. Although evidently a compromise constructed by Grafton to reconcile conflicting opinions within his administration the policy was neither negative nor foolish: at the end of 1768 there seemed good reason to hope that the colonies would back down, that the American problem might simply fade away, for the last few months had seen the peaceful occupation of Boston and the failure of an organized boycott of British goods. Parliamentary approval had been obtained for the measures taken in the summer of 1768 to restore British authority, and ministerial spokesmen themselves had virtually discounted the possibility of Henry VIII's Treason Act being used against colonists.[86] In February 1769 there were many in Britain who thought the administration could simply wait upon events. But others were not satisfied. Hillsborough was only the most significant of those within the ministry who believed that something more positive and constructive was needed: and in the absence of any ministerial move towards conciliation, opposition politicians did not relax their efforts. Already the Parliamentary debates had raised the hitherto gloomy spirits of colonial agents such as Johnson, who on 3 January had sent home this pessimistic comment on the House of Commons. 'It is surprising how few friends we have there, who are so upon real principle. I fear I could not name above five or six, but those who will be so upon the ground of opposition may be pretty numerous, though I fear all too few to stem the present tide, which sets strongly against the colonies.'[87] But the opposition performance in the Commons was commended by Johnson on 9 February. 'It has checked that perverse, peremptory spirit with which administration set out at the opening the sessions. It has put them upon consideration, and shown them that the colonies can yet muster friends, who have given them some trouble, and may yet give them more.'[88] America remained a live issue at Whitehall and Westminster even after the formal completion of the ministry's Parliamentary programme, and even though the remainder of the Parliamentary session was dominated by the Middlesex Elections controversy.

[86] See agent Johnson's comment: *Trumbull Papers*, p. 317.
[87] Ibid., p. 310.
[88] Ibid., p. 317. De Berdt was similarly encouraged: *De Berdt Letters*, p. 358.

7

The British Response: Positive.
February–May 1769

THE Grafton ministry might well have thought that the expulsion of John Wilkes from the House of Commons on 3 February would put an end to the already troublesome episode of the Middlesex Election. Wilkes, still in prison, defied precedent and at once announced that he would stand again for the constituency. He was re-elected without opposition on 16 February, but on the next day the House of Commons at ministerial instigation declared him 'incapable' of election because of his previous expulsion.[1] Wilkes was again re-elected on 16 March, and his return annulled the following day. For the April by-election the ministry contrived to produce an opponent for him, Henry Luttrell. Defeated at the poll on 13 April by 1,143 votes to 296, Luttrell was awarded the Middlesex seat by the House of Commons two days later, on the ground that any votes cast for Wilkes were invalid. A subsequent petition from Middlesex freeholders protesting against this decision was rejected by the Commons on 8 May. The charismatic personality of Wilkes combined with the political and constitutional implications of these decisions to create a political storm of the first magnitude, which saw a safe ministerial majority dropping towards a crisis level. And in the furore over Wilkes, America for most politicians was all but forgotten.

The Middlesex Elections case is a reminder of contemporary perspectives, and an important part of the explanation of why the Grafton administration took no further policy initiatives on America in Parliament, and of why so little attention was given to the colonies at this time. But among those politicians anxious about the American situation there was a great deal of dissatisfaction with the apparent conclusion in February of all official Parliamentary business on America. It was with pardonable exaggeration that Secretary at War Lord Barrington told Governor Bernard of Massachusetts on 12 February that the Address 'though voted by the two Houses I believe is not approved by five men in

[1] *CJ*, XXXII, 228.

either; some thinking it too much and others too little in the present crisis'.[2] Contemporaries were concerned less about the administration's sins of commission than about ministerial sins of omission. Nothing had been done for the colonists. Nothing had been done to them. Advocates of both conciliation and coercion were left unsatisfied by a policy amounting to 'waste paper'. As the perceptive accuracy of that Grenvillite taunt became increasingly apparent pressure mounted on both flanks for further policy initiatives.

Some colonial agents thought that this second American crisis might be the last one. On 9 January De Berdt wrote to Delaware, 'I believe the sense of the colonies are so well known that if this act be repealed no future ministry will attempt another taxation bill.'[3] A month later William Johnson sent home to Connecticut this similar opinion.[4]

I think it evident enough, to an attentive observer, that they wish the controversy was well over, or that they could retreat with tolerable reputation. They have their hands full and see difficulties on every side, both at home and abroad, and could we once get the laws now complained of repealed, we should not, I fancy, very soon see a Minister hardy enough to impose another tax; but their honor, the dignity of government, etc., as I have often mentioned to you, they still insist will not admit of such repeal at present.

Agents differed in opinion as to what course of events would best serve their purpose. Johnson wanted the colonies to maintain a low profile. 'We hope the most prudent measures will be pursued on that side of the water, on which very much depends, for the counsels here will materially vary, according to the intelligence from time to time received from thence.'[5] Benjamin Franklin took a contrary view when writing on 29 January to Joseph Galloway, his political lieutenant in Pennsylvania and Speaker of that colony's assembly. 'It is thought here that if news can come of all the colonies having joined in the determination to buy no more British goods, the acts must be repealed before they rise. It is impossible to say such must be the effect. But perhaps tis the only way in which we can yet contend with this powerful people with any prospect of success.'[6] At the end of that month, so Franklin claimed, eleven ships were sailing empty to Boston and New York

---

[2] *Barrington–Bernard Corr.*, p. 184.
[3] *De Berdt Letters*, p. 354.   [4] *Trumbull Papers*, p. 318.
[5] Ibid.   [6] *Franklin Papers*, XVI, 29.

that would normally have carried an average cargo of £50,000.[7] Franklin's hopes were to be disappointed, and it was ironically his own colony of Pennsylvania that for long prevented any chance of an effective colonial boycott, with Philadelphia failing to respond to the initiatives of Boston and New York. Then a blunder by Hillsborough helped to cause a change in Pennsylvania's attitude. Franklin's dominant Quaker Party had hitherto adopted a conciliatory attitude towards the British government, whoever was in office, in the hope of ministerial support for their long-term objective of changing Pennsylvania from a proprietary to a royal colony. Franklin's own presence in Britain since 1764 was originally and ostensibly to secure this aim. But the American Secretary threw away this tactical advantage at an interview with Franklin in August 1768. Hillsborough's attitude to the proposal was then so cool, and his bias so strong in favour of the Penn family, that Franklin decided to make no further move in the matter while he remained Secretary for America. News of Hillsborough's attitude could have arrived in Philadelphia by 1 November, when that port took the first tentative step towards a trade embargo.[8] A memorial of grievances was then adopted for dispatch to British merchants, including a threat to ban trade if no relief had come by the spring of 1769. On 6 February 1769 a meeting of some sixty Philadelphia merchants cancelled all orders for goods not shipped from Britain by 1 April. On 10 March Philadelphia at last joined the boycott, over 300 merchants voting to stop imports from 1 April until repeal of Townshend's taxation; but this was a decision taken with reluctance under physical and political pressure.[9]

Although all three of the most important colonial ports did eventually decide on an embargo on trade from Britain, this boycott was not only belated but also to prove patchy and incomplete. This absence of significant economic pressure explains why the petitioning movement of British merchants failed to get up any head of steam. Before the end of 1768 Barlow Trecothick had already begun efforts to organize petitions from the merchants of London, Bristol, and Liverpool for the repeal of the Townshend duties.[10] But Trecothick could not make bricks without straw, and

[7] Ibid., XVI, 33.
[8] Franklin reported the interview in a letter of 20 Aug.: ibid., XVI, 189.
[9] Schlesinger, *Colonial Merchants*, pp. 128–31; Gipson, *British Empire*, XI, 183–4.
[10] BL Add. MSS 42087, f. 2; *Grenville Papers*, IV, 408–9.

his campaign was to fizzle out. In January a meeting of London merchants appointed a committee of seven, including De Berdt, to work for repeal of the Townshend taxes.[11] The committee met Hillsborough for an hour-long discussion, only to find the American Secretary against any repeal that session. The committee then turned to the Parliamentary opposition, De Berdt taking a draft petition to Edmund Burke. The Rockinghamite leadership held a meeting to discuss the matter, and was almost unanimous in not advising a petition: the time was unsuitable, and a rejection would prejudice any future move. This discouraging advice, tendered before the end of January, did not kill the idea. The committee of merchants met again, on 15 February, and another unsuccessful approach was then made to the ministry.[12] Trecothick, though not on this committee, was busy in the City of London organizing mass support for repeal. On 10 February 6,000 members of the City Livery assembled to vote instructions to their Parliamentary representatives, of whom Trecothick was one, recommending the encouragement and promotion of trade to the colonies.[13]

Plans for a petition from the colonial agents also failed to come to fruition. The agents held several meetings towards the end of 1768, and some were willing to accept Hillsborough's advice to petition only on practical grounds.[14] De Berdt told the Delaware Committee of Correspondence on 9 January, 'I believe it will be most prudent to keep the matter of right out of sight and only urge the repeal on the footing of inexpediency, upon which all the agents for all the provinces will proceed.'[15] The obvious motive for doing so was the knowledge that all petitions disputing the Parliamentary right of taxation would be rejected out of hand, whereas the purpose of petitioning was to provide the ministry with a pretext for repealing the taxes if it chose to do so. For this reason Charles Garth proposed at a meeting of agents on 24 February that a petition omitting the issue of right should be initiated. The meeting unanimously resolved to submit such a

[11] The others were David Barclay junior, Daniel Mildred, Thomas Powell, Christopher Chambers, Frederick Pigou junior, and Richard Neave: *Middlesex Journal*, 10 June 1769.

[12] *De Berdt Letters*, pp. 355–62. Franklin thought the merchants had consulted the Rockinghamites as to whether to organize 'petitions from the manufacturing towns'. *Franklin Papers*, XVI, 30.

[13] *The Gentleman's Magazine*, 39 (1769), 73–5, 107; *De Berdt Letters*, pp. 360–1.

[14] *De Berdt Letters*, pp. 342, 347, 349, 354.   [15] Ibid., p. 355.

petition, and Franklin was asked to make a draft.[16] Franklin produced one in which the right of taxation was not mentioned, and among other reasons for repeal made the point that some colonies already paid for their government costs.[17] This was approved at a second meeting, but rejected at a third one on 7 March. Two formidable objections had been made: that it must be the presumption that the colonial assemblies which had decided to petition the Crown and ignore Parliament would not approve of a petition to Parliament from their agents; and that such a petition might be used by the administration to claim that the colonies, through their agents, had withdrawn their claim of exemption as of right from Parliamentary taxation. To these arguments there was added the belief that in any case the administration did not intend to enact any further policy decisions on America that session: for the meeting was informed by New Jersey agent Henry Wilmot, a London solicitor who was secretary to Lord Chancellor Camden, that the ministry would repeal the duties next session but 'no consideration would induce them to do it this year'.[18] These observations caused some agents to withdraw their support, and since, as Franklin put it, 'no one cared to sign it unless it was to be signed by all' the matter was dropped.[19] The agents may have decided to refer back to the colonies the question of whether they should submit a petition for repeal on commercial grounds only, for the South Carolina Assembly on 10 July unanimously instructed Garth not to do so.[20]

Agents and merchants were among those critics of government who perceived the American problem as centred on the need to meet colonial objections to Parliamentary taxation. But the administration was also under pressure from those who saw the colonial situation in quite a different light; men who believed the essential need was to rectify what they thought of as the collapse of British authority in America. Two of them were witnesses at first hand, General Gage and Governor Bernard. Both used their friend Lord Barrington as a channel to convey their views to Hillsborough. Bernard's favourite remedy for his predicament he put again to Barrington in a letter of 20 October 1768. 'If the

[16] *Franklin Papers*, XVI, 63; *De Berdt Letters*, p. 364.
[17] For the draft see *Franklin Papers*, XVI, 54–5.
[18] *De Berdt Letters*, p. 367.
[19] *Franklin Papers*, XVI, 62–3. For a similar statement by Johnson see *Trumbull Papers*, pp. 324–5.
[20] *Middlesex Journal*, 31 Aug. 1769.

charter is not so far altered as to put the appointment of the Council in the King, this government will never recover itself. When order is restored it will be at best a republic, of which the Governor will be no more than President. I have sent my Lord H[illsborough] matter enough to support this assertion.' In the same letter Bernard emphasized the importance for the maintenance of British authority in America of the Townshend plan concerning the payment of colonial salaries out of Parliamentary taxation. Officials there would not act 'on behalf of the Crown, when they are left by the Crown to the people for scanty and precarious salaries'.[21] Here was a direct conflict of opinion with the advocacy of repeal.

The impotence of the Governor of Massachusetts when opposed by his own council was confirmed by General Gage in a letter to Hillsborough from Boston on 31 October; but Gage's chief concern was to describe to the American Secretary the difficulties he himself had encountered in quartering the soldiers sent to Boston. The council had claimed that all barracks in the colony, wheresoever situated, ought to be full before any billets were sought in that town, and the magistrates had declined to quarter soldiers in public houses. These and other obstructions led Gage to ask for a revision of the Mutiny Act.[22] In his reply of 24 December Hillsborough assured Gage that he would inform his ministerial colleagues of this request.[23]

On 13 February 1769 the American Secretary submitted to the cabinet a comprehensive list of proposals on America.[24] At one level his aims were simply to solve the practical problems of colonial government raised by men like Bernard and Gage, and to prevent their recurrence. But he also attempted to provide a solution to the crisis created by the imposition of the Townshend duties.

The first group of proposals concerned Massachusetts. Hillsborough responded to Bernard's pressure by suggesting an Act of Parliament to transfer the appointment of the colony's council to the Crown, 'as in the royal governments'. As if this alteration of the Massachusetts Charter was not a bold enough step, it was to

[21] *Barrington–Bernard Corr.*, pp. 177–80.
[22] *Gage Corr.*, I, 202–5.   [23] Ibid., II, 82.
[24] Two identical copies of the proposals have been found, one in Lord Gower's papers as 'Propositions submitted to the cabinet by Lord Hillsborough 13 Feb. 1769'; PRO 30/29/3/2, ff. 118–19. The other was sent afterwards by Hillsborough to the King: *Corr. of George III*, II, 82–4.

be accompanied by a declaration that any resolution by the Massachusetts House of Representatives either denying or even questioning the right of Parliament to legislate for the colony 'in all cases whatsoever' would automatically lead to a forfeiture of the whole charter. It is astonishing that Hillsborough does not seem to have anticipated that this projected legislation might produce any resentment or resistance, for two of his other ideas were based on an assumption that the situation in Massachusetts might well be defused during the next few months. He suggested that his earlier instruction to Governor Bernard, that the next meeting of the colony's assembly should be summoned at Salem or Cambridge and not at Boston, could now be modified to allow the governor discretion whether to hold it in Boston after all. Hillsborough's belief that the crisis was now virtually over was shown even more clearly by his idea that Gage should be positively encouraged to send back to Nova Scotia the soldiers dispatched to Boston from there, and to resume the normal rotation of regiments in America as soon as possible. Governor Bernard should be given a baronetcy, and be instructed to return to Britain for a personal report on his colony, leaving Lieutenant-Governor Thomas Hutchinson to administer the colony during his absence.

Another colony over which Hillsborough suggested direct action was New York. Here the assembly had on 17 December belatedly followed Virginia's lead by voting a petition to the King, memorial to the Lords, and remonstrance to the Commons. These were transmitted to agent Robert Charles. Then on 31 December it had gone even further, passing resolutions which in the opinion of Governor Moore were incompatible with the Declaratory Act. The governor had therefore dissolved the assembly on 2 January, but four of his council had voted in favour of a mere prorogation. This news, sent by Moore in a letter of 4 January,[25] caused evident concern to the American Secretary, who proposed the prompt removal of the four councillors and the reference to Parliament of the papers enclosed by Moore. Hillsborough envisaged two alternative courses of Parliamentary action: either an Address asking George III to instruct the governor to erase the offending resolutions at a joint meeting of council and assembly; or an Act to make all persons concerned in such resolutions 'incur a praemunire, or a disability to serve in any office'.

[25] *NYCD*, VII, 143–4.

A third group of proposals concerned the Mutiny Act of 1765. Colonial obstruction to this, as reported by Gage, had included the claim that the availability of barracks in any part of a colony obviated the need for any other billeting arrangements, the refusal of magistrates to co-operate in finding accommodation, and the refusal of assemblies to vote the supplies for the soldiers as specified under the Act. The American Secretary now proposed to hold over recalcitrant colonies the threat of quartering soldiers on private houses. The Mutiny Act should be altered to direct the quartering of soldiers in public houses, and, when these were insufficient, 'then in private houses, unless the colony build barracks or hire houses at the place to which the troops are ordered for their reception'. A colony must give security for the supply of provisions for soldiers in barracks or hired houses. Penalties would be imposed on officials who refused or neglected to provide quarters for soldiers, and governors were to appoint commissaries authorized to billet the troops. But the colonies were to be offered an alternative to this rigorous enforcement of the Mutiny Act. It would not operate in any colony that passed its own approved legislation for the same purpose. This concession would meet the objections often raised in the colonies to the provision of specified items such as alcoholic refreshment.

All this was no more than a programme for the punishment and prevention of colonial defiance; but the American Secretary's main concern was to obtain a permanent solution of the colonial crisis, and he was prepared to make concessions to achieve that end. Hence his proposals concerning the Townshend duties. His private and public attacks on that measure were now followed by a remedial plan, although not one that followed the line of his previous criticism of the duties as commercially unsound. Hillsborough now took his stand on the professed purpose of Townshend's measure, 'to raise a revenue for the support of the civil establishment of the colonies'. Hillsborough proposed that the Duties Act should be repealed with respect to Virginia and the West Indies, since they had already made ample provision for that purpose. The same concession would be extended to all other colonies that made permanent provision for their costs of civil government.

Hillsborough's wide-ranging and detailed proposals provided his colleagues with much food for thought, and the cabinet postponed any decisions. The American Secretary therefore on 15 February sent a copy of his proposals to the King, knowing that George III was to see ministers individually that day and asking that 'if any part of my ideas are honoured with Your Majesty's approbation you will be graciously pleased to recommend a speedy determination with regard to them'. Hillsborough told George III that he hoped there would be a cabinet on 18 February to make 'a final resolution'. For he expected the New York agent to present his colony's petitions to Parliament in the following week; that step would 'bring on the whole consideration of the state of America, and if administration is not prepared and resolved with regard to their measures, all will be confusion'. Hillsborough was optimistic about the initial response to his proposals. 'The lords of the cabinet, except Lord Chancellor and General Conway, I rather think approve the measures, but none expressed themselves explicitly. The Duke of Grafton still entertains doubts with regard to the alteration of the Council of Massachusetts Bay.'[26]

On America George III had hitherto supported the moderate policy of his cabinet. In commenting to Grafton on the Lords debate of 15 December, after expressing pleasure that it would show the Americans the determination of that House 'to support the superiority of the mother country over her colonies', he had approved the 'desire with temper to let them return to their reason, not with violence to drive them'.[27] Now, when George III was being asked for detailed comments to influence ministerial attitudes, the King's moderation was revealed as something deeper than loyal support of his cabinet. His opinions on Hillsborough's proposals are recorded in a memorandum that was either compiled as a basis for his discussion with his ministers or written up afterwards.[28] George III firmly rejected the proposal concerning the Massachusetts Council despite Hillsborough's emphasis on it. 'The vesting in the Crown the appointment of the Council of Massachusetts Bay may from a continuation of their conduct become necessary, but till then ought to be avoided as the altering charters is at all times an odious measure.' Holding this view, the king therefore condemned Hillsborough's plan for the automatic forfeiture of the Massachusetts charter on further defiance, as 'it rather seems calculated to increase the unhappy feuds that subsist than to assuage them'. George III approved of Hillsborough's other and less important ideas on Massachusetts, and added one further suggestion: 'the dissolving the commission of the peace in the province of Massachusetts seems much called

---

[26] *Corr. of George III*, II, 81–2.
[27] Grafton MSS, no. 531.   [28] *Corr. of George III*, II, 84–5.

for at this time, as the governor cannot remove any of the justices without the consent of the council'. The King accepted Hillsborough's ideas on New York; stressed that governors should be instructed to avoid clashes with their assemblies; made no comment on the Mutiny Act; and ended his notes with this opinion on the central issue of the Townshend duties:

The conduct of the Virginians was so offensive the last spring that the altering the Revenue Act in their favour and in that of the West India Islands this session would not be proper; though any hint that could be given that those colonies which submit to that law and make proper establishments for the governors and other services expressed in the aforesaid act, may another year be exempted from every article of it except the tea duty.

With this royal criticism reinforcing the objections of Camden, Conway, and Grafton none of Hillsborough's more controversial proposals found favour with the cabinet: Lord Barrington ruefully reported to Governor Bernard on 21 March that 'vigorous and proper measures have been proposed to the cabinet, but it is understood they have met with negatives there'.[29] Nothing more was heard of Hillsborough's ideas about Townshend's taxation, and the charter of Massachusetts remained inviolate, for the moment. On 1 March the American Secretary told Governor Moore that no cabinet decision had been taken yet about New York,[30] and it can be deduced from his next letter of 24 March that the cabinet had not adopted Hillsborough's proposals for the colony; for Moore was given no instructions, merely being informed that the King disapproved of the colony's petition as 'tending to deny and draw into question the supreme authority of Parliament to bind the colonies by laws in all cases whatever'.[31] On the same day Hillsborough wrote also to Bernard and Gage with instructions concerning the little that had survived of his proposals. The Massachusetts governor was informed of his forthcoming baronetcy; he was recalled to report on his colony; and either he or Hutchinson as acting governor was given discretion as to whether to summon the assembly in Boston.[32] Gage was authorized to use his discretion whether to retain any soldiers in Massachusetts, and to restore the normal rotation of troops if he judged that 'the general state of America' made this

[29] Barrington–Bernard Corr., p. 185.
[30] NYCD, VIII, 154.   [31] Ibid., VII, 155–6.
[32] CO 5/765, ff. 64–6.

possible.[33] Gage received this letter on 3 June, and promptly issued orders for the withdrawal of two of the four regiments in Boston: one left immediately and the other in July.[34]

These letters of 24 March presumably followed a final cabinet meeting on Hillsborough's proposals. Already the cabinet had rejected his ideas on the Mutiny Act and instructed Lord Barrington, as Secretary at War, to introduce into Parliament a simple renewal of the 1765 Act.[35] He did so, but himself disrupted the smooth passage of the Bill during the Committee stage on 15 March.[36] Barrington then put forward virtually the same idea that Hillsborough had proposed in cabinet: that if the magistrates refused or failed to apply the Act, army commanders should be empowered to quarter soldiers in private houses. Barré at once rose in great indignation to oppose this suggestion, and when Lord North did the same the matter was dropped, although not before William Beckford had 'put in his claim in not having consented to giving free quarters to the troops at Boston'. As an American observer agent Johnson was puzzled at the behaviour of Barrington, 'between whom and the rest of administration there is the closest connection'; but he guessed right when he thought it an indirect warning to the colonies, for Barrington explained his motive to Governor Bernard.[37]

Court and Opposition, who have never agreed in anything else, joined in rejecting my proposal . . . I am as little desirous as any man, that troops should be quartered in private houses; nor was that the intention of my clause, but to engage the Americans to quarter them according to the act, by showing that, if they did not, worse inconveniences would happen to themselves than hiring empty houses and furnishing bedding, etc.

Earlier on the same day the Bill had been significantly altered as a result of an intervention by Thomas Pownall, who proposed two clauses to render the Mutiny Act less obnoxious to the colonists. The first was to exempt from the act any colony that made satisfactory provision itself, the same idea as Hillsborough had unsuccessfully put to the cabinet. After an objection that Pownall's

---

[33] *Gage Corr.*, II, 87.   [34] Ibid., I, 227–9; II, 87 n.

[35] *Barrington–Bernard Corr.*, p. 185.

[36] For the debates on this day see Almon, *Debates*, VIII, 130–2 (from which the quotation is taken), and three letters: (a) B. Franklin to J. Galloway, *Franklin Papers*, XVI, 69–70. (b) W. S. Johnson to Governor W. Pitkin, *Trumbull Papers*, pp. 326–9. (c) C. Garth to South Carolina, *SCHGM*, 31 (1930), pp. 55–7.

[37] *Barrington–Bernard Corr.*, pp. 185–6.

draft clause implied that the colonies were better able to legislate for themselves than Parliament, Charles Garth produced an alternative wording: this simply excused any colony that made its own provision for quartering soldiers. The clause was supported by Trecothick, Conway, and Barré, and accepted by the administration after their procedural expert, Jeremiah Dyson, had added a phrase specifying that approval by the Privy Council would be necessary. Pownall's second clause, empowering army officers and civil magistrates to make mutually satisfactory arrangements, was agreed without alteration or discussion. Gage, when informed of these changes, commented to Barrington that while Pownall and Garth had done their best he did not think the colonists would take the opportunity of making their own billeting laws.[38]

Agent Johnson when reporting these events was scornful about such 'seeming lenity towards the colonies'. Certainly it was evident by March that the ministry had no intention of grasping the nettle of the Townshend taxation issue that Parliamentary session; and by then the efforts of merchants and agents alike had petered out. If the subject was to be raised in Parliament the 'friends of America' there would have to take some initiative themselves. The first move was made by Barlow Trecothick on 14 March, when he produced in the House of Commons the much-postponed petition from New York. In his letter of 15 February to George III, Hillsborough had been concerned that a general debate on America would ensue in consequence, but the discussion proved to be a damp squib. North opposed the introduction of the petition on the ground of its implicit denial of Parliament's right of taxation. Barré made the gloomy forecast that if the colonists could obtain no redress from Parliament 'the whole continent would be in arms immediately, and perhaps those provinces lost to England forever'. Beckford pointed out the financial folly of spending so much on the army to collect so little in revenue. Grenville thereupon said there was no middle way: either Britain must tax, or else with a good grace give up the right entirely.To this Burke made the obvious Rockinghamite retort of the distinction between the right of taxation and the expediency of exercising it. The New York petition was then rejected without a vote.[39] Johnson reported to Connecticut that the Pennsylvania

---

[38] *PCBG*, p. 59.
[39] Almon, *Debates*, VIII, 129–30.

petition would therefore not be presented, and made this scathing comment on the attitude of the administration.[40]

Thus, all the applications of the colonies are rejected as ineffectual. There seems no further hope that anything will be done in their favour this session, and they are left with only a kind of *ministerial encouragement* that, if they are *very quiet* and *quite silent upon the right*, and will *humbly ask it as a favour, perhaps* the offensive acts shall be repealed *next winter*. Such is the attention paid to the united voice of all America, this their boasted readiness to hear all such grievances! That the colonies will resent this treatment of them, nobody can doubt, but I hope wisdom and prudence will still direct all their measures.

The issue of the Townshend duties had still not been raised directly in Parliament. At the agents' meeting on 7 March Richard Jackson, Franklin's co-agent for Pennsylvania, told him that he would himself move repeal of the taxation, 'not with any hope of success, but so as to provide an opportunity for debate'.[41] Johnson understood that the aim of such a motion was 'to take from administration every degree of excuse, and to put them as much as possible in the wrong, that, in case any future ill consequences should follow in America, they might never have it to say that their plan had been acquiesced in, and that nobody had pushed for a repeal of the act'.[42] Jackson did not do so, perhaps because he was forestalled by a motion on 19 April by Thomas Pownall, who proposed that on 24 April the House of Commons should constitute itself into a Committee to consider the Townshend Duties Act.[43]

Pownall put forward this idea on the basis of his own American experience, and avowedly as an independent member. 'I am unconnected. This is no attack upon ministers.' He claimed that there did actually exist a genuine consensus of opinion on the subject. 'Everybody looks out for some mode of policy. Nay. I will venture to say everybody knows what that policy should be. We differ about times, and seasons.' The ministry, he said, could now act from a position of strength. The supremacy of Parliament was unquestioned in Britain, and the Americans were in a state of

---

[40] *Trumbull Papers*, p. 324.   [41] *Franklin Papers*, XVI, 63–4.

[42] *Trumbull Papers*, p. 335.

[43] For this debate see the Cavendish Diary, BL Egerton MSS 219, ff. 286–309 (from which all quotations are taken), and two letters: (a) W. S. Johnson to Governor W. Pitkin, *Trumbull Papers*, pp. 334–41. (b) C. Garth to South Carolina, *SCHGM*, 31 (1930), pp. 58–9. The Cavendish report is printed in Simmons and Thomas, *Proceedings and Debates*, III, 148–53.

submission. 'All is peace. . . . You will never be able to raise the power of this country higher than it is at present.' Pownall then rehearsed the by now familiar arguments against the Townshend duties: they had produced a trifling revenue, had led to a trade boycott, and would encourage colonial manufactures and foreign imports. If the House agreed to the Committee he would propose the repeal of the duties 'upon commercial considerations only'.

Pownall's motion fell on stony ground. It was not supported by any of the opposition factions nor accepted by the ministry. Although William Burke, speaking avowedly as a Rockinghamite, had promptly welcomed Pownall's initiative, Edmund Burke gave it a cool reception later in the debate. 'I never wished to agitate or stir the question, or now to support it.' He was concerned that a confrontation situation might develop over America, based on respective assumptions of oppression and rebellion. 'I never thought America should be beat backwards and forwards as the tennis ball of faction.' In his report of the debate agent Johnson followed his summary of Burke's speech with this comment.

In truth, even this set of men (the Rockingham party), who have generally appeared the most favourable to America, do not seem through the sessions really to have wished the repeal of the act, but rather that it should remain to embarrass the present ministers, and as a means of their destruction, to whom they hope to succeed. They had rather have the honour of doing it themselves, and mean in their turn to govern the colonies, though in a different way; which induces them to assert the supremacy of Parliament in almost as strong terms as the ministerial party, and to avoid giving any encouragement to the colonies which they apprehend may tend to render them untractable and unsubmissive to the dictates of this country, the counsels of which they resolve, if possible, ere long to conduct. Indeed, this must be the case with every party, in some degree: the colonies, therefore, if they are wise, will take care not to become the dupes of any party, nor connect themselves too deeply with any set of men in this country. . . . But to return to the debate.

The first Chathamite speaker, Isaac Barré, suggested the alternative idea of a resolution promising that in the next session Parliament would undertake 'a general revision of all the laws relating to America that have been made in his present Majesty's reign'. Jeremiah Dyson at once asked which motion was the subject of debate, and whether the only constraint upon the Americans was to be their own wishes, for Barré's proposal would encourage them to press for the repeal of all laws. William Beckford supported Pownall's motion as being 'the middle way.

... This is not a promise that we will repeal. It promises that we will look into the grievances of America.' Beckford then reiterated what had always been the Chathamite view, that America ought to be taxed by way of economic regulations and not otherwise.

Early in the debate Lord North had opposed Pownall's motion because of the improper American pressure of a trade boycott; and the conclusion of his speech hinted at what would soon prove to be a difference of opinion within the ministry. 'I see nothing uncommercial in making the Americans pay a duty upon tea.' Despite this implicit acceptance of the case for repealing other duties North promptly disagreed when his fellow cabinet minister Conway later spoke in favour of a declaration of intent, because 'it would convey the idea of a repeal'. Agent William Bollan noted that North, who spoke altogether five times during the debate, 'seemed from first to last determined not to admit any express declaration to be made to the Americans containing any promise of future consideration'.[44]

Repeal of the duties was favoured by several later speakers, among them Liverpool MP Sir William Meredith and Richard Jackson. Newcastle MP Matthew Ridley reminded the House that several towns were suffering from the decline in American trade. Near the end of the debate Sir George Savile reaffirmed Pownall's claim of tacit unanimity by observing that 'not one word has been said in favour of the Act of Parliament'. George Grenville declined to give any opinion until some policy was put forward; but, forthright as ever, he sought to embarrass the ministry by asking, 'If you are ready to repeal the law why keep it an hour?' The debate came to an inconclusive end, Johnson noting that 'nobody would defend the act, nor many urge its repeal', and diarist Cavendish simply remarking that 'nobody thought of making a proposition'. A decision on the motion was avoided by the procedural device of calling for the Orders of the Day, and a few days later Pownall gave notice that he would renew his motion early the next session.[45] It had been too late in the current Parliamentary session, and such opposition speakers as Edmund Burke and George Grenville had said that the ball was in the ministry's court. But the debate had served a useful purpose: as Bollan observed, 'a general sense seemed to prevail in the House that this act was improper'.[46] The ministry

---

[44] *Bowdoin–Temple Papers*, pp. 135–6.
[45] *CJ*, XXXII, 421; *Trumbull Papers*, p. 341.
[46] *Bowdoin–Temple Papers*, p. 136.

now knew that there would be strong support for a policy of concession next year.

Within a fortnight of this debate the cabinet made its decision on American taxation. This was broadly in accordance with the unofficial assurances on repeal emanating from government sources since December 1768, but with what proved to be a crucial exception, the retention of the tea duty. The cabinet held a meeting 'said to be of great importance relative to America' on 24 April,[47] and came to its all-important decision on 1 May.

By that time the bestowal of the Middlesex seat on Luttrell had provided the administration with a temporary breathing-space in the great Parliamentary battle over Wilkes. The impending recovery of Chatham from ill health threatened to pose a question about the future of the ministry, several of whom owed their appointment and professed allegiance to that great man.[48] Trouble threatened on the international scene, where there were ominous indications that Spain had designs on the Falkland Islands, occupied by Britain in 1766.[49] A variety of motives impelled ministers towards a solution of the American crisis before they were troubled by other problems.

Circumstances in both Britain and the colonies were propitious for the attempt, as Pownall had pointed out in the debate of 19 April. British opinion was virtually unanimous on the sovereignty of Parliament over America, but the determination to maintain this was coupled with recognition of the impolicy of the Townshend duties. The apparent success in cowing the trouble-centre of Boston could enable the ministry to portray itself as acting from a position of strength. Other factors in the colonial situation now made a prompt decision desirable and possible. The cabinet must have known by then that the financial statement of the American Customs Board had disclosed a gross revenue from the Townshend duties of only £11,136 for the period up to 5 January 1769.[50] And while the economic consequences of the growing trade boycott were not yet such as to expose the administration to the charge of yielding to colonial pressure, ministers could assume that the news from Philadelphia would mean an intensification of the colonial embargo on imports from

[47] Middlesex Journal, 27 Apr. 1769.
[48] For indications of Chatham's physical recovery at this time see Chatham Papers, III, 355–6.
[49] Goebel, Struggle for the Falkland Islands, pp. 221–72.
[50] Gipson, British Empire, XI, 241–2.

Britain.[51] A timely concession might short-circuit such a development.

When the cabinet met on 1 May the policy decision concerning the Townshend duties was therefore not whether to make a concession but how far to go. Already much political discussion had distinguished the tea duty from the other Townshend duties. The duties on such items as glass, china, and paper were liable to the objection of restricting the sale of British manufactured goods in the colonies, whereas tea was simply a commodity imported from Asia and re-exported to America. Although some contemporaries thought the other duties would encourage colonists to manufacture the taxed goods,[52] the argument that they should be repealed as detrimental to Britain's export trade was one so weak as to be almost spurious, as Edmund Burke was to tell the House of Commons on 9 May 1770. He then pointed out that the economic loss to Britain, even if the export to America of the taxed manufactures ceased altogether, would have been insignificant and 'trifling'.[53]

A second difference concerned the Townshend revenue, for about three-quarters of this came from tea. Grafton when proposing the repeal of all the duties, was well aware of the distinction between tea and 'the other trifling objects of taxation'.[54] Agent Johnson wrote home on 25 May that the tea duty had 'already been considerable', whereas 'all the rest . . . are and must be trifling, and may without injury to the revenue be sacrificed'.[55] The retention of the lucrative tea duty was far more than a token of the right of taxation. Lord North was to make it clear to Parliament that he wanted the revenue in order to implement the original Townshend aim of paying the salaries of colonial officials, and he steadily pursued this policy, already begun in 1768, from 1770 onwards. The symbolic gesture lay in the repeal of the other 'trifling' duties, not the retention of the tea duty.

The cabinet decision of 1 May was therefore a defeat for Prime Minister Grafton rather than a compromise. It is probable that the rumours picked up by Benjamin Franklin a month beforehand represented what Grafton wished to accomplish. On 3 April

---

[51] There is no report in London newspapers for April of the Philadelphia decision of 10 Mar., but earlier news from that port must have been known.

[52] *Trumbull Papers*, pp. 350–3.

[53] Simmons and Thomas, op. cit., III, 306. Britain's china exports to America over the previous three years had averaged £51,000: Chaffin, *WMQ*, 27 (1970), 95.

[54] *Grafton Autobiography*, p. 229.   [55] *Trumbull Papers*, pp. 349–50.

Franklin mentioned in a letter to the Speaker of the Georgia Assembly that 'hints are indeed given, that if everything remains quiet in America, possibly, they may be repealed next year and probably none of the like kind will ever be made hereafter'.[56] The mode of proceeding in the cabinet is not known, although Grafton in his later autobiography did state that he proposed a repeal of all the duties.[57] Of the nine members present, five were in favour of retention of the tea duty: Hillsborough, North, the two Bedfordites Gower and Weymouth, and Rochford. The four who wanted abolition of the tea duty were the three remaining Chathamites: Grafton himself, Camden and Granby, and the former Rockinghamite Conway. What was especially galling to the outvoted Prime Minister was the absence of another Chathamite, Sir Edward Hawke.[58] Nothing is known of any discussion that took place, and it is certainly not evident why ten months later, when this cabinet policy was belatedly being enacted in Parliament, Lord Barrington should put what he regarded as the blame for the repeal of the 'uncommercial' duties on the Lord Chancellor: on 7 March 1770 he told General Gage, 'Lord Camden is the cause of it, for while he was [Lord] Chancellor he got the administration into difficulties which the present ministry cannot yet get rid of.' Barrington was vehemently opposed to any concessions to colonies 'where there have been associations not to receive English goods, or any other kind of resistance to the law'.[59] But what he might have had in mind was not so much the partial repeal of the Townshend duties as the other important decision of the cabinet on 1 May, a public promise that no future taxes would be levied on the colonies. For although Grafton and his supporters had been defeated on the main point at issue, they had secured what the Duke believed to be important concessions.

The intentions of the cabinet as regards both the partial repeal and the decision not to impose future taxation in America were to be made known to the colonies by a circular letter to all the governors. This decision was in accordance with the view Conway had expressed in the Commons debate of 19 April and contrary to the position then taken by Lord North; ironically it was to be North who in 1770 had to defend this action against Commons' critics objecting to the administration's presumption in pledging a future decision of Parliament. The wording of this communication, moreover, was to be moderate and conciliatory in tone: Grafton

[56] *Franklin Papers*, XVI, 79.   [57] *Grafton Autobiography*, p. 229.
[58] Ibid., p. 230.   [59] *PCBG*, p. 70.

long afterwards claimed in his memoirs that 'the majority allowed the first penned minute of Lord Hillsborough to be amended by words as kind and lenient as could be proposed by some of us, and not without encouraging expressions, which were too evidently displeasing to his lordship'.[60]

The American Secretary was to evade this instruction in circumstances that can only be described as highly suspicious. On the pretext of the need to send the circular letter on the first possible packet ship, Hillsborough wrote and despatched it without circulating copies to his cabinet colleagues.[61] The letter, dated 13 May, enclosed the King's Speech made at the end of the Parliamentary session on 9 May, which had commended the support of both Houses for the government measures of 1768.[62] Hillsborough restated this in his letter and commented: 'From hence it will be understood that the whole legislature concur in the opinion adopted by His Majesty's servants, that no measure ought to be taken which can in any way derogate from the legislative authority of Great Britain over the colonies.' Hillsborough then briefly reported the two cabinet decisions, hedged about with qualifications: 'His Majesty's present administration have at no time entertained a design to propose to Parliament to lay any further taxes upon America for the purpose of raising a revenue, and . . . it is at present their intention to propose in the next session of Parliament to take off the duties upon glass, paper, and colours upon consideration of such duties having been laid contrary to the true principles of commerce.' For good measure Hillsborough then added a paragraph of his own, emphasizing that government policy had not been changed.[63]

All this was a far cry from the conciliatory tone agreed upon by the cabinet. When the document was circulated among ministers the cabinet minority perceived, in Grafton's words, that 'the parts of the minute which might be soothing to the colonies were wholly omitted'. Lord Chancellor Camden was particularly incensed, and on 9 June wrote to ask Hillsborough whether the circular had been sent. The American Secretary replied the same day that it had been 'long despatched' and was 'exactly conformable to the minute'. Camden's next letter, which is missing, evidently disputed this and asked for a copy of that cabinet minute.

[60] *Grafton Autobiography*, p. 230.
[61] Ibid.   [62] *LJ*, XXXII, 383–4.
[63] Copies of the circular, with slight variants in the wording, may be found in the *Grafton Autobiography*, p. 233, and *NYCD*, VIII, 164–5.

Hillsborough on 10 June replied that after 'half a day in looking for it' he had been unable to find the original rough minute taken on 1 May. But he had already sent the formal minute to Camden and the other members of the cabinet and to the King, and enclosed for Camden's benefit a copy together with one of the circular letter.[64] Here is the wording of the official minute.[65]

It is the unanimous opinion of the Lords present to submit to his Majesty as their advice that no measure should be taken which can any way derogate from the legislative authority of Great Britain over the colonies. But that the Secretary of State in his correspondence and conversation be permitted to state it as the opinion of the King's servants that it is by no means the intention of Administration nor do they think it expedient or for the interest of Great Britain or America to propose or consent to the laying any further taxes upon America for the purpose of raising a revenue, and that it is at present their intention to propose in the next session of Parliament to take off the duties upon paper, glass and colours imported into America upon consideration of such duties having been laid contrary to the true principles of commerce.

Hillsborough's response did not satisfy the Lord Chancellor, who replied that he did not remember the first sentence as being part of the original minute, and that he had already told the American Secretary so when Hillsborough showed him the official minute 'a day or two after the meeting'. Camden had a more serious objection, that the circular letter 'does not communicate that opinion which is expressed in the second paragraph of the minute . . . The communication of that opinion was the measure. If that has not been made, the measure has not been pursued.'[66] There is no second paragraph in the formal minute! If Camden's version of events is correct, Hillsborough by accident or design omitted the conciliatory part of the original draft minute from both the official copy and the circular letter. And he got away with it. Camden admitted that 'the opportunity of trying what effect that might have been produced, is lost', and he seems to have been the only cabinet member to protest. Even Grafton, who recorded all this evidence in his later memoirs, does not refer to any complaint he himself made at the time, merely to a discussion of the matter 'many years after' between Camden and himself.[67]

---

[64] *Grafton Autobiography*, pp. 230–1.
[65] There is a copy in the Pratt MSS, annotated by Grafton about the voting. This is presumably the copy lent to Grafton by the second Lord Camden and reproduced, without Grafton's note, in *Grafton Autobiography*, p. 232.
[66] Ibid., pp. 231–2.   [67] Ibid., p. 232–3.

Hillsborough's behaviour had greatly weakened the gesture of goodwill that had been intended by way of the circular letter, but there were other motives behind this unwonted publicity given to a cabinet decision. The most obvious was the aim of undermining the growing colonial boycott of British goods, for the ministry hoped that American merchants would resume or continue their orders. The prospect of partial repeal of the Townshend duties might also have the political benefit of dividing colonial opinion about the quarrel with Britain. At home the news would help to allay any discontent among manufacturers and merchants arising from the lack of positive action by the ministry. These were significant benefits that might ensue from making the cabinet decisions known: and in any case, as agent Johnson observed with his usual cynicism, the ministerial promise, conditional as it was, was nothing like as binding as the Parliamentary pledge prevented by the ministry would have been.[68]

[68] *Trumbull Papers*, pp. 347–8.

8

'A State of Suspense Concerning American Affairs'.[1] May–December 1769

THE political scene in Britain during the summer and autumn of 1769 was dominated by the nation-wide petitioning movement arising out of the Middlesex Elections case.[2] Opposition politicians, out of town during much of the long Parliamentary recess, devoted their efforts towards securing as many petitions as possible from counties and boroughs throughout England; and administration supporters sought to counter their endeavours. America was seldom thought of, as the petitioning campaign engrossed political attention in the public press and in private correspondence. Even though the aim was a general condemnation of ministerial measures the attack focused almost exclusively on the constitutional and political issues arising out of the treatment of John Wilkes. That America was mentioned in two petitions was the consequence of initiatives by individual colonists. The national campaign was launched by the Middlesex petition of 24 May 1769, drafted by the radical Bill of Rights Society founded earlier in the year to support Wilkes: one of its members was Virginian Arthur Lee, and he contrived to have this complaint inserted as the final grievance. 'The same discretion has been extended by the same evil counsellors to your Majesty's dominions in America, and has produced to our suffering fellow subjects in that part of the world grievances and apprehensions similar to those of which we complain at home.'[3] But this reference to the colonies was not followed in petitions elsewhere, except in that from Bristol, a port heavily involved in American trade. Bristol merchants, concerned about the threat to this commerce, had in March sent 'instructions' to their MPs asking for support for repeal of the Townshend duties on 'British manufactures exported

---

[1] 'Peoples' mind at present seem in a state of suspense concerning American affairs.' B. Franklin, 4 Oct. 1769. *Franklin Papers*, XVI, 212.

[2] Rudé, *Wilkes and Liberty*, pp. 105–48.

[3] *The Annual Register*, XII (1769), 197–200. London radicals were to champion the American cause throughout the quarrel with the colonies, without any influence on British policy: Sainsbury, *WMQ*, 35 (1978), 423–54.

to America, which have been found highly prejudicial to the nation in general and to this city in particular'.[4] In July Henry Cruger, an American and Wilkite, exploited local anxiety and discontent to organize a petition with nearly 2,500 signatures that, among other complaints, blamed the administration 'for ruining our manufactories by invidiously imposing and establishing the most impolitic and unconstitutional taxation and regulations in your Majesty's colonies'.[5] But no other port took up this refrain. Even the petition from Liverpool concentrated solely on the Middlesex Election.[6] Wilkes still dominated British politics, even though his case had apparently been decided, whereas the American crisis had palpably not been resolved. The Middlesex Election, not America, was to precipitate the fall of Grafton.

The initial effect of the petitioning movement was to harden the existing political alignments. At first Grafton had taken very much to heart his cabinet defeat over the Townshend duties. 'I considered myself no longer possessed of that weight which had been allowed to me before in these meetings especially as the proposal was in a matter of finance, more particularly belonging to my department.' The Duke in his 1804 memoir stated that he had therefore decided to resign 'in the first favourable opportunity that offered. The resistance to any further steps calculated to alienate the colonies would probably have furnished good ground for my retreat: but, while I remained in office, none was proposed.' As the storm of the petitioning movement blew up Grafton changed his mind, thinking that he would be 'blameable' to resign at such a time of political faction.[7] During this new phase of the Duke's administration various circumstances combined to push him into a working alliance with the authoritarian group which had defeated him over the American tea tax. One was Grafton's marriage on 24 June to a niece of the Duke of Bedford, an event that naturally strengthened his personal relationship with that Duke's family and political friends. At the same time Grafton's own hostility to the petitioning movement, which he deemed illegal, led to a growing coolness between him and Lord Chancellor Camden.[8] But what above all drove Grafton closer to the Bedfords, Hillsborough, and North was the re-entry into the political arena of the formidable Chatham.

Chatham's recovery from ill health was signalized by his

[4] London Chronicle, 14 Mar. 1769.
[5] London Chronicle, 25 Nov. 1769.　　[6] Rudé, op. cit., p. 128.
[7] Grafton Autobiography, pp. 234–5.　　[8] Ibid., pp. 238–41.

appearance at Court on 7 July, when he had a private interview with George III.[9] His coldness then towards Grafton was a public indication of his hostility to the administration. Lord Camden had already seen him and reported to the Duke that Chatham was critical of their policy and viewed Grafton's marriage as a political move, whereas it had in fact been a love-match.[10] Although Chatham apparently did not then mention America to Camden, within a month he was understood to include colonial policy in his general condemnation of the ministry. Chatham's political rebirth posed a double threat to the Grafton administration. The great man buried the political hatchet with his brothers-in-law Lord Temple and George Grenville. Temple had already been personally reconciled to Chatham in the previous autumn. Now during the summer of 1769 this relationship was broadened to include Grenville in a political alliance. Rumours and expectations of this event prompted its formal announcement by Temple at the Buckinghamshire county meeting on 12 September at Aylesbury.[11] The Rockinghamite party had already formed a political alliance with the Grenvillites over the Middlesex elections both in Parliament and in the petitioning campaign. Here then was the prospect of a truly formidable Parliamentary opposition, headed by three former Prime Ministers each leading a party, a unique phenomenon in British politics.

Even more alarming as an immediate threat was the disruptive effect of Chatham's recovery on an administration of which he had been the original creator. Chatham's personal hostility to Grafton was further signified by his deliberate refusal to meet the Duke in August.[12] Yet in the same month it was widely believed that the other three Chathamites in the cabinet, Camden, Granby, and Hawke, would quit whenever Chatham gave the nod.[13] This collapse of the ministry did not occur. Royal pressure helped to keep Hawke in office, for George III had a long interview with him on 1 September.[14] Granby was unwilling to resign, for the sake of appearances so Chatham was told: such a step would seem both an admission of his unfitness to command the army, and a retreat in the face of attacks from that noted polemicist Junius.[15] Even

---

[9] This at once led to the rumour that Chatham would replace Grafton: *Middlesex Journal*, 8 July 1769.
[10] *Grafton Autobiography*, pp. 236–7.
[11] *Chatham Papers*, III, 362; *Burke Corr.*, II, 79.
[12] *Grenville Papers*, IV, 457.   [13] Ibid., IV, 433.
[14] *Middlesex Journal*, 2 Sept. 1769.   [15] *Chatham Papers*, III, 363 n.

Camden remained in office, although Burke commented in October that he was 'considered as in open opposition'.[16]

These dangers to the ministry, both external and internal, remained a potential rather than actual threat throughout the rest of the year. No effective challenge from outside could be mounted until Parliament met, and that would not be until January 1770; and personality clashes and disagreements over policy meanwhile put formidable obstacles in the path of a successful opposition alliance. Whereas there had been easy co-operation concerning the issues arising out of the Middlesex Elections, America threatened to be a divisive question, and one that might deliberately be exploited by the ministry to that end. Certainly the proposed repeal of the Townshend duties promised to split the opposition factions asunder. Among the various attempts to guard against this possibility, two informal interviews provided valuable soundings. Early in July Barlow Trecothick called by invitation on Lord Chatham, for a two-hour discussion on America;[17] but not until 15 October did Rockingham tell Burke what had been said then on the colonies.[18]

Lord Chatham expressed dislike of the conduct of administration towards North America, and after saying how bad things were, ended that nothing would tend so much to quiet matters in North America as an administration being formed wherein there were men whom the colonies would confide in. *Our friend Trecothick constern'd* [sic] *that, as an oblique compliment to us.*

Although this was an encouraging omen, it was always likely that Chatham and the Rockinghamites might arrive at a viable agreement over America, as they had done during the Stamp Act Crisis. The real stumbling-block to opposition unity on this issue would be George Grenville; but a meeting between Edmund Burke and Thomas Whately early in September seemed to promise that even that obstacle need not be fatal. Here is Whately's report to Grenville of the conversation.[19]

---

[16] *Burke Corr.*, II, 98.

[17] The meeting was reported in the *Middlesex Journal* of 13 July 1769. 'His Lordship assured him that the American affairs were in a fair way of being settled to the satisfaction of all parties, and that not only a change of men, but of measures also, would soon take place.' The next issue of the paper, on 15 July, stated that this account 'is not true'.

[18] *Burke Corr.*, II, 90–1.

[19] *Grenville Papers*, IV, 449. The meeting took place on 4 or 5 Sept.: *Burke Corr.*, II, 56–7.

He asked whether Lord Chatham and you had gone further than the question of the Middlesex election, and seemed particularly anxious to know whether you have touched upon America. I said that I believed you had discussed many of the present political subjects together; and that with respect to America, your conversation had been satisfactory to each other; he said he did not see what occasion there was for further disputes now about it; that he hoped we should neither of us be caught in the traps which the ministerial people would endeavour to set for us, with a view to create divisions; and that if we differed in speculative opinions, we had no business to bring them into discussion.

I told him that if the repeal of the revenue laws was proposed, we should certainly not agree to it. He answered that as for himself, he hardly thought he should oppose, most probably he should absent himself; for his friends, many of them agreed in his principles, and some of them did not go so far.

Personal rivalries and antipathies presented opposition with more fundamental problems than political attitudes. For the aim of overturning the ministry was to form a new one, and there was the rub. The Rockinghamite group had the numbers, and the Marquess himself would wish and expect to resume the Treasury. But Chatham was not the man to play second fiddle to anyone, while George Grenville was the most formidable opposition spokesman in the Commons. Edmund Burke was therefore sceptical about the possibility of constructing an administration in such circumstances. The pretensions of 'the brothers', Temple, Grenville, and Chatham, would be high, and Chatham was hostile to the Rockinghamites as a party.[20] Even the more optimistic Rockingham could not envisage a ministry composed of all the opposition leaders, replying to Burke on 15 October. 'I think it next to impossible that the *three* brothers and us can form a conjunct administration. They doubtless would have great pretensions, from their age, habits of business, talents of speech, etc. etc. *We* too have our advantages, which in truth I would not barter for theirs.' He would favour an arrangement with Grenville rather than Chatham, who would only produce 'another edition of a court patched up administration' as in 1766.[21] Burke was doubtful even about this possibility. 'I quite agree with your Lordship that Grenville is the most temperate and manageable of the three, but he is no longer George Grenville, a disengaged individual, but one of the Triumvirate, to whom, by the way, he brings all the following that they possess.'[22]

[20] *Burke Corr.*, II, 88.   [21] Ibid., II, 92–3.   [22] Ibid., II, 101.

All talk of new ministries was mere speculation until the Grafton administration was brought down. By the end of 1769 the political world knew that the opposition was planning a determined onslaught on the ministry when Parliament met in January 1770. Chatham had announced that he would attack on 'three grand points; Corsica for foreign affairs; America for home policy; the right of election as a constitutional principle'.[23] Corsica, a dead issue in foreign policy, would offer little political mileage; but the petitioning campaign would provide a platform for a range of motions on the various implications of the Middlesex Elections case. That would clearly be the main basis of the demand for the ministry's removal. Whether the colonial situation would supply much additional fuel with which opposition could roast the administration was for long uncertain: the news from America in the second half of 1769 was confused and contradictory, open to different interpretations.

Since nothing could be known for some months about the colonial response to the government initiative over the Townshend duties, British politicians said and wrote little on America during much of 1769. There were few optimists. Hardliners disliked and disputed the need for any concessions at all. Other critics pointed out that the ministerial offer did not go far enough, being inadequate in itself and ignoring the issue of principle which was at the heart of the colonial objection to taxation.

In order to maximize what was anticipated as the beneficial effect of the cabinet decision the ministry made every effort to publicize it.[24] Immediately after his circular letter of 13 May Hillsborough informed the colonial agents: on 19 May Grenville was told that 'the agents of the colonies have been sent for within those few days and given to understand that in the next session of Parliament the American duties imposed by Mr.Townshend shall be taken off'.[25] It is not evident whether Hillsborough convened a meeting or interviewed agents individually. One not privileged to be informed personally was De Berdt, who on 20 May sent this report to the Speaker of the Massachusetts Assembly. 'They [the ministry] have since industriously spread it about the City that

[23] Ibid., II, 112.
[24] Not until 3 Aug. did the *Middlesex Journal* print it as a news item, and then attributed it to Chatham. It was as late as 24 July that the *New York Gazette* reported Hillsborough's circular letter: *Middlesex Journal*, 5 Sept. 1769.
[25] BL Add. MSS 57818, ff. 164–5.

the obnoxious acts will be repealed next session the first business it enters on if the people of America remain quiet, till then, and have desired several merchants to write out to that purpose. . . . I yesterday waited upon Lord Hillsborough that I might have it from his own mouth, but . . . he was retired into the country.'[26] De Berdt did see Hillsborough before the end of the month, when the American Secretary assured him that the repeal would take place in the next session and detailed the contents of the circular letter.[27] Rockingham knew that members of the ministry, among whom Lord Camden was the most active, were requesting London merchants to inform their American correspondents of the news; but when some of the merchants asked to be authorized to write such assurances this official commitment was not given.[28] There was a widespread misapprehension in London that all the Townshend duties would be repealed, but presumably not among those briefed by ministers: the report sent by Benjamin Franklin to Georgia on 7 June was an accurate account of the ministerial intention.[29]

Before Hillsborough's intimations of the cabinet decision crossed the Atlantic the Virginia and Massachusetts Assemblies again displayed an unrepentant recalcitrance. The Virginia House of Burgesses voted a defiant string of resolutions on 16 May, two among them being that it had the sole right of imposing taxes in the colony and that all trials for treason and other crimes committed in Virginia ought to be held within the colony. The newly appointed governor, Lord Botetourt, thereupon dissolved the assembly.[30] On 11 July Governor Moore of New York confided to Hillsborough his fear that these new Virginia Resolves would, as in 1765, 'add fresh fuel to those heats which have already spread too far over the colonies' and lead the others to follow this example. Delaware had already done this, and so had Massachusetts.[31]

After the stormy events in the latter colony during the summer of 1768 the arrival of soldiers in Boston had produced a mood of caution. The men who had led the defiance of authority came to fear arrest and deportation to Britain for trial, and government officials were sufficiently emboldened as to instigate smuggling

[26] *De Berdt Letters*, p. 373.   [27] Ibid., p. 375.
[28] Wentworth Woodhouse Muniments, R1-1188.
[29] *Franklin Papers*, XVI, 151.
[30] *Middlesex Journal*, 1 and 4 July 1769; *The Gazetteer*, 4 July 1769. Both newspaper reports contain errors. The formal vote was on 17 May.
[31] *NYCD*, VIII, 176.

prosecutions against John Hancock and his associates.[32] In the spring of 1769 news of the Parliamentary resolutions gave fresh heart to the opponents of Britain. This ministerial forbearance was imputed to timidity and not lenity. At the same time the unauthorized publication in Boston in April 1769 of some letters by Governor Bernard, that included his proposal for reform of the Massachusetts Council, produced an outburst of indignation. The assembly when it met on 31 May made its first business a demand for the removal of the army and navy from Boston. A lengthy altercation with Bernard, who pointed out that he had no control over either, ended on 21 June with a resolution that the military presence was unconstitutional.[33] Both council and assembly then demanded Bernard's removal as governor, the assembly in a petition voted on 27 June although dated 15 July.[34] The assembly also voted a long series of defiant resolutions, informing the Virginia Assembly on 30 June that 'we have adopted your resolves, and have added others founded on our own peculiar circumstances'.[35] These last concerned certain events in the colony, such as a declaration that the Convention of the previous September had not been an illegal body. The general resolutions of Virginia and Massachusetts were a direct and deliberate retort to the Parliamentary resolutions and Address of February and, for good measure, the Massachusetts Assembly threw in the charge that 'too many persons in power at home' aimed 'to render the monarchy absolute and the administration arbitrary in every part of the British Empire'.[36] When the assembly then refused to vote any supplies for the soldiers in the colony, in effect the Boston garrison, Governor Bernard prorogued it until the following January.[37] Although no other colony followed Massachusetts in what Gage called this 'flat refusal',[38] disobedience to the strict letter of the Mutiny Act occurred in New Jersey, New York, and South Carolina. Hillsborough frankly admitted to Gage on 9 December that the act could not be enforced as it stood and hoped for legislation on the point in the next Parliamentary session.[39] Ironically by that date, unknown to the American Secretary, the

[32] BL Add. MSS 57817B, f. 54.
[33] *Barrington–Bernard Corr.*, pp. 288–90.
[34] Walett, *NEQ*, 37 (1965), 219–21.
[35] *Middlesex Journal*, 21 Sept. 1769.
[36] Ibid., 24 Aug. 1769.
[37] *Barrington–Bernard Corr.*, pp. 290–2.
[38] *PCBG*, p. 65.   [39] *Gage Corr.*, II, 93.

other three colonies had backed down, leaving Massachusetts solitary in its defiance.[40]

Resistance to the Mutiny Act was in one sense a by-product of the fundamental clash between Britain and her colonies over taxation. Alongside that problem all other issues paled into comparative insignificance. The motive of the British government in giving maximum publicity in the colonies to the cabinet decision of 1 May was evidently to avoid an intensification of the political defiance there, and in particular to prevent any escalation of the trade boycott. The ban on the import of British goods was to be much less effective than its predecessor in the Stamp Act Crisis. But the chief explanation must be found in the natural reluctance of colonial merchants to offer themselves again as sacrificial scapegoats on the altar of American liberty. So far from the news from Britain acting as a deterrent to the boycott, the later part of 1769 saw its continued spread, and there is some evidence that the Grafton ministry's decision was counter-productive.

It was the plantation colonies that in particular saw a clash between the merchants and political activists. When the Virginia politicians, mostly planters, drew up a non-importation agreement on 18 May, at an unofficial meeting two days after the dissolution of the assembly, the colony's merchants refused to implement it. Much the same happened in Maryland after an agreement of 22 June. Nor were boycott attempts effective in North Carolina, where no agreement was even made until 7 November. Only part of Delaware attempted a boycott at all, in August. South Carolina saw a long conflict between the merchants of Charleston and the politicians pressing them for non-importation, a compromise arrangement being made in late July. Savannah merchants were equally loath to sign, and a Georgia agreement finally made on 19 September was only enforced in part. So belated and ineffectual were the boycott agreements in the plantation colonies that imports there from Britain in 1769 actually showed a slight increase of some £32,000 over the total for 1768.[41]

Even New England, despite many meetings and resolutions in the past two years, was slow to implement any significant boycott. Not until July and August did the ports of Connecticut

---

[40] Ibid., II, 533.
[41] *HMC Dartmouth MSS*, II, 75–6; Schlesinger, *Colonial Merchants*, pp. 135–50; Gipson, *British Empire*, XI, 184–6, 266. The British press reported such events in detail: see, for example, the *Middlesex Journal* of 9 Sept. 1769 for South Carolina.

follow the example of nearby New York. Rhode Island was later still, unwillingly falling into line in October after pressure from other colonies that included a New York ban on all trade in September.[42] No non-importation agreement was made in the northerly colony of New Hampshire.[43]

Boston had of course led the way; but the non-importation agreements made there since late 1767 were for a long time largely a matter of political propaganda. When in 1769 the names of about a dozen merchants were publicized as offenders, further inquiry detected some 190 actual importers, among whom were many of those most vociferous against importation.[44] In such an acrimonious atmosphere news of the Grafton ministry's decision was greeted with hostility and suspicion; and a letter from the town on 3 August informed Benjamin Franklin that the government's pledge was regarded as deliberately divisive and that it had had the opposite effect to that intended.[45] On 26 July a meeting of Boston merchants unanimously renewed the existing agreement of August 1768 that had established a tactic of non-importation for 1769, but with the exception of such specified essential items as medicines and school-books: no other goods were to be ordered until the revenue duties were repealed.[46] Commodore Hood understood that the meeting had also considered a demand for repeal of the duties on sugar, molasses, and wine as well as tea, whether or not they were ostensibly for revenue; and he speculated whether the intention was to reject all duties laid by Parliament. 'It seems to be the general opinion at present, that they can force administration and Parliament to yield to them in every respect, and that perseverance in non-importation is all that is necessary to procure them all they want.'[47] The Boston politicians had logic on their side: in the period from September 1767 to January 1770, when the Townshend duties yielded £17,912 in revenue, the duties on wine, imposed in 1733 and 1764, produced £20,130, and the 1766 molasses duty £22,652.[48] Hood's information was evidently correct, for on 17 October the Boston merchants made another agreement, this time not to order any goods from Britain until all these revenue acts had been repealed: and they further

[42] *Middlesex Journal*, 14 Nov. 1769; Gipson, op. cit., 188–90; Schlesinger, op. cit., pp. 150–5.
[43] *DAR*, II, 42–4.   [44] BL Add. MSS 57817B, f. 99.
[45] *Franklin Papers*, XVI, 183.
[46] *Middlesex Journal*, 7 Sept. 1769; Schlesinger, op. cit., pp. 122–3.
[47] *Grenville Papers*, IV, 439–40.   [48] Schlesinger, op. cit., p. 131 n.

intensified the pressure on Britain by deciding to return there any banned goods instead of merely storing them in warehouses as before.[49] They also requested Philadelphia, New York, and other ports to follow this extension of their demand, but all declined on the ground that they had made their orders conditional on repeal of the Townshend duties only. They did, however, accept the Boston agreement so far as to offer future co-operation to secure the repeal of the 1764 and 1766 Revenue Acts. In the interests of unanimity Boston altered its October agreement to conform to those made in other ports, and on 29 December merely sent over to Benjamin Franklin some criticisms of the American trade laws, which he arranged to have published as a pamphlet early in 1770.[50]

At the end of 1769 Gage informed Hillsborough of the reality behind the rhetoric of the colonial boycott. It was notorious, he said, that Boston merchants had been importing on a large scale. Philadelphia had stocked up with a huge quantity of goods before she joined the boycott. Rhode Island had been importing freely until coerced by the other colonies. New York was the port which had adhered to the agreement most scrupulously and was in consequence the greatest sufferer.[51] The broad accuracy of Gage's information is confirmed by a comparison of the value of British goods imported into the colonies for 1768 and 1769 (see table).[52]

	1768	1769
Carolina	289,000	306,000
Georgia	56,000	58,000
New England	419,000	207,000
New York	482,000	74,000
Pennsylvania	432,000	199,000
Virginia and Maryland	475,000	488,000
	2,153,000	1,332,000

Information on the reaction of British politicians to the American news of 1769 is scanty. Surviving political records of the year,

[49] Ibid., p. 122.
[50] *Franklin Papers*, XVI, 272–3.   [51] *Gage Corr.*, I, 242.
[52] These trade figures, which actually relate to the calendar years from Christmas 1767 to Christmas 1768 and then to Christmas 1769, have been frequently printed, as in *Trumbull Papers*, p. 424, and in Gipson, op. cit., 266. The total trade figures usually cited of £2,371,000 and £1,628,000, are the imports for the whole of British North America.

whether private papers or public prints, reflect the contemporary focus of attention on the aftermath of the Middlesex Elections case. There is a dearth of hard evidence, in the form of ministerial correspondence and official papers, as to the attitude of the administration and of individual ministers towards America during these months. Undue reliance has to be placed on the surmises and speculations of colonial agents, whose sceptical interpretations of ministerial views and opinions, as relayed to America, can themselves be held to constitute a factor in the deterioration of the Anglo-American relationship. Agent De Berdt, in a letter of 1 June to Massachusetts, said that Hillsborough had told him 'some time ago' of his desire to alter the Massachusetts charter and, since the American Secretary had hinted that several other charters needed to be changed, gave it as his opinion, one quite unfounded, that the delay of repeal was intended to gain 'time to tamper with the respective provinces'.[53] If such suspicions were mischievous, the portrayal of the alleged unpopularity of the Grafton ministry was misleading in that it had no implications for American policy. Agents cited the petitioning movement in general, and the example of the Wilkite-dominated metropolis in particular: in that same letter De Berdt told Massachusetts that 'people in general are alarmed at their conduct as you will see by the enclosed petition of Middlesex, the most opulent county in England'.[54] In September, Connecticut agent Johnson, on the strength of a tour outside London, claimed to detect a ground swell of public opinion in favour of 'the cause of the colonies'; this he had found among country gentlemen and 'substantial people', from reasons of both political sympathy and economic self-interest.[55] Such misinterpretations of the British political scene served only to stiffen colonial resistance to the Grafton ministry in the unfounded hope of a change of policy.

The first American news concerned the proceedings of the Virginia Assembly in May and the behaviour of the Massachusetts Assembly a few weeks later.[56] Any hope that the Parliamentary resolutions might have instilled some degree of caution into the colonists was shattered, and news of further defiance and disorder provoked a sharp reaction. The destruction at Rhode Island on 19 July of the armed sloop *Liberty*; an alleged tarring and feathering of a customs official in New London, Connecticut; the Massachusetts Assembly's refusal to provide for soldiers; the rejection

[53] *De Berdt Letters*, pp. 374–5.   [54] Ibid., p. 375.
[55] *Trumbull Papers*, pp. 361–2.   [56] Ibid., pp. 358–9.

by the Boston merchants of the cabinet compromise over the Townshend duties: all this, and more besides, aroused the resentment of ministers. Agent Johnson reported to Connecticut on 18 September that 'they now give out doubts' about whether there would be any repeal at all of the offending duties and were hinting at severe measures 'to repress what they are pleased to call the rebellious spirit'.[57] Even the more sanguine Benjamin Franklin commented to his son on 7 October that 'it is very uncertain as yet what turn American affairs will take on the meeting of Parliament'.[58] When De Berdt saw Hillsborough on 1 November he thought the American Secretary uncertain about the repeal of any duties and adamant over retaining the tea tax.[59] There was no foundation for these rumours and suspicions concerning any ministerial rethinking about the cabinet decision of 1 May. On 10 November William Knox reported to Grenville an unchanged administration policy on taxation. Hillsborough was in a fairly optimistic mood, even suggesting as another motive for partial repeal a reason that came close to some opposition and colonial thinking.[60]

Lord Hillsborough gives me hopes that the people in the colonies are in a much more tractable disposition than they appear to be in from the common accounts. His Lordship has no apprehensions of everything doing well, if they be let alone by Parliament, and their affairs not intermixed with opposition points. The duties upon paper and glass, but not teas, are to be repealed from principles of justice, that as the colonies are obliged to take our manufactures, and cannot have others, we ought not to tax them upon their going to them.

Although Governor Bernard had been recalled ostensibly to provide advice and information on Massachusetts, the ministry was predictably reluctant to grasp the nettle of that colony's behaviour. Bernard arrived early in September, and Grafton had a 'long conference' with him on 8 September.[61] But thereafter he was left to cool his heels for a couple of months. It was the time of year when politicians were out of town, and Hillsborough did not return from Ireland until 23 September.[62] As ministerial policy had long since been decided anything Bernard had to offer would be superfluous, and indeed unwelcome: for the Massachusetts Governor made no secret of his opinion that the effect of such

[57] Ibid., p. 359–60.   [58] *Franklin Papers*, XVI, 216.
[59] *De Berdt Letters*, pp. 381–3.   [60] *Grenville Papers*, IV, 480–1.
[61] *Middlesex Journal*, 5 and 9 Sept. 1769.   [62] Ibid., 23 Sept. 1769.

administration measures as the Parliamentary resolutions and Hillsborough's Circular Letter had been to encourage the colonists to defy Britain.[63] Eventually, in November, Bernard and other witnesses were examined on the state of Massachusetts by the Privy Council's Committee of Plantations. The Committee's report painted a sorry picture of the colony, detailing the failure to suppress disorder and to detect offenders, and the unchecked existence of smuggling, trade boycotts, and seditious publications. At an institutional level the authority of the King's government was undermined by seditious town meetings and the refusal of the council to support the governor. The report recommended that the full Privy Council should make a formal examination of the state of the colony, requiring the governor, council, and assembly to send over representatives: any immediate decision was thus effectively postponed. But of especial interest in the report is the clear statement of the underlying attitudes and assumptions on which British policy towards America was based.[64]

That as the riches, strength and power of this kingdom do absolutely depend upon the flourishing state of its commerce, navigations and manufactures, so nothing will, in the opinion of the Committee, more effectually tend to promote these great and important interests than a careful attention to the keeping the American colonies within the due bounds of that commercial and political dependence upon, and subordination to, the Imperial Crown and Parliament of Great Britain, which correspond with the principles and spirit of the constitution, and have been expressly declared by law.

If the ministers paid little heed to Bernard, they did brush aside the assembly's petition for his dismissal, presented by De Berdt to George III on 15 September.[65] The agent warned the assembly three days later that it would be difficult to attack Bernard 'as he is under the immediate patronage of Lord Hillsborough whose orders he did in *many* cases exactly follow and therefore is rather the instrument than the original of several mischiefs, particularly quartering soldiers in the town when the barracks were empty'.[66] The Privy Council on 25 October referred the matter to its Committee on Plantation Affairs.[67] De Berdt was granted several delays in order to obtain evidence from the colony, but when by 7

[63] *Grenville Papers*, IV, 459.
[64] PRO 30/29/3/2, ff. 134–8. This 'sketch of a report', in Lord Gower's papers, is not dated.
[65] *Middlesex Journal*, 23 Sept. 1769.
[66] *De Berdt Letters*, p. 380.   [67] Ibid., pp. 382, 384, 390.

March 1770 he had still failed to procure any, the Committee decided to throw out the complaint; and a week later the Privy Council formally dismissed the petition as groundless, vexatious, and scandalous.[68]

Nothing is known of any ministerial discussion on the colonies at this time except that on 27 November there was a cabinet 'said to be for American business'. Two days before, Chatham's henchman John Calcraft expressed to him concern that Lord Chancellor Camden, whom 'we both understood . . . did not attend councils', was not only going but had pressed Lord Granby to accompany him. 'Fearing neither of our friends are the best politicians, I cannot help harbouring doubts but they may get entangled at this council, for no pains will be spared.' Chatham concurred in this evident fear that his two followers might become involved in colonial policy decisions that would cause later embarrassment when they enrolled openly under his banner.[69]

What happened at this and any other cabinet on America in late 1769 remains unknown. It is also unclear whether Benjamin Franklin ever did fulfil an intention he had near the end of November of submitting to Grafton and other sympathetic ministers arguments in favour of complete repeal, possibly with that same meeting in mind.[70] In the course of this activity Franklin put down on paper a summary of what he deemed the administration's attitude to be. The ministry believed in enforcing the right of taxation 'whatever may be the consequences'. They were sceptical about the effect of the non-importation agreements and thought that they would collapse after the partial repeal of the Townshend duties. The grounds for this confidence were the assurances of officials in America that 'manufactures are impossible there' and the belief that 'the discontented are few, and persons of little consequence'. Franklin therefore concluded that 'no thorough redress of grievances' could be expected in the forthcoming Parliamentary session.[71]

Connecticut agent Johnson sent home a similar forecast on 5 December. The ministers, he wrote, 'seem of late to have resumed and adhered to their first design of repealing the late revenue acts, so far only as they were anti-commercial, and to try the effect that would have before they proceeded further'. They professed to

[68] Ibid., pp. 385–8, 391–7; *Acts PC Col.*, V, 211–14.
[69] *Chatham Papers*, II, 363–5. This was evidently a cabinet meeting, for the Privy Council did not sit that day: *Acts PC Col.*, V, 215–16.
[70] *Franklin Papers*, XVI, 233–5, 243–9.   [71] Ibid., p. 248.

believe that any formal concessions to colonial claims would risk
the entire loss of America, since further demands would follow.
Only the duties deemed contrary to the interests of Britain would
be removed. The administration had been encouraged by recent
setbacks to the opposition petitioning campaign in England, and
especially by the failure of the American non-importation agreements, which had made 'little or no impression upon the
manufacturing and commercial part of the kingdom.That they
have not is, unfortunately, fact.' Johnson believed that this was
due only in part to 'breaches of the agreements', although these
were more extensive than he thought: trade figures would reveal a
decline of only 38 per cent in British exports to the thirteen
colonies for 1769 as compared with 1768.[72] But in any case North
America normally represented only a quite small proportion of the
British export market, about 16 per cent in 1768; and Johnson
noted the expansion of trade at this time to various parts of
Europe, notably Russia, Germany, and even France.[73] But it would
be quite misleading to conclude that economic circumstances
conspired to rob the colonies of their weapon against Britain. For
total British exports in 1769 at £13,400,000 were significantly
down on the 1768 figure of £15,100,000. During the Stamp Act
Crisis the fall had been much less, from £14,600,000 in 1765 to
£14,100,000 in 1766.[74] That in 1769 there was no great outcry
from manufacturers and merchants was due to the political
situation. This time the ministry did not instigate an economic
lobby to serve its political purposes; on the contrary, it was at odds
with the merchants of London, and actively discouraged petitions
from the manufacturing towns.[75]

Opposition politicians in 1769 were in the unusual position of
knowing in advance exactly what the administration policy on
America would be; but this was not a circumstance of which they
could take advantage. While it appeared likely that partial repeal
of the Townshend duties would enjoy the lukewarm support of
the Rockinghamite party, Grenville had at once made it clear that
he would oppose such a measure. Grenville believed, moreover,
that the Americans were encouraged by 'considerable persons in
England'[76] and put the blame on his Rockinghamite allies. If on
the one hand Grenville doubted Rockinghamite determination to
maintain British control over America, he also on the other

[72] See above, p. 152.   [73] *Trumbull Papers*, pp. 383–5.
[74] Ashton, *Economic Fluctuations*, p. 184.
[75] See below, p. 169–70.   [76] *Grenville Papers*, IV, 472–3.

suspected administration motives, remembering what he conceived to have been the authoritarian attitude of ministers since the formation of the Chatham administration.[77] 'I hear', he wrote to Whately on 15 November, 'that the language of the ministry is that they will restrain the Americans by the powers and authority of the Crown without the intervention of Parliament or in other words that they will make them subject to the King though not to the legislature of Great Britain. This special Tory doctrine will certainly fail in its effect as it ought to do.'[78] In his own eyes Grenville was the only true champion of Parliamentary supremacy over America, and he would act accordingly.

Rockingham, although concerned primarily with the petitioning campaign, wished to exploit the colonial crisis as an additional weapon against the administration. On 17 July, before any significant news had come that summer from the colonies, he wrote to Burke from a Yorkshire county meeting. 'The state of affairs in North America will operate and I find much alarm on that subject. This misconduct of administration in respect to North America, will be felt and when it is, and comes in addition to the home jealousies, etc., it will become a very serious topic, and will add fuel to fire.'[79] The Rockinghamite problem was how to exploit the American situation without affording aid and comfort to colonial opponents of Parliamentary supremacy. That was why Rockingham felt obliged to reject a scheme of reconciliation offered to him by Lord Dartmouth in October, one which came from a London West India merchant. 'The general outline of it is a Lord Lieutenant and Parliament in America similar to that in Ireland.'[80] Rockingham's response on 8 November pointed out the many differences between America and Ireland, which for a variety of reasons was under close British control, and he especially questioned the wisdom of any proposal that would unite the colonies still further. 'It has always occurred to me that a fundamental error in *policy*, was in Mr. Grenville's General Stamp Act over *all America*, becuse it *united* them, and also united them in one *common bond* of interest to resist.'[81]

The renewed American defiance posed a problem for opposition

[77] Lawson, *George Grenville*, pp. 228–9.
[78] Grenville Letter-Books, II: Grenville to Whately, 15 Nov. 1769.
[79] *Burke Corr.*, II, 47.
[80] Wentworth Woodhouse Muniments, R1-1240.
[81] Dartmouth MSS D (W) 1778/II/312. For an undated draft copy, see Wentworth Woodhouse Muniments, R1-1244.

as well as administration, Burke commenting to Rockingham on 9 September that 'America is more wild and absurd than ever.'[82] The Rockinghamite line had always been that their party could best give assistance to the colonies 'if America should be quiet'.[83] The colonial behaviour during the summer of 1769 was therefore as exasperating to the Rockinghamites as to other British politicians. Rockinghamite coolness towards America was noted by De Berdt, who sent this comment to Massachusetts on 23 November. 'In my opinion you can make no dependence on any men who are likely to succeed the present in power. Lord Rockingham's party entertain the most favourable sentiments of you; but the conversation of those officers who have arrived here from America has even[84] with them done you great injury.'[85] Two months earlier Johnson had warned his colony of Connecticut to place no reliance on British politicians, and he anticipated no benefit from the expected success of an alliance of the opposition parties.[86]

They have *all* long since agreed that America must be governed by and rendered effectually useful and subordinate to this country, though they have differed in the mode; . . . in the end, if they are to reap the fruits of all our labours, and conduct all our affairs, solely with a view to their own emolument, we shall certainly find the domination of any of them disagreeable enough. How these three seemingly opposite parties may agree upon the subject of America, I have, I believe, before mentioned to you. Mr. Grenville will give up the idea of direct taxation for the purpose of revenue only, to unite with Lord Rockingham in maintaining the right even to that (though not expedient to be directly exercised at present) and effecting the same thing in a less odious manner by commercial regulations, in which Lord Chatham will concur, though he gives up the right of taxation; while he adds to the commercial principle of the two former the dangerous idea of a right to restrain us absolutely from every species of manufacture, even, as we know he expressed it in his speech at the repeal of the Stamp Act, from manufacturing *even a horseshoe*; and whatever he says shall be done, or not done, we know, should he come of power, must be punctually obeyed . . .

At least it is so uncertain which set of men will be most beneficial for us, and so doubtful what principles will be adopted by either of them, that (merely as Americans) I think we need neither anxiously hope nor fear a change, but may firmly stand by and let them squabble it out as they can, while . . . we embark deeply with neither, but attentively mind our own

[82] *Burke Corr.*, II, 77.
[83] Wentworth Woodhouse Muniments, R1-1188.
[84] Text has 'ever'.
[85] *De Berdt Letters*, p. 388.
[86] *Trumbull Papers*, pp. 366–7.

business, get rid as we may of the burdens we are now under, and prepare ourselves to meet the measures of either party which may happen to possess power, or of all of them, whenever we find them inconsistent with the true interest of the colonies.

9

The Tea Tax Retained.
January–April 1770

THE British political crisis simmering throughout much of 1769 came to the boil when Parliament met on 9 January 1770. The background of petitions ensured that the Middlesex Elections would still be the main focus of attention, with the American problem only a makeweight in the opposition campaign. The colonies received little attention in the great Parliamentary battle of January and February when the combined opposition parties of Rockingham, Grenville, and Chatham sought to topple the administration. Not more than thirty petitions had emerged from the constituencies, one recent estimate being that only 14 of the 40 English counties and 12 of 203 Parliamentary boroughs are known to have submitted petitions;[1] but the total of 60,000 signatures did represent about 20 per cent to 25 per cent of the English electorate, and 1769 had seen the new phenomenon of an organized nationwide political movement. The aim was to destroy the government's nerve. But only the Prime Minister himself was to crack. The triumph of the opposition was to be limited to the resignation of Grafton and other Chathamites. Far from ousting the ministry and securing office for themselves, the opposition parties were to find themselves further from power than ever, doomed to over a decade in the political wilderness.

Chatham's political reincarnation proved to be a more significant event than the petitioning campaign. Already by the end of 1769 it was a question of when, rather than if, his followers still in office would resign. During December Grafton was under pressure from George III and from his colleagues to dismiss Lord Chancellor Camden rather than await his potentially damaging desertion during the Parliamentary session.[2] Suspicion about the intentions of the Duke himself also led the King to insure against his resignation by a sounding of Lord North.[3] But Parliament assembled without any changes of office, and in the first day of battle on 9 January 1770 over the Addresses of the two Houses in

[1] Hamer, Thesis, p. 104. [2] Grafton Autobiography, p. 245.
[3] Thomas, Lord North, p. 33.

reply to the King's Speech, administration routed opposition in both Lords and Commons.

The references to America in the King's Speech and in the two Addresses were brief, without any mention of the intended repeal of some of the Townshend duties; and America was only incidentally mentioned in the debates of the two Houses. In the Lords the seconder of the Address, Lord Dunmore, already named as the next Governor of New York, put forward the same opinion that Hillsborough had been voicing in November. 'The Americans, if left to themselves, would soon be quiet.' Chatham rose next, to make his first major speech in the Lords. On America, according to agent Johnson, he began with this declaration. 'I have not altered my general ideas with regard to the principles upon which America should be governed. I own I have a propensity towards that country. I love liberty wherever it is seated.' He favoured leniency although he could not justify the colonial excesses provoked by ministerial policies. Chatham professed himself too ignorant of the current situation in America to suggest any policy initiatives, but he objected to the description in the Speech and the Lords Address of the non-importation agreements as 'highly unwarrantable', since they were not illegal. Chatham proposed an amendment that although essentially concerned with the Middlesex Elections did refer generally to 'the discontents which prevail in so many parts of Your Majesty's dominions'. Lord Cholmondeley retorted that the word 'treasonable' should have been used to describe the behaviour of some Americans. Later in the debate Lord Chancellor Camden spoke for opposition on both America and the Middlesex Elections: according to Johnson, he said 'he was the friend of America, and wished to recover its obedience by lenient measures'. The Duke of Richmond and Lord Shelburne also spoke up for America before the original Address was voted by a majority of 'about one hundred to thirty six'.[4]

The Commons Address included a promise of 'effectual provisions against the unwarrantable measures', as the non-importation agreements were also termed. William Dowdeswell proposed an amendment more sweeping than Chatham's, for it referred to 'the unhappy discontents which at present prevail in every part of his Majesty's dominions'. There was no sustained discussion about the colonies in the ensuing debate, but America was mentioned by

[4] Simmons and Thomas, *Proceedings and Debates*, III, 166–7 (Report by W. Strachan), from which are taken the quotations not ascribed to W. Johnson, *Trumbull Papers*, pp. 397–9.

eleven speakers, including all the big guns of opposition, Dowdeswell, Beckford, Barré, Grenville, and Burke. Agent Charles Garth believed that opposition members were waiting for the ministry to introduce their proposals. For administration Colonel George Onslow, a former Rockinghamite who had stayed on in office from 1766, aimed a barb at Grenville by asking, 'who aggrieved the Americans first?'; and Lord North refuted the potentially damaging charge that Hillsborough's circular letter of the previous May had 'pledged for Parliament'. When the House divided administration triumphed by 254 votes to 138.[5]

After these Parliamentary victories George III thought the crisis over; but it was only just beginning. The King overlooked the significant omen of Chathamite defections. In the Commons, although Sir Edward Hawke and his son had spoken for administration, his fellow cabinet minister Lord Granby and Solicitor-General John Dunning had both supported Dowdeswell's amendment. Camden's behaviour in the Lords had left Grafton with no option but to remove him from the Woolsack. At the Duke's request both Camden and Granby delayed their resignations until 17 January, and Dunning went three days later.[6] Half a dozen other defecting office-holders at this time included two members of the Admiralty Board, but Sir Edward Hawke stayed on as First Lord, soon to become the last survivor of the Chatham cabinet of 1766.

At this moment the administration gained a fortuitous Parliamentary respite. The absence of a Lord Chancellor to act as its Speaker afforded an excuse to defer any sitting of the Lords; and by coincidence the Speaker of the House of Commons, Sir John Cust, resigned through ill health on 17 January and died three days later. Both Houses therefore stood adjourned until 22 January. The breathing-space brought no benefit to the ministry. The most serious set-back was Grafton's failure to find a new Lord Chancellor. His prime target was Charles Yorke, despite Yorke's political link with Rockingham, whose Attorney-General he had been in the ministry of 1765–6. Yorke had not opposed administration over the Middlesex Elections, and was known to be

---

[5] CJ, XXXII, 456. For the debate see Garth to South Carolina, SCHGM, XXXI, 139–40, and Henry Cavendish's Diary, BL Egerton MSS 3711, ff. 1–61, from which the quotations are taken. The parts relevant to America in both sources are printed in Simmons and Thomas, op. cit., III, 169–70.

[6] Grafton Autobiography, p. 246; Chatham Papers, IV, 391–8; Walpole, Memoirs, IV, 37.

ambitious for the Great Seal. He at first refused the offer, because of political embarrassment and family pressure, but on 17 January was bullied into acceptance by George III. Emotional stress undermined ill health, and he died three days later. The loss of Yorke was a body blow for Grafton, who was among those who subscribed to the theory of suicide. The Duke now began to think and talk of resignation, even though the problem of the Lord Chancellorship was avoided by the expedient of putting the Great Seal into commission.[7]

The Prime Minister succumbed to the next Parliamentary onslaught. A vigorous attack in the Lords by Chatham on 22 January was followed by a great Commons debate on 25 January, when a Dowdeswell resolution on the Middlesex Elections was defeated only by forty-four votes, 224 to 180.[8] The next day Grafton decided to resign. George III had already been pressing Lord North to accept the Treasury, and secured his reluctant acquiescence on 28 January, a decision kept secret for two days, since once Grafton's resignation was known other defections might follow.[9] But the Duke himself tried to prevent any such consequence of his resignation and remained an administration supporter. The only important loss was that of Conway, who told North that he would not sit in cabinet with the Bedfords now that Grafton had left; but he did not go into opposition. North's big Parliamentary test came the day after his appointment was known, when on 31 January the opposition mounted another major Commons debate on the Middlesex Elections. North did not duck the challenge by asking for an adjournment, as many had expected. He secured a majority of forty, by 226 votes to 186, at a time when contemporary predictions had ranged between a majority of twenty and outright defeat.[10]

Many contemporaries did not perceive this event as decisive. But George III had struck lucky. Lord North was the man for the occasion. His appointment was popular among government supporters and with independent MPs. Amiable and well liked, North was a man of considerable ability in administration and finance, and one of the best Parliamentary performers the House

[7] Hamer, Thesis, pp. 147–51.
[8] Cobbett, *Parl. Hist.*, XVI, 741–55; Cavendish Diary, BL Egerton MSS 3711, ff. 106–72.
[9] Hamer, Thesis, pp. 152–9; Thomas, *Lord North*, p. 35.
[10] Walpole, op. cit., IV, 51, 57; Cavendish Diary, BL Egerton MSS 3711, ff. 173–246.

of Commons has ever known. But his lack of experience in high office and his diffidence about accepting responsibility made many men doubt his suitability for the role of Prime Minister, and some even thought his appointment a temporary expedient. Events were to dispel such doubts. Within a month he was safe. In the Lords his ministry was virtually unchallenged after Rockingham on 2 February had made the same motion as Dowdeswell in the Commons on 25 January, only to be routed by 96 votes to 47. February saw a succession of opposition attacks in the Commons, but a steady rise in North's majority to one of ninety-seven on 28 February.[11]

America had not been mentioned in any important Parliamentary debate since the first day of the session; but the administration, now secure in office, could at last enact the policy devised ten months earlier. The cabinet headed by North had shed all four of the members who on 1 May 1769 had favoured repeal of the tea duty, and still included all five of the majority for retaining it. What had been a close decision had become a unanimous opinion, and it was to be one retained in the face of views vouchsafed by a number of colonial governors.

Some had written directly to say that the concessions were inadequate. Deputy Governor John Penn of Pennsylvania on 30 September 1769 stated his opinion that colonial fears would not be removed until the duties were actually repealed and the Americans had been convinced that no further taxation was intended. Deputy Governor Robert Eden of Maryland said forthrightly that partial repeal of the Townshend duties would not do. 'While the duty on tea continues . . . the general view is that it will stand as a precedent for laying duties in America on some future occasion.' On 8 November the elected Governor of Connecticut Jonathan Trumbull urged 'total repeal' of the Townshend Duties Act.[12] Two other governors put their own interpretations on Hillsborough's circular letter in order to render it more acceptable to their assemblies. Lieutenant-Governor Colden, in his speech to the New York Assembly on 22 November, announced that all the Townshend duties would probably be repealed in the next session of Parliament.[13] More controversial was Lord Botetourt's speech to the Virginia Assembly on 7 November, when he declared his readiness to make every effort 'to obtain for America that satisfaction which I have been authorised to promise by the

[11] Hamer, op. cit., pp. 194–7.
[12] Rees, Thesis, pp. 210–11.   [13] *DAR*, II, 31.

confidential servants of our gracious sovereign who, to my certain knowledge, rates his honour so high that he would sooner part with his Crown than preserve it by deceit'.[14] Botetourt's speech was criticized in the Commons debate of 9 January 1770 by three opposition members, Barré, Burke, and Thomas Townshend, who voiced the hope that the press report of it was 'spurious'. North deemed it politic to reply that he himself had read the speech only in the newspapers.[15] American Secretary Hillsborough reprimanded both Colden and Botetourt when on 18 January he wrote to all colonial governors, sending them copies of the King's Speech to Parliament and the Addresses of both Houses in reply. There is no record of any answer by Colden to Hillsborough's demand for an explanation. The reproof to Botetourt produced a reply of 14 April, expressing astonishment. Hillsborough thereupon explained on 12 June that his offence had been to use the King's name.[16]

Despite such advice from officials in America and various hopes and fears in Britain, the cabinet never wavered from its declared policy on American taxation: the delay in implementation was caused by the political crisis threatening the ministry's survival and not, as Benjamin Franklin later surmised, by 'irresolution'.[17] American Secretary Hillsborough had publicly reaffirmed the decision to the colonial agents by mid-February, at least in the negative sense of a declaration that he would never consent to take off the tea duty.[18] Lord North said much the same to the House of Commons on 21 February.[19] And the policy of partial repeal was confirmed at a cabinet meeting on 2 March, only three days before the main Commons debate on the Townshend taxation.[20]

What seemed now to be a real possibility was that the partial repeal might be accompanied by some coercive measure. De Berdt told Massachusetts on 1 January that he still feared an attack on the colony's charter.[21] A more evident cause for colonial concern became apparent after the opening of Parliament. Although Charles Garth reported to South Carolina that the debates of 9 January had revealed nothing of administration's intention on

[14] Rees, op. cit., pp. 208–9.
[15] Simmons and Thomas, op. cit., III, 169–70.
[16] DAR, I, 30–3, 88, 118–19; II, 31–2.
[17] Franklin Papers, XVII, 115.
[18] De Berdt Letters, p. 399.
[19] London Evening Post, 22 Feb. 1770. In its previous issue of 20 Feb. this paper had reported that one revenue duty would be retained.
[20] Ibid., 8 Mar. 1770.   [21] De Berdt Letters, p. 392.

America,[22] other observers read a sinister import into some phrases in the Speech and two Addresses. The description of the colonial boycotts as 'highly unwarrantable' and more especially the promise in the Commons Address of 'effectual provisions against the unwarrantable measures' gave rise to immediate rumours that the ministry intended to make or declare the associations illegal. On 11 January Benjamin Franklin told Speaker Galloway of Pennsylvania that 'it is talked . . . that a severe law will be passed with the repeal, to make it highly penal to enter into such agreements not to import goods from hence, as have lately taken place in America'.[23] Three weeks later, on 2 February, De Berdt informed Massachusetts of a strong rumour to this effect,[24] and the next day Johnson sent a similar report to Connecticut. 'They threaten us with some act or resolutions to render agreements not to import criminal, and it seems not unlikely that something of this kind will be attempted.'[25]

There was real cause for this concern. On 21 February Lord North proposed in the House of Commons an Address for an account of all the non-importation associations in America.[26] This was presented to the House on 5 March, the very day of the great debate on the Townshend duties.[27] The subject was not taken further in Parliament; but evidence that the ministry did have some such intention in mind survives in the form of a draft Bill, 'An Act for the more effectually restraining and preventing several unwarrantable combinations and undertakings in his Majesty's colonies and plantations in America'.[28] After the end of the Parliamentary session, Franklin told Galloway that this Bill had never been brought forward, and characteristically gave himself a large part of the credit. In lobbying against this measure, he said, he had emphasized the problems of enforcing such a law: it would be impractical and result in a further display of British weakness and imprudence.[29] There is no direct evidence about ministerial attitudes on this subject. Contemporary doubts did exist concerning the legality of such a ban, but another consideration was probably

---

[22] *SCHGM*, XXXI, 139.   [23] *Franklin Papers*, XVII, 24–5.
[24] *De Berdt Letters*, p. 405.   [25] *Trumbull Papers*, p. 406.
[26] *London Evening Post*, 22 Feb. 1770; *CJ*, XXXII, 745.
[27] *CJ*, XXXII, 745.
[28] *HMC Dartmouth MSS*, II, 50. It is there ascribed to 1766–7, and might also have been drafted in 1774–5 when Dartmouth was American Secretary. I concur in the assumption of 1770 by the editors of the *Franklin Papers*, XVII, 169 n.
[29] Ibid., XVII, 168–9.

more significant. The ministry believed that its strategy of partial repeal would accelerate the collapse of the import boycotts and so obviate the need for such legislation.

In early 1770 those who favoured reconciliation with the colonies by concessions were both divided and politically ineffectual. De Berdt was among the few who favoured the extreme Massachusetts demand of repeal of all legislation imposing taxes or regulating trade, at least before he knew that the colony had itself dropped the demand for tactical reasons.[30] Fellow-agent Johnson regarded such an attitude as an obstacle in the path of the lesser concession of repeal of the Townshend duties. 'What seems most to influence against the repeal is the opinion many have formed (founded, as they pretend, upon the extravagant demands of the people of Boston), that America will not be satisfied with anything less than the repeal of all the Acts of Parliament relating to the colonies, even that of Navigation, and that therefore they had best make their stand where they now are.'[31] For most of the agents, merchants, and politicians active on the colonial behalf, repeal of the Townshend duties was the immediate objective: but there was no grand alliance to put effective pressure on the ministry.

Not much could be hoped for from the politicians in Parliament, so Johnson wrote on 2 February. 'I am not sure that the Opposition will take up our cause with spirit; at least, if they do, I fear it will be only so far as may serve the purposes of pure opposition, not upon the great principles upon which we stand, and if so, what they do will lose much of its weight.'[32] Johnson's pessimism was to prove justified. Of the three main opposition parties, that headed by Grenville would object to any concessions to America at all. The Rockinghamites would lukewarmly support repeal of the tea duty with votes rather than speeches. Chatham, in the Lords, would be unable to join in the main Parliamentary battle, and he was to make public his discouraging opinion that 'the warmest friends of America . . . had . . . pushed matters much too far'. His concern, as always, was with the economic bonds of empire. 'If America was determined to set at defiance all the Acts of trade and navigation of this country, they would not be able to find in this kingdom a more determined opponent.'[33]

---

[30] *De Berdt Letters*, p. 392.
[31] *Trumbull Papers*, p. 406.   [32] Ibid.
[33] *London Evening Post*, 10 Mar. 1770. Chatham's opinion was attributed to a conversation 'on Friday last', 2 or 9 Mar. 1770. The accuracy of this report,

There is no evidence that any of these Parliamentary politicians were involved in any attempt to put pressure on the administration outside Westminster, and only a muted response came from the merchants and manufacturers involved in American trade. Benjamin Franklin added another explanation to the obvious one of the lack of economic pressure when on 11 January he reported to Joseph Galloway his efforts in the London mercantile community. He had been attempting in vain to persuade merchants to present either to the ministry or to Parliament an account of the conditional orders they had received, in order to destroy the widely held opinion, assiduously propagated by the ministry, that American trade was virtually normal. Many of the merchants, he wrote, were so hostile to government that they were unwilling to have anything to do with the ministry.[34]

Several meetings of merchants did take place during January, culminating in what De Berdt described as 'a general meeting' on 1 February, reported by the *London Evening Post* two days later as 'the meeting of the American merchants at the King's Arms in Cornhill'. The gathering was attended by two Americans, from Philadelphia and New York. Their assurances, together with a letter from Boston, convinced the London merchants that colonial trade would be resumed if the Townshend duties alone were repealed, and the meeting decided to petition Parliament for that purpose. It was in vain that De Berdt, attending as a merchant, protested in his other role as an agent that such a step would not suffice to end the colonial boycott on British imports. The merchants freely acknowledged that 'they had no other regard for America' apart from the resumption of trade. Political matters were the concern of the agents.[35] No more help could be expected from that quarter. Johnson commented the next day that the merchants 'do not seem to be very sanguine in their expectations of success. Though they and the manufacturers make some complaints, they are by no means clamorous.'[36] Franklin was later to develop his political explanation of this attitude. The pessimism of the merchants was due to the circumstance of 'the City not being much in favour with the Court at present'.[37] Hence whatever London wanted the government would refuse.

If merchants afforded little help, manufacturers gave none at all.

evidently disliked by some of Chatham's followers, was affirmed in the next issue of the newspaper on 13 Mar.

[34] *Franklin Papers*, XVII, 25–6. [35] *De Berdt Letters*, pp. 396–9.
[36] *Trumbull Papers*, p. 406. [37] *Franklin Papers*, XVII, 112.

Some were annoyed by the colonial attempts to set up manufacturing. Others claimed to have enough work without the American market. And, according to Franklin, ministerial supporters persuaded even those who were to some extent adversely affected by the colonial boycott to do nothing, by the argument that the Americans could not hold out much longer.[38] The North administration therefore adopted a tactic opposite to that used by the Rockingham ministry during the Stamp Act Crisis, when there had been official encouragement of petitions to provide a pretext of British economic distress for the removal of American taxation. Such devices were not needed in 1770, for the cabinet knew that passage of partial repeal was assured, if only because of opposition support. The petition of London merchants merely served to provide an ostensible reason for Parliamentary consideration of the Townshend taxes.

At one time the despondency of the agents about the prospects of a successful repeal campaign had been lightened by what Johnson on 2 January described as 'a tolerable prospect of our receiving some assistance from a quarter whence we did not expect it. The East India Company, it is probable, will petition for a repeal of the duty upon tea, the only article which Ministry themselves wish to retain.'[39] The Company had a well-founded complaint, arising out of the arrangements made in 1767. The political resistance to the Townshend duties as a tax and the consequent fall in legal tea exports to America had confounded all expectations. The Company found itself obliged to pay a substantial annual sum to the government in compensation for lost customs revenue without any prospect of making the profit from increased tea sales that had been anticipated and indeed held out by the ministry as the basis of the 1767 agreement: Thomas Pownall was to tell the House of Commons on 5 March that this indemnification had by then amounted to £126,000.[40] The East India Company therefore had good reason to seek a change in the arrangements. On 6 December 1769 the Company's Court of Directors drew up a list of proposals that included the removal of the American tea duty, 'without which the Company see no possibility of finding a market for teas in America'.[41] According to his later memoirs the Company's Chairman Sir George Colebrooke then had a private

[38] Ibid., XVII, 112–13.   [39] *Trumbull Papers*, pp. 394–5.
[40] Simmons and Thomas, op. cit., III, 218.
[41] East India Company Court of Directors Minutes, B185, p. 330–1. I owe this reference to Dr Huw V. Bowen.

interview with Lord North, and stated that if the ministry wanted an opportunity to repeal the tea duty without the appearance of conciliating America the Company would submit the requisite petition. North declined this offer.[42] It was widely known in January that the East India Company was negotiating with the Treasury about the tea duty.[43] Although agent Johnson doubted whether any benefit to America would result, Franklin hoped that a Company petition would lead to repeal.[44] But after Colebrooke had ascertained North's attitude, the Company decided to apply to Parliament only for an end to the payment of compensation for lost custom duties and not for repeal of the Townshend tea duty. The Company professed to have lost all concern with the colonial market, claiming that it could sell in Europe all its black teas, the sole kind that went to the colonies. So Johnson reported to Connecticut on 2 February, when he said that for all the Company cared the ministry could increase the American tea duty tenfold.[45] Thomas Pownall told the same tale in the House of Commons on 5 March, explaining that it was not in the Company's interest to export tea to the colonies because of the need to pay the 25 per cent compensation for the customs deficiency.[46] Over a month earlier, on 2 February, De Berdt had reported to Massachusetts that the Company would not be applying for repeal of the tea duty.[47]

The London merchants, although neither hopeful nor enthusiastic, wasted no time after their meeting of 1 February in organizing their petition. Two days later press notices informed 'merchants and others interested in the North American trade' that the petition would be 'ready for signing' at a Cornhill notary's office on 5 February.[48] The petition, presented to the Commons on 6 February, was couched in mild terms, emphasizing the importance to Britain of the colonial trade and expressing the opinion that its decline was caused by the Townshend duties. It asked merely for 'such relief' as the House should think fit. The hearing of the petition was fixed for 12 February, when it was adjourned to 21 February.[49] A brief debate arose on that day when Lord North moved a further postponement to 5 March, for a general consider-

[42] *Colebrooke Reminiscences*, I, 174.
[43] Simmons and Thomas, op. cit., III, 216.
[44] *Trumbull Papers*, p. 395; *Franklin Papers*, XVII, 24.
[45] *Trumbull Papers*, pp. 406–7.
[46] Simmons and Thomas, op. cit., III, 218, 235.
[47] *De Berdt Letters*, p. 397.
[48] *London Evening Post*, 3 Feb. 1770.   [49] *CJ*, XXXII, 664–5, 697.

ation then of American affairs. North's professed reason was his recent accession to office; but his speech implied that the administration had not changed the decision to retain the tea duty. Alderman Trecothick, as one of London's MPs, urged that there would be no further delay beyond 5 March. There were two times a year for American trade, he said, spring and autumn. If ships were delayed beyond March the opportunity of the year's spring trade would be lost, for current American orders were conditional upon repeal.[50]

Now that the North ministry was safe, attention could be given to colonial problems. On 5 March the House of Commons was at last asked to confirm the cabinet decision of the previous 1 May on American taxation.[51] Contemporaries were not as well informed as historians, and many MPs did not know what exactly they would be asked to approve. John Yorke told his brother Lord Hardwicke, 'I went to the House today ignorant of the proposition intended to be made (I mean the extent of it) and of the plan for opposing it.' A large attendance signified the sense of occasion, but the quality of the debate did not match its importance. Even Bamber Gascoyne, a past and future Lord of Trade with a keen interest in the colonies, described the discussion as 'cold and indifferent'. John Yorke told his brother that 'the debate was not edifying nor animated, and the subject has been worn so threadbare, that patience is tired, and modes have been so often varied, that there is scarce a choice left'.

The debate was opened by Lord North, to whom Thomas Pownall gave way. Pownall at the time of the defeat of his motion on the Townshend duties on 19 April 1769 had pledged himself to renew the subject in the next session, and early in 1770 gave notice to the House of Commons of this intention: but he accepted the ministerial argument that the Hillsborough circular

---

[50] Ibid., XXXII, 717–18; Almon, *Debates*, VIII, 238–9; *London Evening Post*, 22 Feb. 1770.

[51] For this debate see (i) Henry Cavendish's Diary, BL Egerton MSS 221, ff. 2–53, printed Simmons and Thomas, op. cit., III, 209–28, from which all quotations are taken unless otherwise indicated. (ii) Almon, op. cit., VIII, 245–70. (iii) W. S. Johnson to Governor J. Trumbull of Connecticut, *Trumbull Papers*, pp. 421–3. (iv) C. Garth to the South Carolina Assembly, *SCHGM*, XXXI, 228–33. (v) John Yorke to Lord Hardwicke, BL Add. MSS 35609, f. 282. (vi) Soame Jenyns to Lord Hardwicke, BL Add. MSS 35631 f. 85. (vii) Bamber Gascoyne to John Strutt, Strutt MSS, 6 Mar. 1770. The reports by Almon, Johnson, and Garth are also reprinted in Simmons and Thomas, op. cit., III, 228–42. For a list of other reports see Thomas, 'Sources for Debates . . . 1768–1774', *BIHR* Supp. no. 4, 18–19.

letter of 13 May had committed the administration to bring the matter before Parliament. Lord North knew that many supporters of government would dislike a soft and conciliatory approach. He therefore began by reminding MPs that the dislocation of trade with the colonies was caused not by the legislation complained of in the London petition but by the American challenge to it, deliberately choosing to describe the non-importation agreements as illegal. The Prime Minister then rehearsed the well-worn theme that the Townshend duties imposed on British manufactures were detrimental to the export trade. North said that since he was one of those who had concurred in the dispatch of Hillsborough's circular letter he ought to explain the intention behind it. The letter had been meant to dispel colonial fears that there would be frequent future attempts to assert the right of Parliament by new taxation. But the letter had not had the calming effect that had been hoped for, and the behaviour of America did not merit any further indulgence.

Having established that what he was going to propose should not be construed as a concession to the colonists, North argued that it would be unwise to continue bad taxes simply because of anger at refractory American behaviour. He said that the circular letter had been devised in the light of the Commons debate of 19 April last, which had shown the opinion of the House to be in favour of abolishing uncommercial duties. But there was no comparable reason to justify repeal of the tea duty. Tea was not a British manufacture. It was a luxury. The tax was light. It was productive and increasing, and would go a long way towards paying the costs of government in America, 'the purpose for which it was laid'.

North conceded that 'very possibly' the repeal of the other duties would not satisfy America, 'but I am not clear, that repealing the whole will appease them'. If the House admitted the American distinction between revenue duties and duties for the regulation of trade, 'they will call all duties for the purposes of a revenue, we shall call all for the purposes of trade. . . . It is drawing a line, which does not settle any one dispute.' If Britain repealed the tea duty, the colonies would next challenge the molasses duty. 'Therefore, Sir, upon my word, if we are to run after America, in search of reconciliation in this way, I do not know one Act of Parliament that will remain.'

In order to emphasize that the ministry was not yielding to the colonial boycott North belittled its efficacy. The difference between the export figures for 1768 and 1769 could partly be explained by colonial stockpiling before the non-importation associations were formed, the total for 1768 being higher than for any of the preceding three years. The news from Boston was of violations and of high prices, that of tea having doubled. New York and Philadelphia still held out because they had begun their boycotts later. America simply could not supply herself. Then came his peroration. 'I would be thought what I am, according to the best of my knowledge, a friend to trade, a friend to America. I never was so much amazed in my life to hear talk of the harsh measures of this country to America.' The statute book for the last decade and more had been filled with concessions to the colonies. 'If any proposition is made, we shall consider it. But we shall not repeal, because their conduct is threatening to this country.' North ended by moving for a Bill to repeal all the Townshend duties except that on tea.

The first attack came from William Beckford, currently Lord Mayor of London for a second time. He advanced the argument dear to Chathamite hearts and mercantile pockets that Britain needed a monopoly of colonial trade. The tea duty was unjust and unwise, and unfair to the East India Company. Thomas Pownall then formally put an amendment to add the tea duty to North's motion. 'I do not move it as an American measure, but upon British, commercial ground.' The tea duty was also uncommercial, because it gave a competitive advantage to smuggled tea. Nor would partial repeal meet the colonial grievance, which was based on the threat to their assemblies; these would no longer hold the purse-strings if Parliament raised the revenue to pay for American civil governments.

The issue was now clearly before the House of Commons. Some MPs, notably George Grenville, could support neither the motion nor the amendment, since both courses of action involved concessions to defiant colonists. Grenville therefore took the opportunity to make a scathing speech about the administration's treatment of America. The taxation imposed was repugnant to commercial principles and brought in virtually no revenue, less than a net £16,000 a year. Yet America was in a greater flame than before. After castigating the ministry for having no policy, Grenville mounted his old hobby-horse of the danger of leaving America to the Crown rather than Parliament. 'I will never lend my hand to forge chains for America, lest I forge them for myself. . . . Sir, the Parliament of England is in all cases supreme. I know no other law.' Later in the debate Grenvillite Wedderburn took the same line about the Crown, with respect to the often canvassed alternative method of raising money by requisitions: that would make America dependent on the Crown instead of Parliament.

North was provoked by Grenville's taunts into denying an imputation that his aim was to appease America, and suggested that Grenville should devise a plan, thereby inviting the tart retort that policy-making was the responsibility of the ministry. After a brief intervention from the unwell Alderman Trecothick, who said that the London petition was aimed at the tea tax, Conway rose to make a long speech. He presumably deemed it necessary to explain why he, as an administration supporter newly resigned from the cabinet, should oppose ministerial policy. Conway now put forward in Parliament the same opinion, in favour of complete repeal, that he had voiced in the cabinet of 1 May. Both the Townshend duties and the Stamp Act were unjust because the colonies were not represented in Parliament. 'A system of force over the minds of free people can never be a successful system'.

North also encountered criticism from his own supporters for repealing any duties at all. One who voiced this opinion was Welbore Ellis. 'It is no sound policy to take a measure inconsistent with dignity, honour and authority. When they are using means of violence, to take it up upon anti-commercial principles is laughing at mankind.' Secretary at War Lord Barrington, a man well informed on America through his correspondence with General Gage and Governor Bernard, declared that 'laws must be obeyed, whether they are right, or no'. He announced his disagreement with every other speaker, founding his opinion, he said, on the acceptance of the taxation by the West Indies and much of North America. 'I think you should for the present keep in force all those laws as far as relates to the colonies that have resisted, and repeal all those duties with regard to the colonies that have submitted', an idea approved of by the silent Lord of Trade Soame Jenyns as 'the wisest scheme'.

If the debate revealed this danger that the administration might lose some of its customary support, it also demonstrated the prospect of a solid opposition vote by the followers of Rockingham and Chatham. Although neither William Dowdeswell nor Edmund Burke spoke on this important occasion, another Rockinghamite Sir William Meredith declared that the ministry 'seem disposed neither to tax America nor to restore peace to America'. He argued for complete repeal, since the Declaratory Act obviated the need to retain even the Townshend Act preamble as an assertion of the right of taxation, let alone the tea tax. After Rose Fuller had also called for complete repeal, Barré asked why the duties had not been repealed the previous year, before Hillsborough's letter. 'The language we hold is little short of calling them rebels, the language they hold little short of calling us tyrants.'

John Yorke was probably not the only MP to absent himself from the division early the next morning because he could not make up his mind how to vote. Pownall's amendment was rejected by 204 votes to 142, a margin of defeat that flattered the minority because Grenville had walked out of the House beforehand with Wedderburn and other supporters. Conway and four personal followers voted with the opposition. Lord Barrington and other potential government rebels voted against the amendment, and were spared the embarrassment of a division on North's original motion. There was no Commons debate on the ensuing Bill, which was introduced on 9 March and sent to the Lords on 6 April.[52]

Opposition peers also planned to add repeal of the tea duty to the Bill, and the popular expectation was that Grafton would support this move.[53] But on 8 April Chatham informed Rockingham that gout would prevent his immediate attendance, and expressed the hope that the Committee stage would be postponed long enough for him to be able to support complete repeal.[54] The next day Rockingham failed to counter a motion that the Committee should meet on 10 April, lamely confessing to Dartmouth that he had felt 'so awkward and not well'. Having missed this opportunity, Rockingham was determined to do something, and sought advice from Dartmouth, saying that he thought Lord Egmont favoured complete repeal.[55] In the event Rockingham proposed a postponement of the Committee until 27 April, evidently on the ground of Chatham's absence. The motion was defeated by 15 votes to 9, and the Bill received the royal assent on 12 April; it was to come into effect on 1 December.[56]

It was the obvious hope of the North ministry that the American trade boycott would now collapse, as De Berdt warned Massachusetts on 7 March. 'Your enemies here . . . still entertain

[52] Simmons and Thomas, op. cit., III, 242, 245–7.
[53] *London Evening Post*, 1 Mar. 1770.
[54] Wentworth Woodhouse Muniments, R1-1290.
[55] Dartmouth MSS, D(W) 1778/II/322.
[56] Simmons and Thomas, op. cit., III, 248, 251–2.

warm hopes that you will soon break through all your agreements for the non-importation of goods, and that finally the favourite principle of taxing America must thereby be finally established.'[57] The administration had an early shock when on 8 March a ship arrived at Bristol with a cargo rejected at Boston. News of this and of the sailing of empty ships westward 'a little staggered the Ministry again', according to Franklin, but on 21 March he reported the decision to 'make trial whether the Americans will not . . . be content with what is done, submit to pay the other duties, and go on with the trade as usual'.[58] Johnson wrote in the same vein to Connecticut on 28 March. 'The ministry, I believe, intend to see whether the merchants and people of America have either the resolution or the ability to persevere in their agreements.'[59]

Benjamin Franklin was especially concerned that this ministerial policy might prove successful. On 18 March he therefore wrote to the leading Philadelphia radical Charles Thomson a letter evidently designed for publication, and that was printed in both Philadelphia and Boston at the height of the subsequent controversy in America over the retention of the non-importation agreements. In it Franklin claimed that complete repeal would have been achieved if the ministry had not believed the boycott to be on the point of collapse. 'This, with the idle notion of the dignity and sovereignty of Parliament, which they are so fond of, and imagine will be endangered by any further concessions, prevailed I know with many to vote with the ministry, who otherwise, on account of the commerce, wish to see the differences accommodated.' Franklin then produced this analysis of the British political scene in the American context.[60]

Both the Duke of Grafton and Lord North were and are in my opinion rather inclined to satisfy us, yet the Bedford Party are so violent against us, and so prevalent in the Council, that more moderate measures could not take place. . . . On the other hand the Rockingham and Shelburne people, with Lord Chatham's friends, are disposed to favour us if they were again in power, which at present they are not like to be; though they,

[57] *De Berdt Letters*, pp. 406–7.
[58] *Franklin Papers*, XVII, 116.
[59] *Trumbull Papers*, p. 428.
[60] *Franklin Papers*, XVII, 111–13. The improbable assertion about North's attitude is given some credence by North's statement to the House of Commons on 14 Mar. 1774 that in 1770 'I did hope at the same time to repeal the duty upon tea': BL Egerton MSS 254, f. 106.

too, would be for keeping up the claim of Parliamentary sovereignty, but without exercising it in any mode of taxation.

Merchant opinion in London was divided over the ministerial tactic of partial repeal. The *London Evening Post* reported on 13 March that 'a number of principal merchants, fifteen in number, trading to America, we hear have declared themselves satisfied with the steps that have been taken relative to the colonies'. But pessimism and unease in mercantile circles led Alderman Trecothick to make one last effort in Parliament. On 9 April he moved in the Commons for a Bill to repeal the tea duty.[61] The administration objected to this as contrary to the Parliamentary rule that no decision of the House could be altered in the same session, and reports of the debate show that much of the discussion centred on this procedural point. After Trecothick had recapitulated a wide range of familiar arguments for repeal he grounded his motion on the depressed state of British trade. Of ten or twelve ships in the Thames waiting to sail to New York with orders for £300,000 of goods three had sailed with a mere £10,000 worth and the others were going in ballast. Trecothick predicted that this would be the fate of the entire American trade, and he warned of the delusion of a temporary boom in the European market. He was seconded by Lord Mayor Beckford and supported by Conway, Rockinghamites Dowdeswell and Savile, and Shelburnite Dunning. First to oppose the motion was Peregrine Cust, Deputy Chairman of the East India Company, who declared that the Company did not want repeal of the tea duty. Lord North said that he would not be intimidated into impolitic concessions by threats or coerced by the boycott. After nine members had spoken for the motion and five against, it was defeated in a thin House by 80 votes to 52. Agent Johnson ended the report of the debate he sent to Connecticut on 14 April with this observation.

Thus the matter is fairly brought to this issue, whether the Americans have or have not the resolution, or the ability, to continue and conform to their agreements to decline the trade of this country. Many here think it impossible, and the Ministry are of the opinion that it is now a happy time for them to make the experiment, while their trade to other parts of the

[61] For this debate see (i) Almon, op. cit., VIII, 321–2. (ii) W. S. Johnson to Governor J. Trumbull of Connecticut, *Trumbull Papers*, pp. 430–2. (iii) C. Garth to the South Carolina Assembly, *SCHGM*, XXXI, 254–5. (iv) J. Harris to Lord Hardwicke, BL Add. MSS 35609, ff. 176–7. (v) *South Carolina Gazette*, 7 June 1770. (vi) *London Evening Post*, 17 Apr. 1770. Sources (i), (ii), (iii), and (v) are reprinted in Simmons and Thomas, op. cit., III, 249–51.

world is so flourishing. Not that they have any idea of parting with the trade of the colonies; they imagine it will return of its own accord, and that they shall then forever have done with the embarrassment in their management of the colonies; as the combinations, once dissolved, will never be renewed again, or if renewed will give the people of this country no apprehensions.

10

Massacre at Boston. March–July 1770

The occasion which brought the regiments to Boston rendered them obnoxious to the people, and they may have increased the odium themselves as the disorders of that place have mostly sprung from disputes with Great Britain. The officers and soldiers are Britons and the people found no advocates amongst them. It was natural for them without examining into the merits of a political dispute to take the part of their country, which probably they have often done with more zeal than discretion, considering the circumstances of the place they were in, for in matters of dispute with the mother country or relative thereto government is at an end in Boston and in the hands of the people who have only to assemble to execute any designs. No person dares to oppose them or call them to account, the whole authority of government, the governor excepted, and magistracy supporting them. The people prejudiced against the troops laid every snare to entrap and distress them, and frequent complaints have been made that the soldiers were daily insulted and the people encouraged to insult them even by magistrates, that no satisfaction could be obtained, but the soldiers if found in fault punished with the rigour of the law. Such proceedings could not fail to irritate but the troops were restrained by their discipline, and though accidental quarrels happened matters were prevented from going to extremities.

IN this judicious survey of pre-Massacre Boston, sent to Hillsborough on 10 April,[1] Gage conveyed the deep-rooted resentment of Bostonians at the presence of soldiers in their town, a military occupation nearly eighteen months old by the beginning of March 1770 and one that showed no signs of coming to an end. But the periodic violent clashes and numerous petty quarrels had never exploded into open confrontation.[2] Nor was the Boston Massacre a spontaneous accident. The sequence of events on 5 March points to premeditation, a verdict confirmed by a number of contemporary comments, and not only those in official affidavits. John Adams

[1] *DAR* II, 70–1.   [2] Zobel, *Boston Massacre*, pp. 182–3.

thought the Massacre 'an explosion which had been intensively wrought up by designing men who knew what they were aiming at better than the instruments employed'.[3] What is unclear is whether the clash with the soldiers was motivated merely by a mobbish desire for a fight, or whether there was a deeper plot, master-minded by local politicians intent in creating a situation where the demand for the removal of soldiers from the town would be impossible to refuse.

The Boston Massacre is an oft-told tale;[4] but a brief reconstruction based on the evidence submitted to the British government has the advantage of emphasizing the information on which ministerial policy decisions were to be based. Although witnesses differed in details the broad picture of events they described was consistent rather than contradictory.[5] By seven o'clock in the evening some forty or fifty small bands of men, armed with clubs, were roaming the streets of south Boston. Within an hour a large crowd had assembled, some men apparently armed with guns and swords, although there is no evidence that any military weapons were used against soldiers that night. About nine o'clock the crowd divided into at least three groups, and these paraded past army barracks in vain attempts to provoke soldiers into violence. At the same time there occurred the ringing of the town's alarm bells, customarily used only in cases of fire. One part of the crowd made its way to the Custom House in King Street, where a solitary sentry was on guard. Captain Thomas Preston, the duty officer that night, was informed that the sentry was under threat from a mob of at least 100 people, and despatched a military detail of eight soldiers. Soon afterwards he arrived in King Street himself, to find an ugly scene. The crowd, now considerably larger, was armed with clubs and hurling both insults and such missiles as stones and snowballs at the line of soldiers with fixed bayonets. Captain Preston's summary of the taunting was confirmed by

---

[3] Quoted, Miller, *Sam Adams*, p. 186; Zobel, op. cit., pp. 183–4, cites earlier rumours that 5 Mar. would be a day of battle in Boston, but does not probe the matter further. Miller, op. cit., pp. 183–4, points to such suspicious circumstances as the co-ordinated ringing of bells that night and the prompt response of other towns.

[4] For a lively and detailed survey see Zobel, op. cit., pp. 184–205.

[5] The following account is based on summaries of 24 sworn affidavits taken from soldiers and civilians on 13 to 15 Mar.: Governor Hutchinson's reports to General Gage on 6 Mar. and to Hillsborough on 12 Mar.; Colonel Dalrymple's report to Hillsborough on 13 Mar., enclosing a 'Narrative of the late Transaction at Boston' and the 'Case of Captain Thomas Preston'; and Gage's report to Hillsborough on 10 Apr. *DAR*, I, 67–74, 78, 81; II, 51–3, 58–66, 70–3.

other witnesses. 'Come on you rascals, you bloody backs, you lobster scoundrels, fire if you dare, God damn you, fire and be damned. We know you dare not.' As the mob closed in on the soldiers Captain Preston stepped forward in a vain endeavour to persuade the crowd to disperse. A soldier at the end of the line was struck with a stick and fired in an instinctive response. Captain Preston, turning to reprimand him, was felled to the ground by a club, and while he was temporarily incapacitated several more soldiers fired while under attack by men with clubs and missiles. They afterwards said they had heard the word 'fire', but it was being shouted by many in the mob. Captain Preston later stated that what he said was 'Don't fire. Stop your firing', and that it was false testimony on the part of subsequent witnesses to allege that he gave an order to fire. The crowd fell back as the shooting began, with casualties of three dead, one dying, three dangerously wounded, and five others slightly hurt; the final death-roll was to be five. The whole episode was over in under twenty minutes. Acting Governor Thomas Hutchinson was promptly informed, and hastened to the scene. He later claimed he had prevented further violence by his promise of an immediate examination of the incident by town magistrates, but a more significant factor in cooling the passion of the mob was the immediate deployment in the town streets of the entire military garrison.

A hastily convened meeting of the Massachusetts Council took place the next morning. It was attended by the colonels of the two regiments in Boston, Dalrymple being still the senior officer commanding in the town. The council received a delegation from a town meeting, sent to demand the immediate withdrawal of all soldiers. Colonel Dalrymple proposed a compromise, the removal of the 29th Regiment, whose men had been involved in the shooting. An afternoon town meeting of nearly 3,000 persons deemed this unacceptable, and a second deputation, with Sam Adams to the fore, was sent to inform the council. The threat was made that 4,000 men in Boston ready to take up arms would be swollen to 10,000 from neighbouring towns if the soldiers remained another day. Faced with the certainty of bitter fighting and the distinct possibility that his 600 men would be over-whelmed by sheer weight of numbers, Dalrymple agreed to withdraw all soldiers to Castle William if he received a written request from Hutchinson. The acting governor complied, on the unanimous advice of the council, with several members frankly stating, to quote Hutchinson's summary, 'they knew it to be the determination not of a mob, but of the generality of the principal inhabitants'.[6] After the council a warrant was issued for the arrest of Captain Preston and the eight soldiers; and several reports sent to London expressed great anxiety about their fate at the hands of lying witnesses and a biased Boston jury. Hutchinson and Dalrymple, too, were concerned to emphasize to Hillsborough that they had had no choice but to withdraw the army from the town of Boston. Anxiety that the British government might disapprove such an obvious surrender to duress led Hutchinson to reinforce his explanation by this survey of the earlier inability of the army to play the role assigned to it.[7]

I was sensible the troops were designed, upon occasion, to be employed under the direction of the civil magistrate, and that at the Castle they would be too remote in most cases to assure that purpose: but then I considered they never had been used for that purpose, and there was no possibility they ever would be, because no civil magistrate could be found under whose directions they might act and they could be considered only as having a tendency to keep the inhabitants in some degree of awe and even that was every day lessening and the affronts the troops received were such that there was no avoiding quarrels and slaughter. The troops themselves had also in many instances been very abusive.

Hutchinson's report of 12 March to Hillsborough arrived in Whitehall on 21 April, and news of the Boston Massacre spread the same day.[8] The American Secretary replied on 26 April, stating that the matter was under ministerial consideration and giving immediate instructions that if Captain Preston and the soldiers were convicted and condemned Hutchinson should 'respite the executions' until he had received such directions from the Crown 'as justice and the nature of the case shall appear to require'. The new governor[9] was informed that orders had been sent to the army and naval commanders in North America, General Gage and Commodore Hood, to provide all possible assistance for the preservation of peace and the support of legal authority.[10] Gage was in fact unhappy, for reasons of health, at having two regiments crowded together on the island of Castle William, and he told Hillsborough on 10 April that he could see no useful

[6] For the above proceedings see the official Council minutes, ibid., II, 53–5; and the reports of Hutchinson and Dalrymple, ibid., II, 58–63.
[7] Ibid., II, 60.   [8] Ibid., I, 67; *Chatham Papers*, III, 444 n.
[9] Bernard had resigned in March, and Hillsborough had already notified Hutchinson of his appointment on 14 Apr.: *DAR*, I, 74, 82, 85.
[10] Ibid., II, 85.

purpose in such a garrison 'unless it is to serve in the last extremity as an asylum to which the officers of the Crown might fly for the security of their persons'.[11] Hutchinson had refused to consent to the removal of either regiment, but a fortnight later Gage informed the American Secretary that he proposed to transfer the 29th Regiment to New Jersey, leaving in Castle William only the 14th Regiment. 'If the present object is only to secure the Castle by a garrison of the King's troops, I conceive one regiment will be sufficient for that end: and if his Majesty upon due consideration of all the transactions that have passed at Boston, shall judge it right to take further measures, your Lordship will perceive that a larger force than the two regiments would be required.'[12] He accordingly transferred the 29th Regiment in May.[13] On 12 June Hillsborough wrote to acquiesce in this intention, but also to order Gage to put Castle William into a fit state both to accommodate the 14th Regiment and to be 'a place of strength, and an asylum in the last extremity for the officers of the Crown' should they again have to flee from Boston.[14] That regiment was to remain there another two years, until replaced in the summer of 1772.[15]

Before any ministerial decision or Parliamentary discussions could take place the colonial version of the Massacre appeared in the London press. Most of the front page of the *London Evening Post* for 24 April was taken up by a reprint of the account in the *Boston Gazette* of 12 March. The administration countered this by publication of a version from official sources, for on 28 April the *Public Advertiser* presented a report based on information from Colonel Dalrymple, including a version of Captain Preston's narrative.[16] Parliamentary notice of the event was also prompt. The ministry ascertained that Alderman Barlow Trecothick intended to move for relevant papers in the House of Commons, and both Lord Hillsborough and Lord North failed to dissuade him from doing so by assurances that the papers would be laid before Parliament.[17] On 26 April Trecothick moved for papers relating to any dispute between soldiers and civilians in the colonies since 24 June 1769. North saw no objection, but suggested amendments to prevent the disclosure in the colonies of the opinions of officials there. Colonel Mackay, recently army commander in Boston,

[11] Ibid., I, 73.
[12] *Gage Corr.*, I, 255.
[13] Ibid., II, 542; *London Evening Post*, 14 Jan. 1774.
[14] *Gage Corr.*, II, 103–4.
[15] Ibid., I, 530.
[16] *Franklin Papers*, XVIII, 186.
[17] Almon, *Debates*, VIII, 326.

supported this objection and appropriate amendments were made. Edmund Burke took the opportunity to arraign the ministry for having no American policy, and announced that he would initiate a debate another day on the previous three years of neglect. Grenville expressed the hope that some plan would accompany the papers. Beckford and Barré made comparisons with the use of soldiers against Wilkite mobs in London. This aroused Secretary at War Lord Barrington to defend the army, stating that Boston magistrates were unwilling either to give the protection of law to individual soldiers or to call out troops to maintain order. He then proposed a familiar remedy for this problem. 'There should be an alteration in the constitution. The council would not assist. This arose from the council being of the democratical party. Let it be a royal council.'[18]

A similar Address was passed in the Lords on 30 April, apparently without debate, and a selection of papers was laid before the Lords on 4 May and the Commons on 7 May; further papers from the Admiralty were laid before both Houses on 8 May.[19] Before then, on 1 May, Edmund Burke prepared the ground for his onslaught by asking for copies of Hillsborough's circular of 13 May 1769 together with any resulting speeches of governors and answers of assemblies. George Rice, recently of the Board of Trade, demurred on the ground of Hillsborough's amiable character, and North said the circular letter would be sufficient. But administration did not hold to these objections when Dowdeswell and Grenville both declared that the other papers were needed to demonstrate the colonial consequences.[20]

Before that planned major debate on America took place Thomas Pownall initiated another, on 8 May, making a long-promised motion on the constitutional relationship between the army Commander-in-Chief in America and the colonial governors. Notice had been given two months earlier, but news of the Boston Massacre made the subject one of immediate concern. Reports of that event and its aftermath had disclosed that Hutchinson had had no power to order the withdrawal of the army from Boston or even to order it off the town's streets. A former governor of Massachusetts, Pownall held the opinion that every governor had

---

[18] BL Egerton MSS 222, ff. 17–31; printed in Simmons and Thomas, *Proceedings and Debates*, III, 256–61.

[19] Ibid., III, 262, 265–8.

[20] Ibid., III, 262–4. These papers were given to the Commons on 7 May: ibid., III, 266–7.

the power to overrule that of the Commander-in-Chief within his colony. The question had been a difficult one since the end of the war in 1763. There had been an unresolved dispute in New York between Gage and the late Governor Moore, while former Governor Bernard had disclaimed all power to remove the army from Boston.[21] Lord Halifax, in 1765 when Southern Secretary, had attempted to solve the problem by stating that the Commander-in-Chief and any of his Brigadier Generals outranked governors in military matters.[22] Secretary at War Lord Barrington's private opinion was that only Gage himself did so; but in view of Pownall's contention that even this power was illegal he informed Gage on 2 April of his intention to refer the matter to Attorney-General William De Grey and Solicitor-General Edward Thurlow.[23] These law officers had not yet given their opinion when Pownall raised the matter in the Commons.

Pownall took a high constitutional tone, stating the question to be whether the military was superior to the civil power, and he set the particular issue in the context of the current political crisis in the colonies.[24] Contrasting the current situation with the loyalty and help Massachusetts had afforded during the last war, when he had been the governor there, Pownall tartly remarked: 'Now you are forced to send your troops in order to keep the people in order.' The colonists feared that the Townshend Duties Act would undermine their assemblies. 'They believe . . . that you not only mean to alter their constitution but to establish a military government.' The separation of the military from the civil power had destroyed liberty in France and Hanover. 'If you attempt to force the troops upon them . . . you may drive the people to rebellion.' Some definition of the respective powers of the army Commander-in-Chief and of the governors in America was necessary: but Pownall did not propose one, merely calling on the Privy Council to inquire into the matter.

Supporters of the motion, among them George Johnstone, a former governor of West Florida, explicitly championed the

[21] For discussion of the problem see Shy, *Towards Lexington*, pp. 157–63.
[22] *PCBG*, p. 70.   [23] Ibid., p. 71.
[24] For this debate see BL Egerton MSS 222, ff. 108–43, printed in Simmons and Thomas, *Proceedings and Debates*, III, 270–84. All quotations are from this source. See also Cobbett, *Parl. Hist.*, XVI, 979–1001, and 3 letters from agents. (i) C. Garth to South Carolina, *SCHGM*, XXXI, 283–5. (ii) W. S. Johnson to J. Trumbull, *Trumbull Papers*, pp. 435–6. (iii) B. Franklin to J. Galloway, *Franklin Papers*, XVIII, 169–70. All except the Franklin letter are reprinted in Simmons and Thomas, op. cit., pp. 284–96.

powers of civil governors over the army. The chief administration spokesman was naturally Lord Barrington, who drily observed that General Gage had been surprised to find his orders resisted in West Florida. The Irish analogy invoked by some speakers was invalid, he said, because of the multiplicity of civil governments in America. If there was a Viceroy over the whole continent, he would of course have the supreme military command. Such a power had to reside in somebody. Soldiers would only be used within a colony by order of the civil government. 'Has any man ever heard that the troops at Boston have acted from their own authority? The misfortune is that they have not acted at all.' He then disclosed that he had referred this very question to the law officers of the Crown six weeks earlier. 'What the honourable gentlemen want to be done, is already done', the Secretary at War declared, and he therefore moved an adjournment.

Barrington's announcement killed the debate, but did not end the discussion. Beckford launched into a direct attack on Barrington. Common sense should decide the matter, not the ministry's lawyers. Beckford reminded MPs of Barrington's inclination to quarter soldiers on private houses, warned that force would not succeed in America, and frankly admitted that he had sent to the colonies copies of papers laid before Parliament. Barré claimed that only Pownall's notice of motion had led the Secretary at War to take legal advice, and this remained the assumption of contemporaries even after a denial from Barrington. There was no vote on the motion to adjourn, the critics of administration considering that the reference for legal advice had conceded the substance of the point at issue. But when the legal opinion was given, on 16 May, it proved highly satisfactory to Barrington and Gage. The law officers ruled that the military powers in the commissions of colonial governors applied only to provincial troops and not to the regular army.[25]

On the next day, 9 May, a two-hour speech by Edmund Burke launched the general debate on America that the opposition had been awaiting all the session.[26] This was too late to carry conviction as a serious discussion or even to attract attention.[27] There may even have been the feeling that the opposition was

[25] *PCBG* pp. 78–9.
[26] BL Egerton MSS 222, ff. 146–212, printed in Simmons and Thomas, op. cit., 299–323.
[27] I have found no references to the debate in the correspondence of agents or MPs.

indulging in political shadow-boxing. Lord North on 14 March 1774 referred back to this debate and declared that Burke's resolutions would have done 'a great deal of harm' in America and would not have been proposed unless the opposition had been confident of their defeat.[28]

Burke opened with the remark that he had been 'three years silent upon American affairs': by which he meant that the Rockingham party had not taken any initiative on the subject during that period. Burke's basic premiss was that America could not be governed from Britain, at least in detail. His speech was a broad attack on ministerial measures since 1767, criticizing in succession what he called 'the plan of rigour' and 'the plan of lenity'. When America burst into flames after the imposition of the Townshend taxation the colonists suffered the universal suspension of their assemblies and the despatch of soldiers to Boston. British policy seemed to combine the end of constitutional government in America with the establishment there of military rule. But this hard line had been inconsistent. New York's assembly was suspended for refusing to supply the army in 1767, but not that of Massachusetts in 1768. Half the soldiers had been withdrawn from Boston at the very time when they were most needed there. 'A government without wisdom never will be without woe.'

If the administration's hard line could conveniently be dated from Hillsborough's circular letter of 21 April 1768, the soft line began with that of 13 May 1769. The letter gave Burke the opportunity to play on the prejudices of MPs: Parliament had been insulted, for the Virginia Assembly had been told of ministerial policy first; and 'his Majesty is made the sole mover, to receive all the thanks, and Parliament all the odium of laying them on'. The commercial argument for partial repeal Burke dismissed as 'contemptible', for the trade from which the taxes were removed was 'trifling'. The manner of making the concession had been undignified, so obviously under the threat of colonial trade boycotts that the ministry was 'laughed at from one end of America to the other'. Burke moved a series of eight resolutions that had been previously approved by Grenville and were condemnatory of administration policy both in general and with particular reference to the circular of 13 May 1769.[29]

After Grenvillite Henry Seymour had seconded Burke the

---

[28] BL Egerton MSS 254, f. 106.   [29] *CJ*, XXXII, 969–70.

administration defence was led by George Rice. He urged the House to await the result of partial repeal; defended Hillsborough on the ground that it was the duty of the executive to enforce the law; and said that any opposition proposals should have been made earlier in the session. Subsequent opposition speakers echoed what Burke had said: his survey had been so comprehensive they could do little else. Wedderburn extravagantly declared that Boston was 'no more a part of the British dominions in fact than Calais is'. America had been lost 'not by foreign invasion but by domestic mismanagement'. The appointment of Lord Botetourt as Governor of Virginia was savaged, Thomas Townshend portraying him as a good-natured fool and William Burke as 'a low Lord of the Bedchamber'.

Lord North evidently dozed off during the debate, for William Burke made this aside. 'I wish he had somebody every now and then . . . to keep him awake to the affairs of America.' But the then somnolent Prime Minister was alert enough later in the debate to make an effective reply. He refuted the charge that the administration wished to put America under the King rather than Parliament by pointing out that that was precisely what the colonists wanted. The ministry could at any time have pacified America by conceding that point. The 1768 circular was issued because the King's government thought that assemblies disputing the power of Parliament should be dissolved. The 1769 letter was merely a promise to introduce a measure into Parliament, a promise that had been kept. In humorous vein North asked whether, since a change of administration was apparently the only solution to the American problem, the opposition had decided which ministry should take over, the one that passed the Stamp Act or the one that repealed it. Grenville, in his last Parliamentary speech, replied that the Stamp Act had nothing to do with the question in debate. North was the only Minister who always substituted personalities for argument. The administration had nothing to offer, and Grenville prophetically remarked that 'the loss of America' might result from such idleness. Next year he would charge North with irresponsibility if no policy had been produced: but Grenville was to die in November! After sixteen speeches by eleven members, Burke took the sense of the House on his second resolution, alleging that the ministerial instructions sent to America were a principal cause of the disorders there. It was defeated by a margin of 120 votes, 199 to 79.

The last Parliamentary shot in the opposition locker was fired in the House of Lords on 18 May, when the Duke of Richmond proposed eighteen resolutions, many the same as or similar to those of Burke in the Commons. Chatham did not attend, sending word in the morning that he was ill, but many thought it a political ailment.[30] Richmond arraigned the ministry for having done nothing about America, but Hillsborough then took over the debate and turned the tables on his critics. After declaring that it was his duty as well as his policy to defend Britain's rights in America he took the offensive by asserting that the quarrel between Britain and America would have been healed but for 'the conduct of our patriots who are continually throwing obstacles in the way of reconciliation'. Towards the end of his speech he warmed to this theme, which was a constant refrain in his correspondence.[31]

They are continually exciting the colonies, to demand concessions which the mother country can never consistently allow, and then they exclaim, because our differences are not reconciled. In like manner they are hourly deploring the loss of our American trade, and yet with the very same breath advising the Americans not to deal with us. In fact, my lords, their whole patriotism is a despicable avarice of employment, and their whole labour, an endeavour to distress administration, not a generous solicitude to serve their country.

As soon as Hillsborough finished there were loud cries for an adjournment. Rockingham mildly commented that the administration's reluctance to face an examination of their policies was a self-impeachment. He replied to Hillsborough's charge by observing that it could not be a matter of surprise if the Americans deemed themselves badly treated when many people in Britain thought the same. Power and responsibility should impel Britain to take the initiative in reconciliation. After Temple and Shelburne had also complained of the ministry's desire to avoid a debate, Gower retorted that the opposition, by wasting so much of the time of the House that session on the Middlesex Elections, were themselves to blame for there being no earlier discussion on America. After nine peers had spoken the adjournment was voted by 60 votes to 26, a margin of victory increased by proxies to 75 to 31.[32]

Connecticut agent Johnson was cynical about these belated opposition moves in Parliament. 'It is plain enough that these

[30] *Trumbull Papers*, p. 437.
[31] See, for example, *DAR*, I, 138, 154; II, 186–7, 198–9.
[32] *LJ*, XXXII, 593; Cobbett, *Parl. Hist.*, XVI, 1010–28: both reprinted in Simmons and Thomas, op. cit., pp. 331–42.

motions were not made for the sake of the colonies, but merely to serve the purposes of the opposition, to render the Ministry, if possible more odious. . . . It remains very doubtful whether they would do much better, if at all, than their predecessors.' They had not given 'the least hint' of any future policies, deliberately choosing to be entirely uncommitted. 'The administration were also so cautious of explaining themselves, and continue so close, that there is no saying with precision what course they will pursue.' The only safe conclusion Johnson could come to about the attitudes of British politicians to America at the end of the Parliamentary session was one of general dissatisfaction. 'The truth is, they are none of them pleased with the face of things in America.'[33]

In one sense it was of course quite unfair for the Parliamentary opposition to lambast the administration for having no American plan. The partial repeal of the Townshend duties did constitute a policy calculated to solve the immediate problem of the growing colonial embargo on trade with Britain. Johnson on 21 May reported official optimism on this point. 'They are of opinion that the agreements not to import will come to nothing of themselves, otherwise they would have censured them; and they hope the repeal of the duty on the three articles will give some satisfaction, and, together with the disunion amongst the merchants, effectively open the trade.'[34]

But it was certainly true that nothing had been done about the disorderly state of affairs in Boston, which had been both highlighted and worsened by the events of 5 March. After the end of the Parliamentary session the administration did turn its attention to the practical problems of governing America. The London press in mid-June reported that there had been 'frequent meetings of the ministry' on the subject, but without as yet any policy decisions.[35] One erroneous newspaper rumour was that a Lord-Lieutenancy of America would be created, on an analogy with Ireland, with 'consuls' for the different colonies.[36] Those who, like agent Johnson,[37] believed that the ministry was awaiting further American news were mistaken. More than enough was

[33] *Trumbull Papers*, pp. 437–8.
[34] Ibid., p. 438. The collapse of the boycott of British goods is discussed in the next chapter.
[35] *London Evening Post*, 12 June 1770.
[36] Ibid., 19 June 1770.   [37] *Trumbull Papers*, p. 438.

already known, and the American Secretary had positive ideas as
to what needed to be done.

Hillsborough discussed reform of the civil government of
Massachusetts in a letter of 12 June to Hutchinson, but could not
promise prompt action. 'The consideration of what may be
properly done . . . has opened a large field of discussion, and many
doubts and questions have occurred upon which it will be
necessary to have the advice and opinion of his Majesty's law
servants before any final resolution can be taken.'[38] The American
Secretary had set the ball rolling by instructing John Pownall,
Secretary to the Board of Trade as well as his Under-Secretary of
State, to compile a document entitled 'State of the Disorders,
Confusion and Misgovernment which have lately prevailed and do
still continue to prevail in His Majesty's province of Massachusetts
Bay in America'. This formidable dossier was sent by Pownall to
the Clerk of the Privy Council on 21 June. It recapitulated the
course of events in that colony since 1766, when the first purge of
officials and other supporters of Governor Bernard from the
council had occurred. It concluded that there was good reason to
suspect 'a premeditated design . . . for forcing the regiments to
leave the town' of Boston. The governor, being totally unsupported
by the council, now had 'only the shadow of power'.[39]

The Privy Council next day referred the document to its
Committee on Plantation Affairs.[40] This was the customary
procedure for high-level inquiries into America, and the Committee
meetings were attended by 'all the great officers of state'.[41] The
Committee began to consider the report on 26 June when, after it
and various related papers had been read through, four witnesses
were examined. Captain James Scott, master of the ship *Lydia*
which had recently arrived with goods returned from Boston,
stated that the ship's owner John Hancock had offered free freight
for this purpose. Some merchants had been unwillingly compelled
to reship their goods. Mr Bridgeham, a Boston merchant, said that
many who had not signed the non-importation agreement had
been coerced into obeying it by nocturnal violence. Benjamin
Hallowell, until recently Customs Comptroller of the Port of
Boston, and John Robinson, a member of the American Customs
Board, gave eyewitness accounts of the riots of June 1768.[42] So did
Joseph Harrison, Collector of Customs in Boston, when the

[38] *DAR*, II, 101–2.   [39] Ibid., I, 125; II, 110–28.
[40] *Acts PC Col.*, V, 246.   [41] *Trumbull Papers*, p. 442.
[42] *Acts PC Col.*, V, 246–54.

Committee resumed the next day. He also made the significant observation that the people of Boston had been intimidated more by the warships sent by Commodore Hood than by the presence of soldiers. The last witness was the former Massachusetts governor Sir Francis Bernard, who painted a picture of the complete collapse of all governmental authority. The customs laws could not be enforced. Even after 400 people had taken part in the daylight riot of 10 June 1768 the colony's Attorney-General had failed to obtain evidence against a single one. At the council elections of 1768 every remaining supporter of the governor had been turned out, and in the assembly his four or five possible supporters had absented themselves to permit unanimity. The trade boycott was 'to this hour effected by having a trained mob'. Bernard ended with the pointed observation that it was the opinion 'of the best people there' that Parliamentary intervention was needed to quell the disorder in Massachusetts.[43]

At its third and final meeting on 4 July the Committee again questioned John Robinson, and after passing a series of resolutions on the state of Boston made two practical recommendations: that Boston should be made the naval headquarters for North America instead of Halifax; and that Castle William should be put into a state of defence and then garrisoned by the regular army only, instead of by colonial militia as well.[44]

These precautions the Committee recommend as the means to check further violences and prevent illicit trade and to defend and support the officers of the revenue in the execution of their duty and the magistrates in the enforcement of the law.

But the Committee are of opinion that the weakness of magistracy, and the inefficiency of the law may be most effectually redressed by the interposition of the wisdom and authority of the legislature: wherefore the Committee humbly submit to your Majesty, that it may be advisable for your Majesty to recommend the consideration of the state of the province of Massachusetts Bay to Parliament.

This report was accepted by the Privy Council two days later. By the middle of the month opposition politicians knew of the decisions. On 15 July John Calcraft sent Chatham a copy of the Privy Council minute. 'You will find in it that the ministers have declared war against Boston, and instructions to the military

---

[43] Ibid., V, 254–61.
[44] Ibid., V, 261–4.

commanders are preparing accordingly.'[45] Chatham replied the same day in similarly extravagant language.[46]

The inclosure in your letter is a most melancholy piece of information. I had no idea of it. This poor country seems doomed to the worst species of ruin, that wrought by her own hands; by oppressing, as foolishly as cruelly, the source of our greatness, the devoted colonies. How pregnant is error! And what a fatal progeny one false step in policy, the stamp duty, has brought forth.

Ten days later Chatham went to London and consulted with Rockingham, reporting the unsatisfactory outcome to Calcraft on 28 July. 'I . . . learnt nothing more than what I knew before; namely that the Marquis is an honest and honourable man, but that "moderation, moderation!" is the burden of the song among the body.'[47] The Rockingham lack of concern over ministerial policy for America is evident from a casual remark in a letter from the Marquess to Edmund Burke on 5 September. 'I suspect, some warm measures are intended against the Bostonians.'[48] This attitude reflected the changed political scene in Britain during the second half of 1770. Opposition politicians were disheartened by Parliamentary failure after the high hopes at the beginning of the year; and their attention was diverted from America by both political events within Britain and the growing international crisis over the Falkland Islands. There was also a dearth of information on the formulation of ministerial policy during these months. In part this was a consequence of the tight veil of secrecy the ministry had thrown over their proceedings, reported by agent Johnson to Connecticut on 28 June. 'What the purpose of the inquiry is, is not known, and as they have of late learned to be extremely close in all their proceedings, it is not improbable you may know the result in America before it is made public here.' But by ascertaining what had been asked of the Privy Council witnesses Johnson conjectured that Massachusetts might be subjected to some form of repression.[49]

This was an obvious guess, but one not altogether accurate. The American Secretary certainly favoured such a policy, and at once

---

[45] *Chatham Papers*, III, 467–8. T. Whately informed Grenville on 21 July: *Grenville Papers*, IV, 177.

[46] *Chatham Papers*, III, 468.   [47] Ibid., III, 469.

[48] *Burke Corr.*, II, 153.

[49] *Trumbull Papers*, p. 442. For the ignorance of agents and journalists about what was going on see ibid., p. 451, and the *London Evening Post*, 7 and 12 July 1770.

sent Hutchinson for his private information a copy of the Privy Council resolutions, adding this comment. 'It is now but too plain that the lenity and forbearance of Parliament have had no other effect than to aggravate the evil and to encourage a still further opposition to the supreme legislative authority.'[50] His department had carefully collected and presented evidence to emphasize the immediate necessity of changing the Massachusetts constitution. But the Privy Council resolutions had not endorsed any such policy, and there was good ground for the belief of William Bollan on 9 July 'that some severe measures proposed by Lord Hillsborough had been rejected by the greater part of the [Privy] Council'.[51] The American Secretary now renewed his efforts to win over his colleagues to his intended course of action. His new Under-Secretary William Knox drew up a lengthy document, 'Thoughts upon the Reform of the Constitution of Massachusetts Bay'.[52] This was probably a brief for Hillsborough in the frequent cabinet meetings on America that took place during July. On 26 July the *London Evening Post* purported to reveal the ministry's policy decision. 'That the Bostonians have forfeited their charter, and therefore to support this resolution, Parliament must take away the Charter.' This press report exaggerated the scope of the decision, but is afforded some confirmation by a letter Hillsborough wrote to Gage on 4 August. 'I think I can now confidently assure you, that right principles and purposes with regard to America, are adopted by all the King's confidential servants, and I make no doubt that the measures which will be pursued at the opening of the next session of Parliament will warrant me in this information.'[53] Hillsborough had evidently at last persuaded the cabinet to approve legislation that would alter the constitution of Massachusetts, for the American Department soon began to draft such a Bill.

[50] *DAR*, II, 135.
[51] *Bowdoin–Temple Papers*, pp. 203–4.
[52] *HMC Dartmouth MSS*, II, 75.
[53] *Gage Corr.*, II, 112–13.

11

The Ministry Triumphant.
June–December 1770

BY the mid-summer of 1770 the North ministry had put American resolve to the test. The tea tax had been retained, and with it the preamble to the Revenue Act, so offensive to the colonists because it declared that the purpose of the taxation was to provide finance for their governments: this would replace that voted by their own assemblies and thereby in colonial opinion jeopardize their existence. Would the Americans now accept what was no more than a token gesture of partial repeal and, more important, the promise of no future taxation; or would they continue to insist on the repeal of the entire Townshend Act?

Benjamin Franklin was one who renewed his efforts to ensure the latter response. Early in June, after the end of the Parliamentary session, he informed correspondents in America that the Prime Minister had himself been in favour of repeal of the whole Revenue Act but had been unable to convince his cabinet colleagues. Franklin further reported that 'it is generally given out and understood that it will be done next winter' and even gave details of the face-saving device that would be employed.[1]

A general Act is talked of, revising all the Acts for regulating trade in America, wherein every thing that gives just cause of offence to the colonies may be omitted, and the tea with its odious preamble may be dropt, without hurting the honour of Parliament, which it seems was apprehended if it had been repealed this year.

It would be unwise to discount completely the report of an agent often well informed, but Franklin's claims appear to derive from deliberate deception or wishful thinking; his representations of government views were just what he and many Americans would have liked them to have been. No corroborative evidence has been found to support Franklin's assertions, and they are contrary to what is known about ministerial attitudes. North

---

[1] *Franklin Papers*, XVII, 162, 168. Thomas Pownall was to make the same suggestion in the House of Commons on 25 Mar. 1774: Simmons and Thomas, *Proceedings and Debates*, IV, 128.

himself intended both to retain the tea tax and use the revenue from it; and there can be no doubt about the obvious hope of the administration that the colonial boycott would disintegrate during 1770. The belief that such a collapse would happen was precisely the reason, Hillsborough told Hutchinson on 12 June, why no legislative action had been taken in Parliament as a direct counter to and curb on the non-importation agreements.[2]

The ministerial policy in early 1770 of confirming and enacting the original cabinet decision of 1 May 1769 was undertaken in full knowledge of the expansion and intensification of the colonial boycott that had occurred during the intervening period. It was something of a deliberate gamble, and Hutchinson was soon to tell Hillsborough that the ministry's failure to legislate against the non-importation agreements had worsened the odds. Even before what Hutchinson regarded as this pusillanimity was known in Boston he had informed the American Secretary in a letter of 18 May of the bad effect of 'the opinion which prevails, but which I still hope is ill-founded, that nothing will be done in Parliament to suppress those combinations, and the speeches said to be made in Parliament affirming them to be legal, and letters received by the heads of the combiners from persons of character in England exhorting to perseverance'.[3] In letters of 21 and 27 May Hutchinson reiterated the need for effective suppression of the associations, and on 15 July he reported that both sides in Massachusetts were waiting to hear whether Parliament had taken any action.[4] He had to put a brave face on the news that it had not done so when this information reached Boston on 27 July.[5]

The North administration also now faced the unforeseen possibility that the coincidental event of the Boston Massacre might wreck the ministerial strategy over the Townshend Duties Act. Resentment over the presence of army units in the old colonies had in recent years centred over payment for their support under the provisions of the 1765 Mutiny Act, an issue linked in American minds with the main dispute over taxation. The bloodshed in Boston was quite another matter, and one that at first threatened to alienate colonial opinion. Even in conservative New Hampshire there was an immediate reaction. On 12 April Governor John Wentworth wrote to inform Hillsborough that 'the death of five men killed by the troops at Boston in March last has

---

[2] *DAR*, II, 102.   [3] Ibid., II, 97.   [4] Ibid., I, 107, 143; II, 99.
[5] Ibid., I, 152. It is not mentioned in his letter of the previous day: Ibid., II, 153.

spread a flame like wildfire through all the continent. It is impossible to describe to your lordship the unhappy effect it has produced.' Wentworth, inexperienced in facing political disturbance, was exaggerating greatly. The reaction of New Hampshire proved in the end to be merely the revival by the Assembly of a petition, dormant for two years, asking for relief from the Townshend taxation.[6]

Nor, outside New England, did news of the Boston Massacre have the effect portrayed by Wentworth. Men of moderate opinions had had their eyes opened as to what might lie ahead on the path of resistance to Britain. Awkward questions were soon being asked of Boston. Why was there a mob in King Street that evening? Why did it approach the Custom House? Was it lawful to hurl insults and missiles at soldiers on duty? There developed the widespread opinion that the people of Boston might have been in the wrong. A letter of 15 May from Annapolis, printed in the London press, summed up this attitude with the observation that 'the late riots at Boston are regarded with a very cool eye all over America, except in New England'.[7] Subsequent events were certainly to show that the Boston Massacre had little if any influence on colonial attitudes concerning the trade boycotts.

It would be several months before the ministry knew if its American taxation strategy would prove successful. On 14 April, two days after the royal assent to the amending act, copies of it were sent by John Pownall to all governors in America.[8] This official intimation was supplemented by letters from agents and other correspondents, and had in any case been anticipated by news of the debate of 5 March; for Boston knew of the proposals by mid-April and Philadelphia by mid-May. But colonial responses would await formal notification and then involve consultations between the various American ports. More time still would elapse before London knew what was happening in the colonies. Hard news could not arrive in Britain before the second half of the summer, and the general impression of American reactions was meanwhile a confused one. News reports in the London press, whether purporting to be fact or merely rumour, were vague and conflicting. In their correspondence with Whitehall government officials scattered through America varied in their optimism according to temperament and location, and reports even from

[6] Ibid., I, 74.
[7] *London Evening Post*, 28 July 1770.
[8] *DAR*, I, 81.

the same man might be contradictory in their implications.[9]

It had always been evident that the real decision would be made by the three major ports of Boston, New York, and Philadelphia.[10] Within them there was an important difference in the process of decision-making that explained in part the more uncompromising stand of Boston. In the Massachusetts capital meetings of 'the trade' were attended by shopkeepers and all others involved in any kind of commerce as well as the merchants actually trading with Britain. In both New York and Philadelphia there was a sharp distinction between the mercantile interest and the other inhabitants: there the international merchants could not be intimidated in mass meetings, manipulated by radical politicians, as happened in Boston. In that town, Hutchinson's reports had long made clear the ministry could expect no change of attitude. When after 1 January a few merchants thought themselves free to sell British goods mobs soon persuaded them otherwise. On 28 February Hutchinson warned the ministry that the boycott enjoyed general support, and after the Massacre the movement expanded to include virtually every town in Massachusetts.[11] In Boston on 25 April a meeting of merchants, as a direct riposte to news of the retention of the tea duty, voted that all goods imported from Britain should henceforth be returned there and no longer be stored in local warehouses.[12] Any prospective importers were coerced by fears for their safety and property, and the ministry by the end of June could evidently abandon any hope of an early end to the non-importation agreement in that town.

Outside Massachusetts it was a different story. The ministerial tactic of partial repeal soon produced results sowing dissension and doubt among many who had hitherto supported non-importation agreements. The concession offered an excuse to merchants anxious to end the boycott. The first of the big ports to make a move was Philadelphia, whose Committee of Merchants organized a meeting on 14 May. This decided to suggest to other ports an end to the boycott on British goods except tea, but to take no decision until another meeting on 5 June so as to act in concert

[9] Compare the reports of Lieutenant-Governor Robert Eden of Maryland on 21 Feb. and in June, DAR, II, 46–7, 129–40. The above general remarks are based on a perusal of the London press for 1770 and official correspondence, ibid., vols. I and II.

[10] For a detailed survey of events in these ports and elsewhere see Schlesinger, Colonial Merchants, pp. 217–33.

[11] DAR, I, 94; II, 33, 50–1; London Evening Post, 14 June 1770.

[12] Ibid., 16 and 19 June 1770; DAR, II, 96–7.

with merchants elsewhere. Four days later a meeting of New York merchants decided to postpone any decision in the hope still that the tea duty would be repealed. But when news of the Philadelphia initiative reached Boston, about fifty merchants welcomed the idea at a hastily convened and private meeting. This response so alarmed the organizers of the Boston boycott that they called a public meeting for 23 May. This voted 'almost unanimously' to adhere to the agreement of 29 October last not to import any goods from Britain before complete repeal of the Townshend Duties Act. Hutchinson sent a tart comment to Hillsborough on this disappointment. 'I find many of the merchants are very much dissatisfied that their trade should be so regulated by people not concerned in trade and without property, but their timidity is such that a meeting of such great numbers of people in opposition to them immediately discourages them from pursuing what seemed to be their determination.'[13] There had meanwhile occurred in Philadelphia on 23 May a meeting of 'inhabitants', many of whom decided to adopt the Bostonian tactic of swamping the meeting of merchants arranged for 5 June. That meeting was also influenced by the example of Boston and by the well-publicized letter of 18 March from Benjamin Franklin to Charles Thomson urging a continuation of the boycott until complete repeal was achieved. The decision, with only four dissenting voices, was to retain the boycott agreement of 10 March 1769.[14]

The key to the unlocking of the Townshend Duties Crisis proved to be the behaviour of New York, and that was influenced by both the North administration and the Rockinghamite opposition. Towards the end of the Parliamentary session the ministry granted a unique concession to New York, permission to issue new paper currency that would be legal tender for public debts in the colony, contrary to the 1764 Currency Act. At the end of 1769 acting Governor Colden had explained to Hillsborough that Britain would derive two advantages from such a concession. Without it the New York Assembly would be unlikely to vote provisions under the 1765 Mutiny Act for army units in the colony; while the granting of the request would influence opinion there towards ending the non-importation agreement.[15] Although the Privy Council in February 1770 had to disallow New York's

---

[13] Ibid., II, 97–9.
[14] *London Evening Post*, 21 July 1770; *DAR*, II, 139–44; *Franklin Papers*, XVII, 110–13.
[15] *NYCD*, VIII, 189–91.

own legislation on the subject Hillsborough informed Colden that the ministry intended to pass an Act of Parliament to the same effect, and Colden reported this to the New York Council on 20 April.[16] The legislation was formally initiated by a petition from the colony's agent Robert Charles, instructed by the assembly and urged on by the new governor Lord Dunmore.[17] During its Parliamentary passage Charles Garth vainly attempted to obtain the same concession for all the colonies.[18] The circumstance that even New Jersey, also using the argument about payments under the Mutiny Act, was not granted the same favour emphasizes the political calculation about the trade boycott behind the ministerial decision.[19]

Further British influence on the New York decision to end the boycott came from the Parliamentary opposition, through the close link between Rockingham and the politicians now in power in New York. There the faction headed by the De Lancey family had won the 1769 assembly elections, and acting Governor Colden was their ally: in his reports to Hillsborough, Colden portrayed the argument over non-importation in terms of local politics, with the opposition faction depicted as adopting the Boston line of non-importation.[20] Rockingham was in constant correspondence with the De Lancey family, and in discreet fashion used this connection to seek an end to the confrontation between Britain and America. In a letter of 11 April to James De Lancey, after mentioning that there was 'too much heat both on this side and on your side', Rockingham concluded: 'I preach moderation here, and so it is but fair in me to preach it on both sides.'[21] It is of course impossible to assess the effect of such exhortations, and they did accord with the inclinations and interests of the De Lancey party, for the merchants of New York comprised an important part of the De Lancey political coalition. That the local mercantile community was to be successful in the New York struggle over importation can be attributed in part to this political connection.

The initial response of New York promised no such outcome.

[16] DAR, I, 42, 46, 136; II, 25–7, 40–1; Smith Memoirs, I, 80–1.
[17] Franklin Papers, XVII, 121–2. Charles became so concerned over the responsibility and expense that he committed suicide: ibid., 170–1.
[18] SCHGM, 31, 285–6; Simmons and Thomas, Proceedings and Debates, III, 253–5, 296.
[19] Franklin Papers, XVII, 62, 120–1, 173–4; Ernst, Money and Politics, pp. 264–81.
[20] DAR, II, 96.   [21] Wentworth Woodhouse Muniments, R1-1292.

On 6 June, the day after the Philadelphia meeting confirmed that port's boycott, a meeting of 'inhabitants' resolved to do the same in New York until there was complete repeal of the revenue duties.[22] But the merchants here were not disposed to accept such dictation from the mob. At a meeting on 11 June they decided, in the words of Postmaster Alexander Colden, that 'proper persons should go through the several wards of the city with two subscriptions, the one for non-importation, the other for importation, in order to collect the sentiments not only of the merchants but of the mechanics and every inhabitant relative to importing goods as formerly'.[23] In this survey of public opinion importation was defined as excluding tea and other dutied goods, a convenient distinction for a port that did not buy much British tea, relying on its Dutch connections for smuggled tea from Holland.[24] The result of this house-to-house canvass, the acting Governor was pleased to report to Hillsborough, showed that '1180, among which are the principal inhabitants, declared for importation, about 300 were neutral or unwilling to declare their sentiments, and a few of any distinction declared in opposition to it'.[25]

On 16 June the New York Committee appointed to enforce the non-importation agreement thereupon sent express messengers to Boston and Philadelphia requesting their concurrence in the proposal to end it in this manner. The letter described the partial repeal as a 'conciliatory measure', and stated that since this amending legislation would not come into effect until 1 December all the items taxed by Townshend would be excluded until then and tea afterwards. If the other towns rejected the plan the sense of New York would be taken again.[26] Boston and Philadelphia promptly did reject it, and New York's neighbours, New Jersey and Connecticut, announced their refusal to trade with her unless the boycott was maintained in full.[27] Postmaster Colden reported to London that 'the principal and most thinking merchants' were nevertheless not deterred from pursuing their scheme, well aware that many families in the town, especially those of 'the mechanics', were nearing destitution. Opposition came only from a small but

[22] *London Evening Post*, 21 July 1770.

[23] *DAR*, II, 143. For the date see *London Evening Post*, 28 July 1770.

[24] See Hutchinson's sharp comment to Hillsborough on 26 July, *DAR*, II, 153.

[25] Ibid., p. 140. Colden's letter did not reach Whitehall until 17 Aug. Ibid., I, 138; but news of the canvass had arrived in London by 23 July. *London Evening Post*, 24 July 1770.

[26] Ibid., 28 July 1770.   [27] Ibid., 18 Aug. 1770.

noisy faction, led by Isaac Sears and Alexander McDougall, 'the American Wilkes'.[28] Acting Governor Colden told Hillsborough that during the first week of July these men used such means as rioting, clamour, and threats to deter any further steps by the merchants, but their efforts were in vain.[29] The merchants acted on 7 July, a sense of urgency being engendered by the circumstance that mail for the next packet-boat to Britain closed the following day. A merchant meeting, held at a tavern in the evening, agreed to send orders for all goods except tea. Sears and his allies promptly summoned a general meeting for noon the next day: this pledged opposition to any importation, and Sears apparently threatened death and destruction of property to enforce this ban. A simultaneous mass meeting of merchants decided on a more democratic proceeding: 'persons of note should again be sent through the several wards to take the sense of all the inhabitants'. The merchants, with the support of acting Governor Colden and General Gage, then persuaded the Postmaster to detain the packet until 11 July, so that orders for goods could be sent at once if the boycott ended.[30] Once again, the Governor reported, 'persons on both sides of the question were appointed to go from house to house to collect the sentiments of the inhabitants'.[31] By 9 July there was a large vote in favour of importation, and the New York merchants busied themselves in compiling orders before the packet-boat sailed on 11 July. But this second sounding of opinion had been hasty and irregular: only 704 inhabitants had supported the decision, and opponents were afterwards to claim that the majority had taken no part in it.[32]

News of the New York decision, along with orders for goods, reached Britain by the middle of August.[33] It was thought to be the fatal blow to the boycott, and rumours soon circulated that the ministry would not now call a meeting of Parliament until after Christmas, 'on account of the American affairs being likely to terminate so well'.[34] Connecticut agent Johnson was utterly dismayed when writing to Governor Trumbull on 20 August.[35]

---

[28] *DAR*, II, 144.   [29] Ibid., p. 143.
[30] Ibid., p. 145.
[31] Ibid., p. 143.
[32] *London Evening Post*, 4 Sept. 1770.
[33] Ibid., 18 Aug. 1770. Letters from Gage and A. Colden arrived on 17 Aug. *DAR*, I, 139–40.
[34] *London Evening Post*, 11 and 13 Sept. 1770.
[35] *Trumbull Papers*, p. 450.

I cannot express to you with what astonishment and confusion, on one hand, and with what exultation and triumph on the other, the news that the merchants of New York have agreed to open the trade has been received here. The exception of tea and other dutiable articles is esteemed of little consequence. It is expected the merchants in all the other colonies will immediately follow the example, and that the American controversy is now at an end. The Ministry are confirmed in their system, their prudence and firmness are applauded, the advocates for the colonies are confounded, and hardly dare show their faces.

Subsequent American news at first made these initial reactions appear over-hasty. For a while it seemed as if New York might be alone. Before the end of August it was known in London that Philadelphia had on 11 July rejected an approach from the New York Merchants Committee and condemned New York for 'a measure which we think will be prejudicial to your own and the liberties of all America. . . . We think you have, on the day of trial, deserted the cause of liberty and your country.'[36] Eight days later a mass meeting of Philadelphia inhabitants resolved to maintain the non-importation agreement as 'a safe, peaceable and constitutional way of asserting our rights'. Other resolutions dismissed the New York arguments of necessity and of the partial tax repeal: 'the claim of right to tax us without our assent is still kept up, and the duty on tea retained as a test of that right'.[37] Deputy Governor John Penn, when on 5 September he belatedly sent Hillsborough a copy of these resolutions, commented that opinion in the town still remained the same.[38]

Bad news for the ministry had also been arriving from other colonies. On 13 August Whitehall was informed by the Governor of Virginia, Lord Botetourt, that on 22 June a new non-importation agreement had been signed by 165 merchants and members of the House of Burgesses.[39] North Carolina was to adopt the Virginia agreement on 17 September, and early that month there came from South Carolina the report of a Charleston meeting on 23 June that had simply assumed a continuation of the boycott by banning trade with Georgia and Rhode Island for breaking it.[40] Newport responded to such hostility by agreeing to resume its boycott of British goods on 20 August, until a majority of colonies decided otherwise.[41]

---

[36] *London Evening Post*, 28 Aug. 1770.
[37] *DAR*, II, 149–50.   [38] Ibid., pp. 176–7.   [39] Ibid., I, 128.
[40] *London Evening Post*, 8 Sept. and 3 Nov. 1770.
[41] Ibid., 18 Oct. 1770.

This qualification was an omen of the changing colonial situation. Merchants elsewhere would not and could not be expected to allow New York to appropriate their trade. On 13 September Boston, in an evident attempt to prevent a complete collapse of the boycott, proposed a meeting of delegates from the various colonies to discuss whether any alterations should be made in the non-importation agreement, this invitation being authorized by 'a meeting of the trade' attended by 1,000 persons.[42] Nothing came of this initiative, partly no doubt because Boston itself was widely suspected of honouring the boycott in word rather than deed. The colonial press elsewhere depicted the Boston boycott in terms of a sealed warehouse with a secret back door opened at night.[43]

With New York open and Boston reputedly cheating, Philadelphia took action a week later. A decision to open the port on the same terms as New York was voted by a majority of 89 to 45 at a meeting of subscribers to the boycott agreement on 20 September. The meeting defeated a proposal to consult other colonies, but voted that no goods should be landed before 15 January 1771 in order to put everyone on an equal footing. A week later a meeting of 'a large body of inhabitants', evidently called in protest, resolved rather tamely that 'it would have been for the honour of this city' if the merchants had first consulted other ports.[44] In Philadelphia, as in New York, the merchants actually involved in trade with Britain had taken matters into their own hands.

News of the Philadelphia decision reached Britain by 2 November, and the complete collapse of the colonial boycott was soon being prematurely reported in the London press.[45] Not until the end of the month did news arrive that on 11 October the merchants of Boston had unanimously resolved to follow the example of New York and Philadelphia.[46] News from the southern colonies came even later. Information on events in the northern and middle colonies took some time to reach there, and news from them much longer to arrive in Britain. In mid-December a report reached London that Annapolis had renewed its boycott agreement as late as 1 November.[47] But on 25 October Baltimore had decided to follow the lead of New York, and Charleston did the same on 13

---

[42] Ibid., 3 Nov. 1770.
[43] Miller, *Sam Adams*, p. 224; Gipson, *British Empire*, XI, 270–1.
[44] *London Evening Post*, 6 and 10 Nov. 1770.
[45] Ibid., 3 and 17 Nov. 1770.
[46] Ibid., 29 Nov. 1770.   [47] Ibid., 18 Dec. 1770.

December. Elsewhere boycott associations often collapsed without any formal decisions being taken. News of these events continued to arrive in Britain until well into 1771.[48] The North ministry could derive satisfaction not only from the actual collapse of the non-importation campaign but also from the manner in which it had occurred: the sequence of events left a legacy of mutual antipathy between the various colonies that would render any future co-operation more difficult.

If the American situation did not now necessitate the meeting of Parliament in November, the Falkland Islands Crisis certainly did. Throughout 1770, and indeed earlier, there had been growing concern in Britain about the evident Spanish intention to enforce an old claim of sovereignty against a new British settlement at Port Egmont in West Falkland. Matters came to a head during the summer of 1770. On 2 June a Captain Hunt arrived home with news of a Spanish ultimatum. Three months later, in mid-September, news reached Britain of the actual Spanish seizure of Port Egmont. Government attention thereafter was taken up with diplomatic negotiations to avoid war and preparations to fight one. The latter included many dispatches to North America, for that was an obvious potential area of conflict. A Spanish war would put the two Floridas at risk and threaten British and colonial shipping in West Indian waters; while the Mississippi formed a common boundary between the British and Spanish territories in North America. In that continent the war scare lasted for several months, until the various British colonies gradually received Hillsborough's circular letter of 22 January 1771 announcing an agreement whereby Spain agreed to evacuate the Falkland Islands.[49]

This international crisis might have been expected to influence the relationship of Britain and her American colonies in different ways. But it proved too brief for the sense of a common danger to stimulate colonial appreciation of the value of having a British army and navy in America. And the prospective theatres of war were too distant from the trouble-centre of New England to produce any significant patriotic response there. General Gage was to tell Lord Barrington on 5 May 1771 that the Massachusetts Assembly 'showed little inclination to co-operate in any measures

[48] *DAR*, I, 234; II, 297; Schlesinger, *Colonial Merchants*, pp. 233–6; Gipson, *British Empire*, XI, 271.
[49] *DAR*, I, 255.

against Spain, had war been declared'.[50] Moreover, as Gage reported to the Secretary of War on 4 June, Rhode Island had evaded and Connecticut had ignored Gage's requests for quarters for regiments moved south from Nova Scotia during the war scare.[51] The New England contribution to the Canadian campaigns in the mid-century wars, which advocates of those northern colonies never ceased to extol in the current quarrel with Britain over taxation, was revealed to have been motivated by self-interest rather than patriotism. Boston politicians even thought that advantage might now be derived from Britain's predicament: Samuel Cooper, writing to Benjamin Franklin on 1 January 1771, when for all Americans knew war with Spain might have already begun, commented that 'the circumstances of Europe . . . are sufficient to show the propriety of securing the affections as well as the submission of the colonies'.[52]

Although this would not seem to have been the time to embark on controversial policies for North America the Falkland Islands Crisis did not deter Hillsborough and his American Department from going ahead with the projected Massachusetts legislation. In August 1770 both Hillsborough and John Pownall wrote to request information from Governor Hutchinson and to sound out his opinion on proposals under consideration, notably a change from an elected to a nominated council. In a hasty answer written to catch the packet-boat of 9 October Hutchinson warned that there would be violent opposition to this change: nor would a council nominated by the Crown be able to function efficiently, since the assembly would probably ignore it. As an alternative he suggested a new charter, to be devised in consultation with the colony. At the very least there ought to be a year's delay to give proper notice and a chance to hear the colony's opinion. He himself thought that any change should simply extend from one to three years the term of office for councillors, and he opposed any alterations in the judicial system and even in the method of town meetings.[53]

Preparations for a draft Bill were well advanced by the time this discouraging response arrived in London on 7 November. William Knox recalled the circumstances at the time of the 1774 Massachusetts Government Act. It was Sir Francis Bernard who had prevailed on Lord Hillsborough to initiate legislation to alter the

---

[50] *Gage Corr.*, II, 576–7.
[51] Ibid., p. 579.   [52] *Franklin Papers*, XVIII, 3–4.
[53] Bailyn, *Hutchinson*, pp. 189–92. Hutchinson's letter does not appear to survive in the official correspondence.

Massachusetts charter, a course of action he had earlier been urging from Boston when governor. A consultative meeting therefore took place of Hillsborough, Bernard, and the two American Under-Secretaries Pownall and Knox. The latter recalled that 'I gave my opinion then against any alteration but that of the Council. The others were for all.'[54] The American Department then prepared a 'Draft Act to amend the Charter of Massachusetts Bay'.[55] This anticipated many provisions of the 1774 Massachusetts Government Act. The council was to be nominated by the Crown from among the inhabitants of the colony, to number between twelve and thirty-six, and the members were to hold office during royal pleasure. Another clause provided for juries to be named by sheriffs and no longer elected.

On 3 October Hillsborough, back from his annual Irish visit, wrote to Hutchinson in terms expressing his determination to proceed with the measure. 'I am persuaded that all those who wish well to the community and who do not mean to concur in the dangerous design of a few desperate men will see the necessity of such a further explanation and reform of the constitution of Massachusetts Bay as shall have the effect to restore the dignity of the King's government and the authority of the supreme legislature.'[56] But Hutchinson's own letter, crossing in the post with this missive, provided ammunition for opponents of such a provocative step. An angry and dismayed Bernard on 15 November wrote to tell him that 'the intention has cooled since the receipt of your letter', for there was a strong inclination within the ministry to grasp any excuse to avoid troublesome business.[57]

By the time Parliament met on 13 November the ministry, aware that both New York and Philadelphia had abandoned their embargo on British imports, could make an optimistic appraisal of the colonial scene. The King's Speech referred to the ending of the boycott in 'most' of the American colonies, but also mentioned that 'unwarrantable practices' and violence were still prevalent in Massachusetts. The Commons Address in reply, also drafted by the ministry, promised that the House would neglect 'no means of securing the commercial interests of the Kingdom or of providing

[54] HMC Knox MSS, p. 257.

[55] A copy survives among the papers of Lord Gower, then President of the Council: PRO 30/29/3/2, ff. 112–17. It is undated, but a clause voiding the appointment of all JPs for Suffolk County appointed before 1 Jan. 1770 ties the draft to this year.

[56] DAR, II, 199–200.   [57] Bailyn, op. cit., pp. 192–3.

for the protection of your Majesty's good subjects'.[58] These assurances were widely interpreted as a promise of legislation on Massachusetts. The ensuing debate naturally focused on the implications of the Falkland Islands dispute with Spain, and America was mentioned only by a few speakers. Lord Greville, mover of the Address, commented that the colonial combinations had sowed the seeds of their own destruction by producing scarcities, and George Rice exulted in their collapse. Sir William Meredith pointed out that since 'commerce is of a free nature' the boycotts had not been illegal. He then raised the issue of the apparent threat to the Massachusetts charter. 'When the people are willing to be at peace with you, is this a time to revive this language, that caused those combinations?' He challenged the ministry to tell the House whether 'there is a design of taking away what is their birthright'. Edmund Burke was scornful about the ministerial self-congratulations over America. 'You, however, keep up the duty upon tea in order to preserve the right. They forbid, in order to deny the right. This is the matter, upon which we are to cry victory.' He also linked the American situation with the international crisis, recalling the help given to Britain by the colonies in earlier wars. 'Before you are going to war, consider what circumstances you stand in with regard to the colonies.'[59]

Agent Johnson noted that in this debate Lord North refused to commit himself on the subject of America, and wryly observed that 'the mercantile combinations are esteemed to be at an end, and will have no further weight in the present deliberations than may be derived from the resolution not to import tea and other dutiable articles, and how far that is like to go, after what has happened, you will easily judge'. Johnson added that the colonies were thought to be 'effectually divided amongst themselves, and not likely to be again very soon united. What then, in this state of things, has Massachusetts Bay to expect? Certainly that whatever Ministry propose will be adopted.' He then reported the rumour, based on ministerial activity and strengthened by the Commons Address and debate, that 'a Bill is preparing . . . not, it is said, absolutely to take away their charter, but to introduce some new regulations only'.[60]

This projected Massachusetts legislation never came before

[58] *CJ*, XXXIII, 3–4.
[59] BL Egerton MSS 222, ff. 213–56. Extracts relevant to America are printed in Simmons and Thomas, op. cit., III, 342–3.
[60] *Trumbull Papers*, p. 466.

Parliament. One reason was the dispute with Spain. The possibility of war remained a real one until January, with Hillsborough warning Gage on 11 December not to relax his military preparations.[61] One man who attributed overriding importance to the Falklands factor was Benjamin Franklin, on 24 October chosen by the Massachusetts Assembly to replace the recently deceased De Berdt as agent. In his acknowledgment to Speaker Cushing on 24 December, Franklin was able to convey good news. 'I have the pleasure to acquaint you, from good authority, that the project formed by the enemies of the province, for bringing into Parliament a Bill to abridge our charter rights . . . is now laid aside.' The reason, he thought, was obvious. 'I rather think a disposition prevails of late to be on good terms with the colonies, especially as we seem to be on the eve of a war with Spain.'[62]

There were other motives for this political forbearance more creditable to the administration. Johnson gave considerable weight both to protests against the Bill, 'the representations of the injustice and the ill consequences which would attend it', and also to, 'let me add, to do justice . . . the moderation of *some* of his Majesty's Ministers'.[63] Undoubtedly the gradual collapse of the trade boycott helped to convince those in administration who had no desire to provoke further controversy that it would be unwise to launch an attack on the constitution of Massachusetts. More directly relevant was the significant improvement of the situation within that colony. Ironically for Hillsborough his favourite project was killed by the success of ministerial policy in other respects.

The deployment of naval and military forces had succeeded in overawing Boston. Commodore Hood sent to that port as many ships as Governor Hutchinson and the Customs Board deemed necessary.[64] Castle William, although the fort belonged to Massachusetts and was garrisoned still in part by colonial militia, was transferred to the royal army in September without disturbance. Consternation but not commotion was Gage's summary of Boston's reaction.[65] This firm line by the British government at the very time when Boston thought it had virtually freed itself from imperial control had a chastening effect on the inhabitants. On 15 November Hillsborough informed Gage of the ministry's satisfaction that the Privy Council's directions of 6 July had been

[61] *DAR*, I, 228–9.   [62] *Franklin Papers*, XVII, 258, 275–83, 308.
[63] *Trumbull Papers*, p. 471.   [64] *DAR*, I, 144, 156.
[65] Ibid., I, 159, 162, 165, 167, 180; II, 135, 184–5.

successfully executed. 'The good consequences with which it has already been attended in awing the licentious and encouraging the peaceably disposed inhabitants of Boston, fully evince its propriety.'[66] On 5 December Hutchinson wrote that the situation in Boston was more favourable than for eighteen months,[67] and two days later Gage sent this report. 'The people of Boston have been cavilling and quibbling which shows they still retain a sour disposition, but I have not heard of any noise or tumults amongst them. The King's troops taking possession of the Castle has mortified them a good deal and I believe alarmed many.'[68] By the end of the year even the unpopular Customs Board had left the refuge of Castle William and resumed its meetings in Boston.[69]

This restoration of law and order in Boston had a background influence on both the breakdown of the trade boycott there and the trials of the soldiers involved in the Boston Massacre. Ever since 5 March the possibility of death sentences had been a black cloud on the British horizon. Both administration and opposition had sought to prevent such a catastrophe. Barlow Trecothick, on the advice of the Duke of Richmond, exploited his Boston connections by a suggestion to James Bowdoin, one of the town's foremost politicians, that if any accused were sentenced to death Boston itself should petition the Crown for a pardon. Trecothick seemingly put forward this idea of a conciliatory gesture by Boston as the advice of the Parliamentary opposition. But Gage, when reporting this news on 16 August, pointed out that the inhabitants of Boston were then so far from accepting this idea that they were threatening to hang Preston if he was acquitted.[70]

Successive postponements of the trials soon ensured that the instructions sent to Hutchinson on 26 April would prevent the immediate enactment of any death sentences. Although this worst fear had been removed, the ministry sought as long a delay as possible, for the prospect of impartial trials would improve as the political temperature in Boston dropped. This tactic succeeded. The trial of Captain Preston was eventually fixed for the end of October, and news of his acquittal reached London on 8 December.[71] On 30 December Hillsborough was notified that six of the eight soldiers involved had been acquitted, but the other two convicted of manslaughter on clear evidence that their shots had resulted in

---

[66] *Gage Corr.*, II, 120–1.
[67] *DAR*, I, 220.   [68] Ibid., II, 291.
[69] Ibid., I, 241.   [70] *Gage Corr.*, II, 118 n.
[71] *DAR*, I, 88–9, 116, 190; II, 85, 156–7, 241.

deaths.[72] These verdicts were as satisfactory as ministers could expect, and the result of a fair trial. It was all too apparent from the evidence that the soldiers had not fired until under attack, and the court gave permission for its publication so that the true facts would become widely known.[73]

Before the end of the year the administration derived the additional satisfaction of confounding opposition prophecies by an important expansion of the payment of colonial salaries out of the tea duty. Already in 1768 a tentative start had been made in this direction by the payment of salaries to the Attorney-General of New York and the Chief Justice of Massachusetts. In 1770 the method was introduced of implementing this policy as new appointments were made. On 21 June Hillsborough notified the Treasury Board that Lord Dunmore had been named Governor of New York at a salary of £2,000 payable out of the tea duty. When Dunmore was given his formal instructions on 16 July he was expressly forbidden to accept a salary from the Assembly. On 7 December Hillsborough informed the Treasury Board that the same arrangements would apply for Thomas Hutchinson and Andrew Oliver as Governor and Lieutenant-Governor of Massachusetts, with respective salaries out of the tea duty of £1,500 and £300.[74]

For the North ministry 1770 therefore ended on a note of triumph concerning America. The token concession of cancelling unremunerative duties had seemingly sufficed to destroy the colonial embargo on British goods that had comprised the practical resistance to the Townshend taxation. The only significant revenue duty had been retained and afforded every prospect of providing sufficient income in due course for the accomplishment of Charles Townshend's scheme for the payment of colonial salaries, at least for those men in key executive and judicial positions. North had adopted that plan as his own, and had made clear to Parliament his view that the tea tax revenue was therefore important in itself. And, as contemporaries knew and historians have long perceived, there was also symbolic significance in the

[72] Ibid., I, 220–1. Their punishment was merely to be burnt on the left thumb, since they pleaded benefit of clergy. This medieval law could not have been invoked in convictions for murder, hence the earlier anxiety in Britain: Baker, *Introduction to Legal History*, pp. 423–4.

[73] Knollenberg, *Growth of the American Revolution*, p. 340; Gipson, *British Empire*, XI, 281.

[74] *DAR*, I, 125, 143, 223.

retention of an actual tax, even though critics of the administration contended that the Declaratory Act of 1766 was symbol enough. In the wider context of the imperial relationship 1770 had seen the restoration of British authority not only in respect of the collapse of the non-importation agreements but also with regard to the problem town of Boston. The Massacre had not in the short term had the consequence either of destroying British control of the Massachusetts capital or of alienating colonial opinion elsewhere. American opposition to Britain was altogether at a low ebb as the year closed, and the North ministry had good reason to regard the colonial crisis as virtually at an end.

12

'A Pause in Politics'. 1771–1773

THE beginning of 1771 completed the transformation of the British political scene from the instability and confusion of the previous decade. In the 1760s frequent changes of and within administrations had rendered difficult any consistency of policy, whether on America or any other subject. Ministries had faced major political crises, formidable overseas and factious at home, that on several occasions threatened to topple them from power. The early 1770s were by contrast a period of stability and calm. Although issues relating to Wilkes, India, and America troubled North's ministry his tenure of office was never in doubt. Having weathered the Parliamentary storm of early 1770 North was able to embark upon a consolidation of his ministry before the end of the year. The death of George Grenville on 13 November 1770 removed a redoubtable Commons adversary and was followed within a few weeks by North's acquisition of his most important followers as part of a wider ministerial reconstruction. Lord Suffolk joined the cabinet, as Lord Privy Seal and then as Northern Secretary; Alexander Wedderburn became Solicitor-General when Edward Thurlow moved up to be Attorney-General in January 1771; and Thomas Whately enjoyed a final sojourn in office at the Board of Trade. This political reshuffle completed what was almost a polarization of British politicians with regard to America. 'The Stamp Men' were in office, the self-styled 'friends of America' in opposition and powerless to influence policy. Chatham played increasingly little part in politics during the next few years, leaving the initiative to his lieutenant, Shelburne. Since the Wilkites made little noise outside the City of London, it was left to Rockingham and his followers to constitute the only significant and not very formidable opposition group in Parliament.

The earlier 1770s, with the North ministry safe in office and virtually free from crises at home and abroad, appear in retrospect as a last and lost opportunity of averting the American Revolution. At the time such an opponent of Britain as Boston clergyman Samuel Cooper thought the administration had an opportunity to act from a position of strength, as when he wrote to Benjamin

Franklin on 1 January 1771. 'There seems now to be a pause in politics. The agreement of the merchants is broken. Administration has a fair opportunity of adopting the mildest and most prudent measure respecting the colonies without the appearance of being threatened or drove.'[1] In his autobiography the Duke of Grafton took full advantage of hindsight when he wrote, under the date of 1771, 'in the next and subsequent sessions there was nothing done, or even attempted, that could soothe the discontented minds of our American brethren'.[2]

Contemporary or retrospective criticism of the lack of any constructive ministerial policy for America at this time founders on the rock of political reality. Ministers, then as now, would not voluntarily embark on troublesome and embarrassing measures of conciliation to avoid possible problems in the future, especially when a quite different line of policy had apparently been successful. For what Cooper and other critics of government had in mind was presumably at least the repeal of the tea duty, so as to remove the main bone of contention between Britain and America. That idea was totally to misunderstand the attitude of the ministry. Lord North saw the tea tax as the practical solution to the problem of interference by assemblies in the administration of colonial government. During the next few years the payment of salaries to officials and judges in America was extended as far and as fast as possible. When by 1773 the revenue from the tea duty proved inadequate for this purpose the North ministry sought ways to increase it. Benjamin Franklin understood this policy perfectly well, ending an otherwise optimistic survey of British attitudes to Speaker Cushing on 5 February 1771 with this warning.[3]

There is no doubt of the intention to make Governors and some other officers independent of the people for their support, and that this purpose will be persisted in, if the American revenue is found insufficient to defray the salaries. Many think this so necessary a measure, that, even if there were no such revenue, the money should issue out of the Treasury here. But this, I apprehend, would hardly be the case, there being so many demands at home.

[1] *Franklin Papers*, XVIII, 3-4.
[2] *Grafton Autobiography*, p. 266. This comment was unfair. The Duke was Lord Privy Seal from 1771 to 1775, but refused to sit in the cabinet and give ministers the benefit of his advice.
[3] *Franklin Papers*, XVIII, 29. Franklin said much the same to Samuel Cooper on 30 Dec. 1770, when he mentioned that 'on this point, I think all Parties are against us': *Franklin Papers*, XVII, 312.

After 1770 the North ministry was content to do as little about America as possible, in the way of either coercion or conciliation. Any measures to counter the non-importation agreements were now unnecessary, and by the beginning of 1771 the plan to alter the constitution of Massachusetts had been dropped. Ironically this idea was now advanced by Governor Hutchinson, whose own letter of the previous October had helped to kill the project and who urged it upon Hillsborough in a letter of 22 January. 'The change in the temper of the people has been brought about sooner and to a greater degree than anybody could expect, and we seem now to be as well-prepared . . . to receive such a change in the constitution as we probably shall be at any time hereafter.' Hutchinson thought that an alteration of the Massachusetts Charter, since it had been granted by the Crown, would be done with more propriety by order of the Privy Council than by an Act of Parliament. The specific change he had in mind was the obvious one, an end to the assembly's right of choosing the council.[4] Hillsborough replied on 1 April, only two days after the letter arrived. He ignored the governor's suggestions and merely expressed satisfaction at the Massachusetts situation.[5]

Blind eyes were being turned towards America by the ministry. No American Secretary who read the correspondence from governors and other officials in the colonies, and both Hillsborough and his successor Dartmouth meticulously replied to such letters, can have been unaware of the simmering discontent at British assumptions of sovereignty that occasionally boiled over into open defiance. Hillsborough, for example, did nothing about a complaint from three plaintiffs in a court case in Rhode Island. In March 1770 a defence plea that a judgement of the Privy Council could be set aside as 'contrary to law, reason, equity and justice' had been refused by the colony's judges only on a three to two majority. At the 1770 election these three judges had been turned out by the assembly, the new Chief Justice being Stephen Hopkins who 'had several years past publicly declared that the King and Parliament had no more right to pass any Acts of Parliament to govern us than the Mohawks'. The new judges had then set aside the Privy Council decision.[6] Rhode Island was a colony with its own conception of an independent role within the British Empire, but knowledge of a widespread colonial attitude made a pessimist out of General Gage, whose sources of information were better

---

[4] *DAR*, I, 255; III, 32–3.
[5] Ibid., III, 73–5.   [6] Ibid., I, 374–5; III, 139–45.

than those of any other official correspondent. 'Something is generally out of order in this part of the world', he wrote privately to Barrington on 13 April 1772. A claim by the South Carolina Assembly to have sole power to vote taxes was the incident that occasioned this comment and led Gage to these reflections.[7]

Democracy is too prevalent in America, and claims the greatest attention to prevent its increase, and fatal effects. It is necessary too that Great Britain should not only assert, but also support that supremacy which she claims over the members of the Empire, or she will soon be supreme only in words, and we shall become a vast empire, composed of many parts, disjointed and independent of each other, without any head.

Responsibility for the formulation of colonial policy lay in the office of the Secretary of State for America, although cabinet initiative often stimulated action there and cabinet approval was needed before its enactment. It has therefore been assumed that the personalities of the American Secretaries were of great significance in the coming of the American Revolution. Historians have almost invariably contrasted the unyielding and formal Hillsborough with the pious and pliant Dartmouth, who succeeded him in August 1772, and found there a key to the alienation of the colonies. Hillsborough's reputation, both then and later, suffered from the enmity of Benjamin Franklin, who passed this savage comment on him in 1771. 'His character is conceit, wrongheadedness, obstinacy and passion. Those who would speak most favourably of him allow all this; they only add, that he is an honest man, and means well.'[8] Yet the final breach with America came when he was out of office, and he regarded himself as a friend of the colonies.[9] He on occasions vigorously attacked British control of the American economy.[10] And despite his advocacy of Parliament's right to tax the colonies he had both opposed the Stamp Act and publicly criticized the Townshend duties, albeit on grounds of inexpediency. Only in his antipathy to paper money, so essential to the economic well-being of the colonies, was Hillsborough in a policy issue personally identified in American minds as an enemy.

It was Hillsborough's stiff insistence on what he conceived to be the correct forms of conducting business that put him in a worse

---

[7] *PCBG*, pp. 103–4.　　　　　　　　[8] *Franklin Papers*, XVIII, 24.
[9] *De Berdt Letters*, pp. 335–7.
[10] As in his Irish interview of 1771 with Franklin: *Franklin Papers*, XIX, 48–9.

light than his views on colonial policy warranted. In particular he held the view that the appointment of a colonial agent was not a matter for the assembly alone: the council and governor must concur. This issue came to a head at an interview on 16 January 1771 when the American Secretary refused to accept Franklin as De Berdt's successor as agent for the Massachusetts Assembly. 'The House of Representatives has no right to appoint an agent. We shall take no notice of any agent but such as are appointed by acts of assembly to which the governor gives his assent.'[11] Franklin put a sinister interpretation on Hillsborough's pedantry, claiming that by appropriate orders to governors the American Secretary would acquire a power of veto over the appointment of agents.[12] This fear was without foundation. Barlow Trecothick, a Parliamentary critic of administration, had been accepted as New Hampshire agent in 1769, since his appointment conformed to the requisite criteria. So had Charles Garth much earlier, and he was no more inhibited in his conduct than Franklin himself as agent for Georgia since 1768 and also for New Jersey, after the latter had been appointed to represent that colony in an ironic episode later in 1771. In June Hillsborough forbade Franklin's son, Governor William Franklin, to agree to any appointment of an agent by the assembly alone: the political skill of the son contrived to obtain the constitutionally correct appointment of the father as agent in December.[13]

That 1771 did see pressure on this issue from the American Department is confirmed by a report of Edward Burke to New York, whose assembly under De Lanceys influence had unanimously elected him as agent in December 1770. Burke, aware of Hillsborough's attitude, left the administration to make the running, and not until December 1771 did he inform the colony of a recent conversation with John Pownall, who had put forward the view that the governor and council ought to participate or at least have a negative voice in the choice of a colony's agent. 'He speaks of it rather as a scheme under deliberation than as a point actually determined.' Pownall contended that only the consent of assembly, council, and governor could give an agent authority to represent a colony and would give him more weight to do so. Burke had

---

[11] See ibid., XVIII, 12–16, for Franklin's purportedly verbatim account of the interview. The instruction of 28 Mar. 1771 to Governor Hutchinson on his formal appointment forbade him to agree to the payment of any agent not appointed by the whole legislature: Acts PC Col., V, 264.

[12] Franklin Papers, XVIII, 27–8.   [13] Ibid., XVIII, 260–2; XIX, 3, 51.

replied that the agent represented only the legislature and not the executive, and that there might be a clash of a complaint against a governor by his assembly.[14]

Hillsborough remained adamant on the point, Franklin informing James Bowdoin on 13 January 1772 that 'at present no attention is paid by the American Minister to any agent here, whose appointment is not notified by the Governor's assent.[15] Dartmouth proved less punctilious and raised no objection to Franklin acting as Massachusetts agent.[16] But the new American Secretary's goodwill could not rescue the system of colonial agencies from irreversible decline. They had ceased to have a significant role in the British political world. There had always been defects: inadequate, irrelevant, or impossible instructions from America; financial stringency; conflicting interests of different colonies, as in boundary disputes; and inability to recruit men of weight, not even Burke being as important in the London political scene as colonists might imagine. These perennial elements of weakness were now compounded by the increasing irrelevance of agents as the quarrel between America and Britain polarized over the sovereignty of Parliament. The colonies now almost always instructed agents to transmit petitions directly to the King, and so American grievances seldom came before Parliament. Symbolic and symptomatic of the demoralization of the agents was the end of joint action: that became virtually a thing of the past, as regular meetings of agents, common in the 1760s, ceased from 1770.[17]

Dartmouth's accommodating attitude concerning the status of agents confirmed the favourable impression Franklin had already formed of him, one that was almost universal at the time in the colonial context. Grafton was to comment later that Dartmouth was 'the only one [in the North cabinet] who had a true desire to see lenient measures adopted towards the colonies'.[18] Dartmouth's role as President of the Board of Trade in the Rockingham ministry of 1765–6 gave him admirable credentials for the post in the eyes of professed friends of America. Edmund Burke naturally welcomed his appointment in a letter of 20 August 1772 to James De Lancey. 'He has certainly talents for it. When he had the first place at the Board of Trade he acted with those who were real

[14] *Burke Corr.*, II, 289–93.
[15] *Franklin Papers*, XIX, 12.   [16] Ibid., XIX, 361.
[17] Kammen, *Rope of Sand*, pp. 145–6. On the decline of the agencies see ibid., pp. 127–281, and Sosin, *Agents and Merchants*, pp. 108–61.
[18] *Grafton Autobiography*, p. 267.

wellwishers to the colonies. He did not then differ with his colleagues, and I hope he still perseveres in sentiments so proper for his situation.'[19]

Yet no significant alteration in colonial policy followed the change of American Secretary. Circumstances both immediate and long-term precluded any such consequence. Dartmouth was appointed during the *Gaspée* crisis; he had little room to manœuvre, and it served immediately to damage his reputation in the colonies.[20] In any case there can be little doubt that Dartmouth lacked the force of character and personal weight necessary to effect a major shift in colonial policy in the face of the hardline attitudes of his cabinet colleagues. His overt piety may even have proved politically counter-productive in alienating some of them: on 10 October Rochford told Gower that 'Lord Dartmouth is at his prayers. May he pray and be damned.'[21] It should not be forgotten either that Dartmouth was Lord North's step-brother and brought into the cabinet merely to bolster the Prime Minister's position and not, as some thought, to initiate a new line of policy. There is even considerable doubt as to how far he was master in his own house. He retained the two Under-Secretaries he had inherited from Hillsborough, a decision criticized by Rochford to Gower when expressing hope for a change in attitude by 'our new American Board, . . . though I cannot say I am much edified by his keeping Pownall and Knox for his two Secretaries, for I own I fear they are but bad advisers'.[22] Certainly they were both men lacking in warmth of sympathy towards the colonies. It was, moreover, Hillsborough's protégé, Bamber Gascoyne who was the dominant personality at the Board of Trade and who conducted the Board's business in the House of Commons. Piqued at his Department's declining influence, John Pownall sent this picture of Dartmouth's impotence to the absent and ill Knox on 23 July 1773.[23]

Our business has hitherto been as light as you could wish, and I think it is likely to continue so, for what can Lord Dartmouth have to do whilst Bamber Gascoyne is minister for America at the Board of Trade and Lord Suffolk at the Council Office, where they will not let us have anything to say, all Councils for American business being in Lord Gower's absence held by Lord Suffolk.

[19] *Burke Corr.*, II, 326–7.
[20] For this episode see below, pp. 226–30.
[21] PRO 30/29/1/14, ff. 667–8.
[22] PRO 30/29/1/14, ff. 663–4.
[23] *HMC Knox MSS*, p. 110.

The improvement in the relationship between Britain and her American colonies between 1770 and the Boston Tea Party was superficial and accidental. But in those years, as the sense of confrontation faded, practical answers were produced to problems and disputes arising out of such earlier legislation as the Currency Act of 1764 and the Mutiny Act of 1765.

No solution to the problem over colonial currency came before the resignation of Lord Hillsborough, that long-standing enemy of paper money. After New York in 1770 had obtained permission to issue paper currency that would be legal tender at its own treasury, Benjamin Franklin was given to understand that he could obtain, on petition, similar concessions for each of the colonies he represented as agent. He declined to do so, because of the cost involved. New York had paid out £180 in fees for what, in a Parliamentary sense, had been private legislation. Franklin took the view that since the 1764 Currency Act had been a public measure any defects in it ought to be corrected free of private expense.[24] As New Jersey agent Franklin argued at the Board of Trade against disallowance of legislation passed by that colony's assembly, contending that the Currency Act could not have been intended to prevent a colony treasury accepting its own paper money as legal tender. The Board of Trade view was that 'the business of the Board was to follow the letter of the Act'.[25]

It was in fact a widespread colonial practice for local treasuries to accept paper money for payment of public debts. Maryland and Pennsylvania had even been allowed to issue currency under conditions similar to that denied New Jersey.[26] Late in 1771 Hillsborough considered disallowing a Virginia measure to issue £30,000: but the act was approved by the Privy Council because it did not specifically make the currency legal tender.[27] Although occasional concessions were made to individual colonies, as when North Carolina was permitted in 1771 to issue £60,000 as legal tender at its treasury to pay the cost of the campaign against the rebel Regulators, Hillsborough blocked any general legislation to alter the Currency Act. After his resignation, Charles Garth led the pressure on Dartmouth to extend to all the other colonies the provisions of the New York Currency Act. But Benjamin Franklin

[24] *Franklin Papers*, XX, 340–1. Franklin did not state that any application would have been a tacit acknowledgment of Parliament's right to legislate for the colonies.
[25] Ibid., XIX, 67.   [26] *DAR*, II, 194; *JCTP 1768–1775*, p. 184.
[27] *DAR*, I, 434–5; *Acts PC Col.*, V, 586.

thought that the decisive factor in persuading the ministry to act was not this lobbying but the complaints of British merchants about a fall in trade and payment difficulties arising from the shortage of colonial paper money.[28] On 22 April 1773 the Board of Trade decided on legislation to extend the New York concession of 1770 to the other colonies affected by the Currency Act, and entrusted Bamber Gascoyne with responsibility for the measure.[29] The Bill, drafted by Richard Jackson, passed without debate in either House.[30]

The Mutiny Act of 1765 posed a more complex problem. The practical defects in its operation had been all too evident from the beginning.[31] The care to avoid the political objection of billeting soldiers in private houses had placed a weapon in the hands of the assemblies, by the stipulation that they should vote supplies for any army units stationed within their colonies: Gage explained this to Hillsborough in a private letter of 2 July 1771. 'The execution of the act depends upon the temper of an assembly. When they take it in their heads to be offended with the King's Ministers, or displeased with their governor, they immediately show their resentment by refusing to supply the barracks.'[32] It was on Gage as army Commander-in-Chief that the immediate problems fell, and he commented privately to Secretary of War Lord Barrington on 6 November 1771 that the matter was a regular bone of contention. 'It is an annual demand, or rather requisition of the governors, in whose provinces the troops are stationed. It is become a main point of government, and almost the only thing the governors have to ask of their assemblies.' Gage regretted that the act had not been so worded as to imply that troops would be billeted in private houses unless assemblies voted supplies to them in barracks, for the colonists would obviously then have chosen as an option what was resented as compulsory.[33]

It was easier to state the problem than to find an answer. On the renewal of the Mutiny Act in 1769 one colonial complaint had been met by the omission of the clause itemizing the requisite supplies, for many Americans had resented voting money for such purposes as alcoholic refreshments: and a new clause allowed the

---

[28] *Franklin Papers*, XX, 346.   [29] *JCTP 1768–1775*, p. 353.
[30] Simmons and Thomas, *Proceedings and Debates*, III, 493, 495, 503. For a fuller survey of the currency question in these years see Ernst, *Money and Politics*, pp. 282–311.
[31] Shy, *Towards Lexington*, pp. 250–8.
[32] *Gage Corr.*, I, 302.   [33] Ibid., II, 592.

civil authority to make arrangements with commanding officers 'by mutual agreement . . . to provide quarters . . . in any manner most convenient'.[34] But the basic grievances remained: the demand for money fell unequally, being consequent on the location of army units, and it was sometimes interpreted as a variant of Parliamentary taxation. On 4 June 1771 Gage told Barrington that he feared 'a long contest'; it was ominous that no assembly had taken advantage of the clause in the 1769 act allowing the passage of a colony's own alternative legislation.[35]

Barrington now revived a previous suggestion of his own, that colonial obstruction could be avoided by the judicious placing of soldiers in those newer colonies where the question of assembly co-operation did not arise, 'except when the old colonies are either in actual rebellion or call out themselves for military assistance'.[36] Gage in reply accepted this as one possibility, and suggested the threat of quartering on private houses in the event of non-compliance with the act, but on the whole thought it best to make no change as yet.[37] Barrington then proposed on 24 December 1771 a variant of his earlier idea, withdrawal of soldiers from recalcitrant colonies. 'I do not see the use of having any soldiers in the Massachusetts where no civil officer will employ them.'[38]

The American Secretary was meanwhile feeling his way towards a solution along similar lines. On 19 July 1771 Hillsborough wrote to Gage about the current refusal of the New Jersey Assembly to pay for a regiment of soldiers. 'There are in fact but two measures that can be trusted to as effectual; the one is to interpose the authority of Parliament, the other to withdraw the troops out of the colony, which last measure, if it can be adopted without prejudice to the King's service and in such a way as to avoid the appearance of yielding to the disobedience of the assembly, would perhaps be under all circumstances the most eligible.' He asked for Gage's opinion before putting the matter to the cabinet.[39] Gage in reply merely reported that the regiment stationed in New Jersey had now left.[40] This military evacuation was a factor in Hillsborough's pragmatic answer to the problem, based on the view that the threats of such withdrawals would prompt appreciation by colonies that the economic and military benefits of the presence of soldiers outweighed the financial burden of a contribu-

[34] See *Franklin Papers*, XVI, 70, 126–7, and above, pp. 131–2.
[35] *Gage Corr.*, II, 579.   [36] *PCBG*, p. 94.
[37] *Gage Corr.*, II, 592.   [38] *PCBG*, pp. 100–1.
[39] *Gage Corr.*, II, 135.   [40] Ibid., I, 312–13.

tion to their maintenance.[41] This opinion was confirmed by a letter he received from Gage on 9 March 1772 saying that New York had voted its contribution and that no difficulty was expected in Pennsylvania, the only colony with soldiers never to have refused to obey the Mutiny Act. 'The people here', Gage wrote from New York, 'upon a report that all the troops would be removed out of the Middle Colonies are alarmed at it, and say the town should never be without a regiment'.[42] To which Hillsborough made this complacent reply on 18 April. 'I always was of opinion that the advantages which the colonies derived from the troops would finally operate to remove these difficulties and disputes which the providing quarters for them had given rise to, and I am happy to find the event has justified that opinion.'[43]

Although the problems arising from such earlier and limited legislation as the Currency Act and the Mutiny Act were in some sense resolved in the early 1770s, the issue of the trade laws was more intractable. American politicians might pay lip-service to Parliament's right to decide such matters, but colonial merchants usually took little notice of rules and regulations interfering with their commercial enterprise. Customs officials were frequently bribed or coerced into compliance. Resort to violence was an age-old smuggling practice, in Britain as well as America; but in the colonies customs officers all too often obtained no support or even protection from the civil authority. By mid-1771 even a reluctant North administration was coming round to the view that something had to be done about so outrageous a situation, ministers being especially concerned over physical attacks on customs officers attempting to do their duty and the failure of governors to support them. On 13 July 1771 Secretary to the Treasury John Robinson sent to John Pownall thirteen papers concerning violent incidents since 1768 in Boston, Philadelphia, Rhode Island, and elsewhere.[44] The list did not include the worst episode, when at Newport in Rhode Island in July 1769 the sloop *Liberty* had been burned by a mob successfully intent on freeing a ship and cargo impounded for smuggling; the perpetrators had escaped with impunity.[45] The most recent outrage had also occurred at Newport on 2 April 1771; an assault on the Collector

---

[41] Ibid., II, 139. Shy, op. cit., p. 339, suggests that a regiment might spend £6,000 a year in pay, quite apart from its maintenance costs. It was said that the soldiers in Boston in 1769 were spending £250 a week: ibid., p. 309.

[42] *Gage Corr.*, I, 302, 316–17.   [43] Ibid., II, 143.

[44] *DAR*, I, 369–70.   [45] Ibid., VI, 162.

of Customs, Charles Dudley, after he attempted to seize the *Polly* on its arrival from the Dutch island of St Eustatius.[46] Hillsborough responded to the Treasury prompting, writing to Governor Joseph Wanton of Rhode Island about the *Polly* incident on 19 July. Wanton replied on 2 November, blaming drunken sailors for the incident and denying that the customs officers had applied for protection.[47] The American Secretary also wrote on 19 July to the Proprietors of Pennsylvania about violent attacks on Philadelphia customs officers who had made lawful seizures in April and October 1769. The belated reply of Thomas and John Penn on 24 December defended the governor and magistrates of their colony: the violence had been unexpected and short-lived, and no information was subsequently forthcoming.[48] Before the end of 1771 violent resistance to enforcement of the trade laws had occurred in Falmouth, Massachusetts, and in New Hampshire, where prompt action by the governor quelled the disorder.[49]

Despite all the evidence of open and widespread defiance of the trade laws, the British government took no positive measure until the outrage of the *Gaspée* affair, the particular circumstances of which made it a significant trigger-point in the coming of the American Revolution. Rhode Island, even before the recent incidents at Newport, had long been a colony notorious in Britain both for its disregard of customs regulations and for its political system: all officials from the governor downwards were subject to annual election and therefore at the mercy of public opinion. Matters came to a head when in February 1772 the *Gaspée*, a naval schooner commanded by Lieutenant Dudingston, arrived in Rhode Island waters with instructions to prevent smuggling from Rear-Admiral John Montagu, the new naval commander for North America. According to the inhabitants Dudingston at once began to stop and search every vessel in sight. On 21 March Governor Wanton therefore sent, through the local county sheriff, a peremptory request for his authority to do so, since Dudingston had neglected the formality of showing his papers to the civil government. Dudingston complied with this demand the next day, but in reporting the matter to Admiral Montagu in Boston he mentioned rumours that some colonists were 'arming a vessel to prevent my carrying any seizure to Boston'. On 8 April Montagu thereupon sent a sharp letter to Governor Wanton, reminding him of his duty to help the King's officers and threatening to hang

[46] Ibid., III, 78–82.   [47] Ibid., I, 372–3, 421.
[48] Ibid., I, 373; III, 275–6. [49] Ibid., I, 431–2; III, 234–40; IV, 13.

'as pirates' any men taken in an attempt to rescue captured smugglers. Wanton's reply was tart. 'I hope you will not hang any of his Majesty's subjects belonging to this colony from such false information.'[50]

The scene was set for the events of 10 June. On the previous day the *Gaspée* went aground on a sandbank six miles from Providence while pursuing a suspect vessel. Soon after midnight she was surrounded by a flotilla of small boats, containing some 150 armed men, on the pretext that the sheriff demanded access. When Dudingston refused because of the time of night, he was shot and wounded. The ship was captured, and burnt after evacuation of the crew. News of this outrage reached London on 16 July, but made little public impression: the *London Evening Post* two days later merely reported it in a short paragraph. Admiral Montagu's letter to Hillsborough enclosed an affidavit from midshipman William Dickinson, who stated that a mob had been collected in Providence by the beating of a drum.[51] Governor Hutchinson was concerned about the proximity of Providence to Boston, less than fifty miles away. 'If some measures are not taken in England in consequence of so flagrant an insult upon the King's authority, I fear it will encourage the neighbouring colonies to persevere in their opposition to the laws of trade and to be guilty of the like and greater acts of violence.'[52] Governor Wanton's account arrived six days later. He promised an inquiry and had offered a £100 reward for information. But much of his letter emphasized the provocations allegedly suffered by Rhode Island merchants, and he blandly cited the fact that only two out of 200 ships entering Newport since 1 March had been seized for smuggling as evidence that 'the trade of this colony stands upon as fair and legal a footing as the trade in any part of His Majesty's dominions'.[53]

The cabinet considered 'the Rhode Island business' on 30 July, doubtless one occasion when First Lord of the Admiralty Lord Sandwich, furious at the destruction of a navy ship, demanded the revocation of the Rhode Island charter.[54] Lord Hillsborough was instructed to order Governor Wanton 'to exert himself seriously and actively to discover the perpetrators of the burning of the sloop *Gaspée*, and not content himself with the mere official conduct of issuing a Proclamation'. The governor was to be warned that unless the criminals were arrested the matter might

[50] Ibid., III, 95–6; V, 51, 62, 99–100.
[51] Ibid., IV, 102; V, 121–3.
[52] Ibid., V, 118.
[53] Ibid., IV, 109; V, 125–7.
[54] Bargar, *Dartmouth*, p. 76.

be taken up by Parliament. A reward of £500 was to be promised for each offender convicted. Admiral Montagu was to be ordered to go himself to Rhode Island to detect the culprits and tighten the check on smuggling. Finally Hillsborough was directed to obtain the opinion of the government's law officers, Attorney-General Thurlow and Solicitor-General Wedderburn, as to whether the offenders could be tried in England and for what crime.[55] Hillsborough, who had by then already resigned over the Vandalia issue, duly wrote to the law officers on 7 August, enclosing not only the evidence but also a copy of the 1772 Naval Dockyards Act.[56] That legislation had been enacted because of arson in dockyards within Britain, but it did contain a clause authorizing the transfer to Britain of any trial for such a crime in the colonies.[57] Thurlow and Wedderburn dismissed its relevance in their reply three days later. It applied only to the burning of ships in dockyards and 'not to ships upon actual service'. But, neatly hoisting Governor Wanton with his own petard, they ruled that since according to his statement the *Gaspée* had been within the colony of Rhode Island the attack on the ship had not been mere piracy but 'an act of high treason'. The offenders could therefore be indicted in either Britain or Rhode Island.[58] There seemed every prospect that at last the 1769 threat to use Henry VIII's Treason Act against Americans might be implemented.

Further correspondence drafted by Hillsborough on 7 August arising out of the cabinet meeting included letters to the Admiralty, General Gage and Governor Wanton.[59] They were never sent. One reason, according to John Pownall, was that they went 'beyond the minute of cabinet and the first order in Council'.[60] But there is evidence that some ministers had been having second thoughts: Rochford commented on 'the Rhode Island business' to the absent Gower on 15 August that 'it grows serious. I mean as to what part to act with safety. The Attorney General is for taking the offenders, bringing them here and trying them for high treason. Some of us I believe think this rather a violent measure and yet something must be done.'[61] The replace-

---

[55] Cabinet minute; Dartmouth MSS, D(W) 1778/II/372.
[56] *DAR*, IV, 146.
[57] Gipson, *British Empire*, XII, 28–9. The act has often been erroneously linked with the *Gaspée* affair, by both contemporaries and historians. The cabinet had ordered that a copy be sent to Governor Wanton.
[58] *DAR*, V, 163–4; Bargar, op. cit., p. 76, misread this report.
[59] *DAR*, IV, 146–7.   [60] Dartmouth MSS, D(W) 1778/II/400.
[61] PRO 30/29/1/14, ff. 663–4.

ment of Hillsborough as American Secretary by Dartmouth would in any case obviously necessitate his involvement in any decisions he would have to implement. On 20 August the cabinet considered the matter again, and decided to recall or cancel the letters from Hillsborough to Governor Wanton, the Admiralty, Admiral Montagu, and General Gage: they were countermanded two days later.[62] The ministry instead decided to establish a formal commission of inquiry, empowered to offer pardons and rewards to anyone identifying the culprits.[63] Next day the Privy Council directed the Attorney- and Solicitor-Generals to prepare the relevant documents, and formally approved their drafts on 26 August.[64] The Order in Council appointed a five-man Commission of Inquiry, and instructed General Gage to protect and Admiral Montagu to assist this Commission. It also approved a Proclamation offering a reward of £500 for the discovery of any person involved and a further £500 for the person called High Sheriff, with pardons to accompany these rewards. Governor Wanton was appointed to head the Commission, despite numerous warnings about his behaviour from such men as Admiral Montagu and Governor Hutchinson. The four other members were American judges, all on Treasury salaries: Chief Justice Daniel Horsmanden of New York, Chief Justice Frederick Smyth of New Jersey, Chief Justice Peter Oliver of Massachusetts, and Robert Auchmuty, Judge of the Boston Vice-Admiralty Court, whose jurisdiction encompassed all New England. Governor Wanton was instructed to hand over to Admiral Montagu any persons arrested for the *Gaspée* incident, so that they could be sent for trial in England.[65] Dartmouth issued the formal instructions early the next month, writing to Governor Wanton on 4 September a letter that was to be widely publicized in America. For in it the American Secretary stated that the offence was high treason and not piracy, and announced that it was the government's intention to bring any accused persons to England for trial. They were therefore to be handed over to Admiral Montagu, together with witnesses on both sides.[66] This information was grist to the mill of colonial propagandists.

The role of Dartmouth in this policy decision is difficult to

[62] *DAR*, IV, 157.   [63] *HMC Dartmouth MSS*, II, 88.

[64] *Acts PC Col.*, V, 356–7; *HMC Dartmouth MSS*, II, 89.

[65] *DAR*, IV, 158; V, 173–5.

[66] Ibid., IV, 165–7; V, 186–9. Dartmouth's instructions to the Admiralty ordered that Montagu should send any such 'delinquents' on board a naval ship to England: ibid., V, 189–90.

ascertain. The Commission of Inquiry was a more formal procedure than that conceived under Hillsborough, and a method that was to provoke widespread resentment in America. Was the new American Secretary pushed by his colleagues into a hardline measure before he was aware of the implications? His Under-Secretary John Pownall sent this warning letter to Dartmouth on 25 August. 'I am convinced that this proceeding is meant to pledge the American minister in coercive measures, and your Lordship will judge what other people will think of this proceeding when I tell you that the Attorney-General said to me himself this morning that he thought it five times the magnitude of the Stamp Act [Crisis].'[67] By September the American Secretary was reported to be saying that his office would not issue orders for bringing to trial in Britain any persons accused of the *Gaspée* outrage.[68] Yet by that time the appropriate authority had already been given and the matter was out of Dartmouth's hands.

By then in London it already seemed that a breakthrough had occurred in the problem of identifying the culprits. On 27 August a letter arrived from Admiral Montagu enclosing a statement from Aaron Biggs, a negro indentured servant. It identified five men involved in the attack on the *Gaspée* and named one of them, John Brown, as having shot Dudingston.[69] A formal affidavit by Biggs arrived on 3 October, with a letter from Montagu affirming his belief in the evidence. The Admiral also enclosed a statement from Charles Dudley, the Collector of Customs maltreated in 1771, asserting that 'the attack upon the *Gaspée* was not the effect of sudden passion and resentment but of cool deliberation and fore-thought. . . . It had been long determined she should be destroyed.'[70]

The news from Rhode Island, when it arrived after a long winter of waiting, proved a bitter disappointment for ministers. The first report came on 26 March 1773, a letter from Chief Justice Smyth. He predicted that the offenders would not be brought to justice in such a colony, where 'the popular charter' was the root cause of all the disorder and defiance. The governor had even claimed that his duty to the inhabitants had caused him to make public Dartmouth's letter of 4 September. Hundreds of people in the colony must know who the perpetrators were, but 'all our enquiry has been ineffectual to fix with certainty upon any particular person

[67] Dartmouth MSS, D(W) 1778/II/400.   [68] Bargar, op. cit., p. 78.
[69] Dartmouth MSS D(W) 1778/II/369; printed *DAR*, V, 141–2.
[70] *DAR*, IV, 161; V, 146–7, 149–50.

concerned in the outrage, and to keep the matter secret is now become a common cause'. Smyth then warned that since the administration seemed to think the evidence of Aaron Biggs 'a discovery of consequence' he had to report that 'the credibility of his testimony is exceedingly questionable in every article'. It was full of mistakes and contradictions, and he was a runaway servant hoping to avoid punishment by providing whatever testimony was desired.[71] The official interim report of the Commission, dated 21 January from Newport, arrived on 29 March. It merely stated that witnesses and papers had been examined from 5 January, and that proceedings would be resumed in May.[72]

The ministry had already sought to assist the inquiry by sending Dudingston and Dickinson as witnesses; although the former was too ill to go, Dickinson sailed in mid-March in the belief that he could identify some of the culprits.[73] But he could provide only descriptions and not names. The final report of the Commission, dated 22 June and received in Whitehall on 4 August, was a complete anticlimax, with Governor Wanton's influence clearly stamped on much of the document. It began with the statement that the attack had been a spontaneous action, because of the accident of the *Gaspée* going aground. As if in further alleviation of the offence, it rehearsed the colony's previous record of violent resistance to the trade laws, and blamed Dudingston for 'an intemperate if not a reprehensible zeal'. The testimony of Biggs, the only witness to name individuals, had been completely discredited. The evidence had been submitted to the scrutiny of the Rhode Island judges, who affirmed that it did not fix 'a probable suspicion' on any individual. Since there was 'no probability' of new evidence the inquiry would be concluded.[74]

The Commission of Inquiry had failed in its objective, and the mere fact of its appointment led to a further intensification of colonial animosity towards and suspicion of Britain in a manner potentially very ominous. It was as a direct consequence that on 12 March 1773 the Virginia Assembly set up a 'Standing Committee' of eleven members, whose business would be to obtain prompt information on all British government decisions relating to America and to correspond with other colonies about

---

[71] Ibid., IV, 249; VI, 82–5.   [72] Ibid., IV, 237–8; VI, 47–50, 52–3.
[73] Ibid., IV, 251, 253, 254.
[74] Ibid., IV, 336–7; VI, 160–4. Soon afterwards Chief Justice Horsmanden obtained information that confirmed beyond all reasonable doubt that Biggs had given false testimony: ibid., VI, 195–6.

them. The Virginia Speaker was instructed to write to the Speakers of the other colonial assemblies asking for the appointment of similar committees. The colony's governor, Lord Dunmore, showed a remarkable lack of political perspicacity when he forwarded the relevant journals to Whitehall with this comment: 'I thought them so insignificant that I took no notice of them.'[75] The North ministry was properly concerned, and on 1 July the Board of Trade completed a report for the Privy Council.[76] This described the Virginia Assembly's behaviour as being of 'a very extraordinary nature and we think that the inviting the other colonies to a communication and correspondence upon such matters as are stated in these proceedings is a measure of a most dangerous tendency'. The Privy Council was therefore advised to take 'proper and expedient' action.[77] Nothing was done, and the anticipated consequences ensued. Hutchinson, who had himself promptly sent Dartmouth a copy of the Virginia resolutions,[78] reported on 10 July that Massachusetts, Rhode Island, and Connecticut had already appointed Committees of Correspondence, and the other assemblies were expected to do the same.[79] By March 1774 all the colonies had appointed such committees, and a communications network of resistance to Britain had come into existence as a direct result of the *Gaspée* incident.

One way and another the whole affair had been a political disaster for the North administration. British authority was further discredited in America. By the time news of the final outcome of the inquiry arrived in Britain the ministry had no inclination to pursue the subject further. More urgent matters in Massachusetts required attention.

[75] Ibid., VI, 109.
[76] *JCTP 1768–1775*, pp. 365–6.
[77] *DAR*, VI, 168–70.
[78] Ibid., VI, 299–300. This copy arrived on 29 May, before Dunmore's letter on 9 June.
[79] Ibid., VI, 183–4.

13

Massachusetts Challenges Britain.
1771–1773

By the end of 1770 Boston had been overawed by the presence of a naval squadron in its harbour and an army regiment in Castle William. But this British riposte merely changed the nature of the political contest. Although the leaders of the popular party in Massachusetts had been deprived of the weapon of physical coercion, they never lost sight of the constitutional issues raised in the controversies of the previous decade. Soon the news from the colony was the familiar story of discontent and defiance.

On 29 June 1771 the assembly, through Speaker Cushing, replied to agent Benjamin Franklin's letter of 5 February, in which after general reassurances about British attitudes and policies towards America he had warned of the ministerial determination to retain the tea tax and pay colonial salaries from the revenue obtained.[1] Cushing's letter announced that the assembly could not regard Parliament's right of taxation as given up while the tea duty remained. Since silence by colonial legislatures might be construed as tacit consent 'it is therefore our duty to declare our rights'. The assembly professed not to be dismayed by the collapse of the trade boycott. 'We have reason to believe that the American colonies, however much they may have disagreed among themselves in one mode of opposition to arbitrary measures, are still united in the main principles of constitutional and natural liberty.' The refusal of Governor Hutchinson to accept any grant from the assembly was implicit confirmation of Franklin's comment on Treasury payment of colonial salaries, the purpose of which was interpreted as 'making governors of the colonies and other officers independent of the people for their support'.[2] Massachusetts politicians may well have been puzzled at the British government's stand on that point, for even at the height of the controversies with Governor Bernard the colony's assembly had never threatened either to reduce or to delay his salary.[3]

---

[1] *Franklin Papers*, XVIII, 26–30.
[2] Ibid., XVIII, 147–53.   [3] Ibid., XVIII, 172–5.

Franklin was baffled when speculating about the matter on 13
January 1772 and could think of no reason 'unless it be with an
intention to influence him [the Governor] by with-holding it
when he declines executing arbitrary instructions', a characteristically sinister motive for Franklin to attribute to Hillsborough,
whom he wrongly portrayed as the man behind retention of the
salary policy.[4]

In 1771 the Massachusetts Assembly did not take up the salary
issue, but it did revive other grievances. After a protest at being
summoned to meet again at Cambridge instead of in Boston,[5] the
assembly renewed an attempt to tax the salaries of the American
Customs Board, based at Boston but paid directly from Britain. In
1770 the ministry's own law officers had ruled that royal officials
were liable to such taxes,[6] but Hillsborough's instructions of
March 1771 forbade Hutchinson to accept any tax on royal
officials whose office did not relate exclusively to Massachusetts.[7]
Hutchinson, although unhappy about this order, duly vetoed the
colony's tax legislation. The assembly thereupon asserted that the
royal instruction infringed their charter right, and Hutchinson on
6 July reported 'the most open denial of the authority of
Parliament to appoint Commissioners of the Customs or to raise
any monies from the colonies. It is not the first time this principle
has been avowed. It has for some years been gaining strength
among the people in this and other colonies, which made it less
difficult for the representatives of the people of this province to
avow it in this open and public manner.'[8] Not a man to mince his
words or flinch from a crisis, Hutchinson later sent this private
comment to John Pownall. 'This doctrine of independence must
sooner or later become a serious affair, and the same spirit which
denied the authority of Parliament to make laws now denies the
authority of the King to give instructions to his Governor.'[9]

Not until Hillsborough dispatched routine letters to colonial
officials on 4 December did he comment to Hutchinson on the
defiance in Massachusetts. The administration chose 'to consider
what passed on that occasion as the result of a rash intemperate
moment', and so the matter would not be put before Parliament.
But Hutchinson was told to conform to his original instructions.[10]

---

[4] Ibid., XIX, 13–14.   [5] *DAR*, III, 122.
[6] *JCTP 1768–1775*, pp. 169–70.   [7] *DAR*, I, 280.
[8] Ibid., III, 133. See also *Franklin Papers*, XVIII, 179–80, and Gipson, *British
Empire*, XII, 45.
[9] *DAR*, III, 155–6.   [10] Ibid., III, 246–8.

And that the ministry, though preferring a low profile, was not unmindful of the potential danger, was shown by an order of 11 January 1772 to General Gage that he should ensure the safety of Castle William because of a revival of faction in Boston.[11]

During the first months of 1772 the ministerial attitude appeared to be one of common sense, as the political situation in Massachusetts calmed down. On 24 January 1772 Hutchinson wrote that the enemies of government there had been disheartened both by the news that the Parliament opposition in Britain was at a low ebb and by a breakdown in their correspondence with Pennsylvania and New York.[12] On 27 April the Governor reported that 'the Assembly have gone through their business with more decency and propriety than any Assembly has done for seven years past';[13] in other words, before the Stamp Act Crisis had initiated the first major quarrel with Britain. So confident was Hutchinson about the drop in the political temperature in Massachusetts that he decided he would permit the assembly in June to meet again in Boston, after an absence of more than three years.[14] He was soon to be disillusioned. Gage, replying on 13 April to the order about Castle William, reminded Hillsborough that 'principles repugnant to the British constitution are too prevalent in that province';[15] and a letter of 27 April from Hutchinson announced the assembly's refusal to pay adequate salaries to the judges.[16]

This was an omen of a new area of controversy. In his reply to Hutchinson on 6 June Hillsborough stated that he had consulted Lord North, who 'entirely concurs with me in the propriety of recommending to His Majesty to give adequate salaries to his law-officers in the Massachusetts Bay'. Hillsborough had not then had the opportunity to put the matter to George III, but he hoped that news of this intention would prevent the resignation of any judges. 'I think, however, I ought to add that an adequate provision for so large a number of judges as five may amount to more than the revenue can bear.' It might therefore be necessary to reduce the number of judges to three unless 'the Assembly should grant a permanent provision for the two junior judges'.[17] The ministry did find the requisite finance. On 27 July Hillsborough informed the

<hr />

[11] Ibid., IV, 17.
[12] Ibid., IV, 24.
[13] Ibid., V, 77–8.
[14] Ibid., IV, 96, 106; V, 104.
[15] Ibid., V, 69–70.
[16] Ibid., V, 77–8.
[17] Ibid., V, 112–13. Hutchinson replied on 4 Sept. that he did not think the Assembly would provide the two salaries in such circumstances: ibid., IV, 166. But the point did not arise.

Treasury Board of the decision to pay royal salaries of £400 to the Chief Justice of Massachusetts, £200 to each of the four Associate Judges, and £150 and £50 respectively to the colony's Attorney-General and Solicitor-General. 'These several salaries should be paid them out of the duty upon tea imported into America' and would date from 5 July.[18]

The issue of the payment of colonial salaries by the Crown was the next spark to ignite the tinder-box of Massachusetts politics. Even before the North ministry had decided to pay the Massachusetts judges out of the Treasury the colony's assembly had voted a petition to the King, on 14 July, protesting against the royal payment of Governor Hutchinson's salary. This was claimed to be a breach of the colony's charter, since that gave the assembly full power to levy taxes for the support of government: and that had been the practice ever since, for over eighty years.[19] Hutchinson himself was not inclined to take the matter too seriously when he wrote to Hillsborough the next day. 'The attempt to find a new cause of grievance from the payment of the Governor's salary by order from his Majesty will rather serve than hurt the cause of government.'He noted the analogy of the complaint about the King's instructions to the governor, an issue that had faded away.[20]

By the time news of the petition reached London, Hillsborough had been replaced as American Secretary by Dartmouth, whose reply to Hutchinson on 2 September clearly demonstrated that there would be no change of policy on the salary dispute. Dartmouth did not accept that the assembly's doctrine was founded upon either 'any powers or authorities conveyed in the charter or any just principle of the British constitution, and I must confess that I have been always taught to believe that the providing for the support of the American Governors and other officers of the Crown in the colonies independent of the people is a measure equally for the honour and dignity of the Crown and for the welfare of those colonies'.[21] Dartmouth's teacher in this matter had doubtless been his step-brother, Lord North.

Two months later, early in November 1772, Dartmouth was given the assembly's petition by agent Franklin, and the new American Secretary was in a dilemma. Knowledge of its contents would offend and outrage much British opinion, while rejection of

---

[18] Ibid., V, 152. Hutchinson was notified in a letter of 7 Aug.: ibid., IV, 147–8. The judges took their 1772 salaries from the Assembly, but agreed to be paid thereafter by the Crown: ibid., VI, 221.

[19] Ibid., V, 142–4.   [20] Ibid., V, 144–5.   [21] Ibid., V, 182.

the petition would have similar consequences in Massachusetts. All this he explained to Franklin in an interview reported by the agent on 2 December to Speaker Cushing.

After a long audience he was pleased to say, that notwithstanding all I had said or that could be said in support of the petition, he was sure the presenting it at this time could not possibly produce any good. That the King would be exceedingly offended, but what steps he would take upon it was uncertain; perhaps he would require the opinion of the judges or government lawyers, which would be surely against us; perhaps he might lay it before Parliament, and so the censure of both Houses would be drawn down upon us; the most favourable thing to be expected was, a severe reprimand to the Assembly by order of his Majesty; the natural consequence of which must be, more discontent and uneasiness in the province. That possessed as he was with great goodwill for New England, he was extremely unwilling that one of the first acts of his administration with regard to the Massachusetts should be of so unpleasant a nature.

Dartmouth therefore asked Franklin to hold back the petition, in the hope of its reconsideration by the assembly. Franklin replied that any change of mind was unlikely in view of 'the great majority' there had been for the petition, and he commented that the earlier treatment of colonial petitions by Parliament had led to 'a questioning of their authority'. That was why petitions came only to the King, who 'appears to be now the only connection between the two countries': this comment was an implicit but clear denial of the authority of Parliament over America. But, Franklin told Speaker Cushing, he agreed to Dartmouth's request, for two reasons: that there had been a favourable change of American Secretary, and that the assembly wished now to complain about other grievances.[22]

It was with this missive of 2 December that Franklin enclosed the bundle of letters known to posterity as 'the Hutchinson letters', private letters written in the later 1760s to Thomas Whately by American correspondents, chiefly Thomas Hutchinson and Andrew Oliver, now Governor and Lieutenant-Governor of Massachusetts. Whately, at the time a Grenvillite opposition MP, had died on 26 May 1772. How Franklin obtained the letters and why he sent them have been matters of conjecture and speculation ever since.[23] Franklin himself maintained that his motive was to improve relations between Britain and the colonies by showing

---

[22] *Franklin Papers*, XIX, 409–11.
[23] For an admirable discussion of this point see *Franklin Papers*, XIX, 401–9. The letters are conveniently reprinted in *Franklin Papers*, XX, 539–80.

Americans that their real enemies were in Boston and not London. This claim is born out by his comment to Cushing at the time that his perusal of them had greatly moderated his own resentment at government policy.[24]

Long before this explosive packet arrived in Boston the political situation there had so changed as to jeopardize all hope of reconciliation between Massachusetts and Britain. On 10 September 1772 the radical *Massachusetts Spy* published a vicious attack on the King, comparing George III with Charles I for enforcing laws and imposing taxes without consent. Hutchinson failed to persuade the Massachusetts Council to order the arrest of the printer, and in any case doubted whether a prosecution before a Boston jury would secure a conviction.[25] When news of the proposed payment of Treasury salaries to the colony's judges arrived in October 'the most inflammatory pieces' were published in the Boston press, and a Boston town meeting asked Hutchinson about the truth of the report; the Governor refused to confirm or deny it.[26] On 2 November Boston appointed a Committee of Correspondence to write to the other towns in Massachusetts, and when informing Dartmouth of this ominous development Hutchinson made a deliberate comparison with political events in Britain. 'The inhabitants of Boston, like the livery of London, have been for a long time used to concern themselves with all the affairs of government.'[27] Hutchinson's letters to Dartmouth can have left the American Secretary in no doubt of the challenge to Britain that was building up in Massachusetts, as when he wrote on 23 October.[28]

The source, my lord, of all this irregularity is a false opinion, broached at the time of the Stamp Act and ever since cultivated until it is become general, that the people of all the colonies are subject to no authority but their own legislatures and that the Acts of the Parliament of Great Britain, which is every day in print termed a foreign state, are not obligatory.

Hutchinson was penning this observation against a background of Boston town meetings that culminated on 20 October in the

---

[24] *Franklin Papers*, XIX, 411–13. Cushing acknowledged this letter on 24 Mar. 1773 (*Franklin Papers*, XX, 123), but the 'Hutchinson Letters' were not made public until June. The subsequent controversy is not here discussed. For it see Bailyn, *Hutchinson*, pp. 238–59.

[25] *DAR*, V, 190–3, 200.

[26] Ibid., IV, 193; V, 205–6.   [27] Ibid., V, 206.

[28] Ibid., V, 204–5. Dartmouth received this on 10 Dec. (Ibid., IV, 188), soon after the interview when Franklin had implied much the same views.

adoption of resolutions that matched the law of nature against the British constitution. The authority of Parliament was refuted and that of the Crown limited by the natural rights of the colonists to life, liberty, and property. These rights nullified the claim of Parliament to tax or legislate for the colonies or regulate their economy, and the royal prerogative did not extend to breaches of the charter or to such other powers as the maintenance of a peacetime army in America, the payment of colonial officials, and the use of admiralty courts and writs of assistance to enforce the trade laws. This Bostonian behaviour Hutchinson described privately as 'a declaration of independency', and he decided it was his duty to check the spread of such dangerous doctrines.[29] He did so by a surprise speech to the next meeting of the Massachusetts General Court on 6 January 1773, informing Dartmouth the next day that he had taken this step because many Massachusetts towns had followed the example of Boston in denying the authority of Parliament, and he had been afraid that the assembly might issue a similar circular to the other colonial assemblies.[30] With hindsight, Massachusetts opponents of Hutchinson came to suspect that his motive was also, by forcing a public controversy, to prevent any repeal of the tea duty.[31] Certainly the news from Massachusetts in early 1773 was to contribute to the hardening of ministerial opinion.

Hutchinson's speech set out the historical basis of Parliament's authority, and he then buttressed his case with constitutional theory. 'I know of no line that can be drawn between the supreme authority of Parliament and the total independence of the colonies.' If the supremacy of Parliament was not denied, the exercise of its authority could not be a grievance. Hutchinson ended by inviting the General Court to debate the subject with him. Since he could not conceive that independence was the aim, he asked what other form of constitutional dependence would be possible.[32] Hutchinson admitted privately to John Pownall that 'I was afraid of being charged with bringing on a fresh dispute, although it was inevitable a short time after'; but he evidently thought he had struck a stout blow for government. 'At the delivery of the speech the members seemed to be amazed, three-quarters of them having taken for granted that all that had been done by Parliament was arbitrary and unconstitutional without

[29] *Franklin Papers*, XX, 82–3.   [30] *DAR*, VI, 44–5.
[31] *Franklin Papers*, XX, 252–4.
[32] For the text of his speech see *DAR*, VI, 39–44.

having ever been informed what is their constitution. I flatter myself that it will be of service.'[33]

News of Hutchinson's speech met a mixed reception when it reached Whitehall on 22 February.[34] Benjamin Franklin told Thomas Cushing on 9 March that it had been 'printed and industriously circulated here by (as I think) the ministerial people, which I take to be no good sign'.[35] The omen was misleading. Publication of the speech was probably on the initiative of American Under-Secretary William Knox, who was to be suspected of leaking official papers to the press in 1774.[36] Dartmouth would certainly not have welcomed Hutchinson's move, for the American Secretary had been hoping for a period of quiet improvement in the colonial situation, so he had told Franklin in a conversation in December 1772. Dartmouth then professed goodwill to America and promised consideration of colonial grievances. 'If the Americans continued quiet, and gave no fresh offence to government, those measures would be reconsidered and such relief given as upon consideration should be thought reasonable.'[37] Franklin soon perceived that the cabinet had not welcomed the controversy Hutchinson had provoked, for he informed Joseph Galloway on 15 March that 'the Ministry are a good deal chagrined with the Boston proceedings, but seem not to know what to do with them'.[38] Dartmouth had sent a cool answer to Hutchinson on 3 March. He accepted the need for the governor 'to speak out upon the occasion. But how far it was or was not expedient to enter so fully in your speech into an exposition of your own opinions in respect to the principles of the constitution of the colony I am not able to judge.'[39]

Hutchinson's reply of 1 June to this mild reproof claimed wide support for his initiative.[40] One man who approved was General Gage in New York. He told Barrington on 7 April that Hutchinson 'had good reason for what he did, and that he has defeated the intentions of the leaders to invite the assemblies of the other provinces into a public avowal of the same sentiments and a consultation upon measures to maintain them. . . . Many in other

---

[33] Ibid., VI, 45.   [34] Ibid., IV, 233.
[35] *Franklin Papers*, XX, 98. The speech was printed in the *London Chronicle* for 27 Feb., and the *Public Advertiser* for 4 Mar., two newspapers inclined to support government. It did not appear in the opposition *London Evening Post*.
[36] Simmons and Thomas, *Proceedings and Debates*, IV, 397.
[37] *Franklin Papers*, XX, 8. This conversation took place 'a day or two' after 8 Dec. 1772.
[38] Ibid., XX, 109.   [39] *DAR*, VI, 94–5.   [40] Ibid., IV, 321.

provinces who wish and think like the Bostonians say the measure is untimely so they mean to leave it to their children.'[41]

The controversy in Massachusetts lasted from January to March, when the governor prorogued the assembly. Hutchinson had deliberately taken the General Court by surprise, and the position he had adopted put his opponents in a quandary, as Speaker Cushing was to tell Franklin on 6 May. 'In justice to the Americans, I would observe, that the colonies from the first of this dispute acquiesced in the distinction between taxation and legislation and were disposed to confine the dispute to that of taxation only and entirely to waive the other as a subject of too delicate a nature but the advocates for the supreme authority of Parliament drove us into it.'[42] No immediate reply was made by either council or assembly, and not until 1 February did the governor send news of their rejoinders. The council on 25 January challenged the authority of Parliament by implication, the assembly next day did so more directly. After arguing that Parliament had never been empowered to override the colony's charter, the assembly answered Hutchinson's question. 'If there can be no such line the consequence is either that the colonies are the vassals of the Parliament or that they are totally independent.' Before any line could be drawn the consent of the other colonies in a Congress would be necessary. The assembly's answer fell short only of a claim of independence, ending with the assurance that 'after all we have said we would be far from being understood to have in the least abated that just sense of allegiance which we owe to the King of Great Britain, our rightful sovereign'.[43] American denial of Parliamentary authority therefore preceded the Intolerable Acts of 1774, at least in the pace-setting colony of Massachusetts, and Gage was warning that many Americans elsewhere held the same opinion.

News of the assembly riposte belatedly arrived in Whitehall on 29 March,[44] to be followed nine days later by another letter from Hutchinson, who claimed that subsequent events in the colony justified his speech of 6 January. Whereas at least 80 out of about 250 Massachusetts towns had declared against the supremacy of Parliament before then, only one or two had subsequently called meetings.[45] On the advice of 'friends of government' he had replied

---

[41] *Gage Corr.*, II, 640.   [42] *Franklin Papers*, XX, 204.
[43] *DAR*, VI, 58–77.   [44] Ibid., IV, 242.
[45] Hutchinson's optimism was unjustified, and his information wrong. Many towns still supported Boston from January onwards. By April at least 119

to the answers of the two Houses 'further to expose the absurdity of the strange principles in government'.[46] Dartmouth's reply on 10 April accepted that persuasion would not now suffice to secure obedience to Parliament; announced that the ministry would take the state of Massachusetts into consideration; and enjoined Hutchinson to avoid further debate in the meantime.[47]

The American Secretary was under pressure from within the administration to adopt a hardline policy. Secretary at War Lord Barrington thought that Massachusetts had played into the hands of men like himself, for he wrote to General Gage on 4 April: 'I am very glad the people of the Massachusetts have pulled off the mask, which I hope will put an end to that supineness here that has already proved so detrimental, and which will prove so fatal if it continues.'[48] What some of the cabinet had in mind was to be revealed to Hutchinson by Lord North in a private interview on 7 July 1774. The Prime Minister then remarked that a measure such as the recent Massachusetts Government Act 'ought to have been done the last session, upon the Declaration of Independence, both by the Council and House; that the delay had been occasioned by the state of affairs here in England'.[49]

Such legislation was not what Dartmouth had in mind. Franklin informed Cushing on 3 April that the American Secretary was anxious to find some means to 'heal the breach. I took the freedom to tell him, he could do much on it if he would exert himself. I think I see signs of some relenting in others.'[50] In an interview with Franklin on 5 May Dartmouth was astonishingly frank in his complaints of the difficulties caused for the administration by Hutchinson's 'imprudence'. If Parliament had to take official notice of the assembly's declarations, as would happen if copies of the governor's letters were requested by either House, the ministry feared that 'measures may be taken that will widen the breach'. Franklin advised the American Secretary to let the matter rest. The dispute was one of 'words only', he claimed, for 'Acts of Parliament are still submitted to there. . . . Force can do no good.' Dartmouth replied that he had been thinking not of force but of legislation 'to lay them under some inconveniences' until the

of 260 towns had responded, and 25 more did so later in the year. Many of the others were small and new. Brown, *Revolutionary Politics in Massachusetts*, pp. 90–9.

[46] *DAR*, IV, 256–7; VI, 89–90.
[47] Ibid., IV, 295. *HMC Dartmouth MSS*, II, 146.   [48] *PCBG*, p. 112.
[49] *Hutchinson Diary*, I, 181.   [50] *Franklin Papers*, XX, 139–40.

declaration was rescinded. Franklin commented that that would never happen and that Massachusetts would probably retaliate by 'inventing some method of incommoding this country'. Dartmouth retorted that his information was that many colonists shared Hutchinson's opinion but did not dare to say so. Franklin thought the source was Dartmouth's previous visitor that day, the former Governor Bernard.[51]

Correspondence from Massachusetts increased the pressure on Dartmouth to come to some decision. On 12 May there arrived a letter from Hutchinson, warning of the need to take positive action. 'I am informed that they are apprehensive of disagreeable consequences from the declarations of the towns and the vindication of them by the Assembly, and that their dependence is in the Opposition in England. If all which has been done should pass without notice the Opposition here will triumph more than ever.'[52] At about the same time Dartmouth received a letter of 5 March from Speaker Thomas Cushing on behalf of the Massachusetts Assembly. After expressing pleasure at Dartmouth's appointment the letter requested his support for a second petition voted that day. The American Secretary was also asked to secure the restoration of the colony's 'charter rights' and the repeal of all American revenue acts. 'In a word, all that is desired by the people of the province is that they may be restored to their original standing and all controversy between both countries may then cease and determine.'[53] Such demands were already beyond what any British politician, even Dartmouth, could begin to contemplate as practical policy.

The second Massachusetts petition, necessary because of Franklin's referral back of the first one at Dartmouth's request, extended to the salaries of the judges the same arguments that the first petition had put forward about the governor's salary, alleging that impartial administration of justice would be endangered by their dependence on the Crown for salaries as well as tenure of office.[54] The question had surfaced again during the constitutional debate between Hutchinson and the General Court, with the assembly voting increased salaries for the judges, a rise from £160 to £300 for the Chief Justice and £250 each for the other four. Hutchinson consented to these grants, but vetoed an even more obvious attempt to forestall the British government decision by

[51] Ibid., XX, 197–203.
[52] *DAR*, IV, 282; VI, 104–6.
[53] Ibid., VI, 96–100.   [54] Ibid., VI, 100–2.

paying the judges a year's salary in advance.[55] Franklin formally delivered both petitions to Dartmouth on 14 May, and the American Secretary informed him of their fate on 2 June. He had read them to the King, who had announced that it was his royal duty to preserve the power of Parliament to make laws for 'his subjects in America in all cases whatsoever' and that he was 'greatly displeased' with the petitions for questioning that right.[56]

This royal rebuff was to be the only decision taken about Massachusetts. No positive policy concerning that recalcitrant colony was initiated; and if a difference of opinion within the ministry formed part of the explanation, a more significant reason was the crisis within the East India Company that virtually monopolized political attention at this time. Parliamentary investigation into alleged malpractices by the Company's servants, notably Lord Clive, coincided with the passage of legislation to assist and regulate the Company.[57] Ministerial activity was almost entirely taken up with these urgent matters, and the problem of Massachusetts was postponed.[58] On 2 June Dartmouth wrote to assure Hutchinson that it was the unanimous opinion of the cabinet, in which the King concurred, that the authority of Parliament should be supported, and that Parliament should take into consideration the declarations of the council and assembly: but he ended tamely that this could not be done during the current session of Parliament.[59] On reflection, in a letter of 7 July to the Massachusetts Assembly, Franklin thought he knew why, apart from the pressure of East India Company business, Parliament had risen for the summer recess without 'meddling with the state of America. . . . The King's firm answer (as it is called) to our Petitions and Remonstrances, has probably been judged sufficient for the present.'[60]

In the absence of an official policy initiative Dartmouth made a personal attempt to resolve the impasse, albeit one that revealed a lack of political realism. On 19 June the American Secretary sent a private letter to Speaker Cushing. After stating his personal opinion that Parliament's right of taxation 'should be suspended and lie dormant', he asked whether the Massachusetts Assembly

[55] Ibid., VI, 90.

[56] *Franklin Papers*, XX, 223–4.

[57] See below, pp. 251–4.

[58] Franklin thought another reason was the European situation, arising from the current Russo-Turkish War and the recent partition of Poland: *Franklin Papers*, XX, 200.

[59] *DAR*, IV, 321.

[60] *Franklin Papers*, XX, 279.

could reconsider its repudiation of Parliament's authority. While he could not give up that principle he would then make every effort to redress colonial complaints. The assembly's doctrines, Dartmouth said, 'appear to me to be a most serious (I had almost said, an insuperable) Bar to the return of that state of union and tranquility which I so anxiously wish to see restored to the British Empire'.[61] This letter was greeted with hilarity and jubilation by the assembly politicians, and with dismay by supporters of Governor Hutchinson, whose opponents had been encouraged in their aim of securing his removal.[62] Cushing's reply on 22 August blamed Hutchinson for having provoked the assembly's declaration, and, reminding Dartmouth of 'the interest which every part of America takes in this important question', said that the assembly would never be persuaded to retract. In any case it would not meet until January. Cushing countered with the suggestion that Parliament should 'take up American affairs upon their own principles, without any apparent attention to the applications made by the Americans for redress, and from great national considerations place America upon the same footing in which she was at the conclusion of the late war. By this means the entangling question of the right of Parliament . . . will be kept out of sight, and the colonies by such a voluntary act of justice and benevolence will be highly gratified.'[63]

This was to ask the impossible of any British politician by this time; and Dartmouth's lack of influence within the administration was now apparent to Benjamin Franklin. Writing confidentially to his son William on 14 July he portrayed the American Secretary as a political disappointment. 'He is truly a good man, and wishes sincerely a good understanding with the colonies, but does not seem to have strength equal to his wishes. Between you and I, the late measures have been, I suspect, very much the King's own, and he has in some cases a great share of what his friends call *firmness*.'[64] In this picture of Dartmouth as a man of goodwill towards America unable to have his way over policy Franklin may have had in mind the American Secretary's recent behaviour over the payment of colonial salaries. During a debate in the House of

[61] Stevens, *Facsimiles*, XXIV, no. 2025.

[62] *HMC Dartmouth MSS*, II, 173. Stevens, op. cit., XXIV, no. 2029.

[63] Stevens, op. cit., XXIV, no. 2028. For this incident see Bailyn, *Hutchinson*, pp. 215–18.

[64] *Franklin Papers*, XX, 308. For a quite different view of the King's role, one of him as a prisoner of the contemporary British political system, see Franklin's letter of 7 July to the Massachusetts Assembly. Ibid., XX, 280.

Lords on the Committee stage of the East India Company Regulating Bill, which took place on 17 and 18 June, Shelburne, when pressing for the judges in India to be appointed for life, expressed the wish 'that the same policy might be extended to America'. He reported to Chatham that in response on 19 June Dartmouth 'in terms of very great personal civility declared his determination to support such a proposition for America, and, as I understand him, to place his existence in ministry upon it'.[65] Dartmouth followed up this announcement by drafting a letter to Governor Hutchinson, in which he stated that whenever the Massachusetts Assembly decided to establish permanent and adequate salaries for the judges the King would not only withdraw the royal salaries but also give the judges security of tenure by introducing the British practice of appointment 'during good behaviour' and not any longer 'during pleasure'. He would also allow the governor to receive his salary from the assembly, provided it was not less than £2,000.[66] Such concessions would have met the ostensible Massachusetts grievances in the salary dispute, but the letter was never sent, presumably because Dartmouth was unable to obtain cabinet approval for the proposals.

Massachusetts was the only colony where the Townshend Duties Act was fully implemented, with all the top officials in both the civil government and the administration of justice paid by the British Treasury. In the two other colonies where the Act had been carried out in part there was little hostile reaction. Governor William Franklin of New Jersey told Dartmouth on 5 January 1773 that he had attempted to persuade his assembly into voting higher salaries for the colony's officials by the threat that otherwise the Crown would take over their payment 'as had been done for some time past in most of the King's other colonies' and recently for their own Chief Justice.[67] The assembly's response had professed an indifference founded on two assertions: that the clamour in Massachusetts had arisen because some politicians there wished 'to keep their party alive and to give themselves consequence'; and that in New York the assembly had made no opposition and that that colony had suffered no inconvenience.[68]

[65] *Chatham Papers*, IV, 282. Chatham commented on 17 July, 'I rejoice that America, at least, has a chance to have independent judges. . . . Lord Dartmouth does himself honour, by this just and liberal sentiment.' Ibid., IV, 285.   [66] *HMC Dartmouth MSS*, II, 152–3.
[67] Hillsborough had notified Governor Franklin of this decision about New Jersey's Chief Justice in a letter of 6 June 1772: *DAR*, IV, 100.
[68] Ibid., VI, 28–9.

This claim about New York was in fact misleading. There may not have been any protests when the Attorney-General received a Treasury salary from 1768, the Governor from 1770, and the Chief Justice from 1772: but the assembly had asked both Lord Dunmore and his successor Governor Tryon to accept salaries from itself and not the Crown.[69]

The New Jersey Assembly had even counter-attacked on the salary question, querying the propriety of Governor Franklin's request on the ground that they were already being taxed by Parliament for that very purpose under the Townshend Duties Act. The governor was writing to enclose a memorial from the colony's Attorney-General about the inadequacy of his salary, stating that he had told the assembly that most salaries were disgracefully low.[70] Dartmouth replied on 3 March that he would recommend higher salaries for Crown officials in New Jersey:[71] but on 4 August he had to report that there had been insufficient revenue under the Townshend Act to make possible the proper provision of government salaries in New Jersey, although he would not lose sight of the matter.[72] The proceeds of the tea duty were by this time already over-committed to the payment of salaries elsewhere.[73]

Only part of the American complaint against the Townshend Duties Act concerned the use made of the revenue from the tea duty to pay colonial salaries. More significant was the older grievance about the imposition of Parliamentary taxation, and it was this that led directly to the Boston Tea Party. Although the decisions ending the boycott of British goods in 1770 had specifically excluded duted tea from importation, only Philadelphia and New York, the two ports with a tea smuggling tradition, effectively carried out this undertaking. Whereas in 1768, the first full year of the tea tax, duty was paid in these ports on 352,000 lbs. and 147,000 lbs., by 1772 the respective totals were 350 lbs. and 128 lbs.[74] Elsewhere the import of taxed tea was resumed along with the purchase of other British goods. Boston imported 373,000 lbs. of dutied tea between 1 December 1770 and 5 January 1773.[75] Other colonies, even Rhode Island and especially Virginia and South

[69] *NYCD*, VII, 299–300.   [70] *DAR*, VI, 28–9.
[71] Ibid., IV, 269.   [72] Ibid., IV, 357–8.
[73] Dickerson, *NEQ*, 31 (1958), pp. 241–2.
[74] Dickerson, *Navigation Acts*, p. 100.
[75] Schlesinger, *Colonial Merchants*, p. 246.

Carolina, contributed to official import totals of 479,000 lbs. in 1770, 525,000 lbs. in 1771, and 258,000 lbs. in 1772.[76]

These totals fell far short of all estimates of colonial consumption, and there was no lack of correspondents anxious to open ministerial eyes to the full enormity of what was going on. Governor Hutchinson told Hillsborough in a private letter of 25 August 1771 that 'the consumption of tea in America exceeds what anybody in England imagines. Some persons capable of judging suppose five-sixths of what has been consumed the two last years has been illegally imported.'[77] On 10 September he drew attention to the loss in taxation, by a calculation that the tea duty should yield £76,800 a year.[78] This implied the import of 6,144,000 lbs., a higher rate of tea consumption than in Britain. Another Hutchinson estimate was 6,528,000 lbs., but Samuel Wharton thought 5,000,000 lbs. near the mark.[79] In 1773, at the time of the Tea Act, London tea merchant William Palmer put the American market at something over 3,000,000 lbs.[80]

Hutchinson offered advice as well as information. Since customs officials were being intimidated by 'the rage of the people', one remedy would be to increase incentives: even naval officers were not willing to incur unpopularity for trifling rewards. But Hutchinson did not see stricter enforcement of the trade laws as a real answer to the problem. The only permanent solution would be a competitive price for British tea. 'Unless the East India Company bring the price of their teas so near to the price in Holland as to make the profit of importing teas from thence not equal to the risk, in a short time there will be scarce any teas imported from England.'[81] The 1767 legislation had made it possible for the East India Company to reduce the cost of its tea below that of smuggled Dutch tea. This had not happened because the Company, in a mistaken and unsuccessful attempt to remedy an already precarious financial position, had taken advantage of its monopoly within Britain by setting too high an upset or reserve price at its London tea sales.[82] A change in the Company's pricing policy was evidently what Hutchinson had in mind. When in 1773 such an alteration was made, the widespread assumption in America was that it represented a deliberate ministerial initiative to cripple tea smuggling, with government supporters seeing it as a lenient

[76] Dickerson, op. cit., p. 100.   [77] *DAR*, III, 172–3.
[78] Ibid., III, 180–1.   [79] Schlesinger, op. cit., p. 249.
[80] Labaree, *Boston Tea Party*, pp. 73–4.   [81] *DAR*, III, 172–3, 180–1.
[82] For comparative tea prices see Labaree, op. cit., pp. 332–3.

alternative to rigorous enforcement of the trade laws.[83] But the alteration in the arrangements for the sale of tea in America did not originate from political motives: it arose out of the financial crisis in the East India Company.

Parliamentary action concerning the American tea trade was precipitated in 1772 by the consequences and expiry of the 1767 legislation. This had allowed the East India Company to export tea to the colonies free of the 25 per cent British duty, but on condition that the Company compensated the Exchequer for the lost revenue. Calculation of this sum had led to a running battle between the Company and the Treasury, and the whole arrange-ment was due to end in 1772. On 11 February a copy of the offer made by the Company to the Treasury for payment of this debt was laid before the House of Commons. Lord North then moved for a Bill accepting this proposal. He recapitulated the difficulties and disputes that had arisen over this compensation and said he would settle for the immediate offer of £117,000 instead of the £247,000 claimed by the Treasury. The measure passed without any subsequent debate.[84]

The rebate of the British 25 per cent duty that had given rise to this compensation was not taken into Parliamentary consideration until 13 May, when Lord North proposed instead a rebate, on tea re-exported to America, of only three-fifths of the British duty. But the East India Company was now to be relieved of future liability for any deficiency in the tea tax revenue. The Prime Minister represented this new arrangement as a concession that would enable British merchants to compete with Dutch and other smugglers in the American market, but he did tacitly admit that the Treasury might not have assessed the situation correctly. 'How far right, time only can determine. Grant it only for five years.'[85] Parliament duly enacted these changes without further discussion.[86] But the consequence of what was in effect a 10 per cent duty on tea going to the colonies in addition to the politically obnoxious 3d. tax levied at the American ports proved a disastrous blow to Britain's tea trade across the Atlantic. Legal exports of tea to the colonies had recovered in 1771 to 359,000 lbs. from 109,000 lbs. in the boycott year of 1770; but they slumped to 263,000 lbs.

[83] Oliver, *Origin and Progress*, p. 101.
[84] Simmons and Thomas, op. cit., III, 406–8, 416, 420.
[85] Ibid., III, 440–1 (misplaced under 12 May).
[86] Ibid., III, 442–3, 447.

in 1772 and to 139,000 lbs. in 1773, when the Tea Act for that year worsened the situation still more.[87]

This fall in the American market was only a minor factor in the sharp growth of the Company's tea mountain in 1772 and 1773. The 1772 legislation also ended the 1767 cancellation of the 1s. a lb. duty on tea sales within Britain: these now fell from 7,512,000 lbs. in 1772 to 4,134,000 lbs. in 1773. Continuing large-scale imports meanwhile raised the tea surplus stored in Company warehouses from 13,627,000 lbs. in 1771 to 17,756,000 lbs. in 1772 and 21,233,000 lbs. in 1773.[88] In this context the decline of the existing American tea market had little immediate effect in creating the problem. But the contemporary estimates of the illicit tea trade in the colonies do suggest that it would never have arisen at all but for the smuggling of foreign tea into America: and that was the opinion of Benjamin Franklin when writing to Joseph Galloway on 2 December 1772. 'For the five years past we might probably have otherwise taken off the greatest part of what the Company have on hand and so have prevented their present embarrassment.'[89]

As the growth of the Company's tea mountain both coincided with and helped to cause its financial crisis, the American market was one obvious outlet for the surplus. Politically motivated observers thought this the opportunity to get rid at last of the Townshend duty, but Franklin was not optimistic in his letter to Galloway. 'Although it is known that the American market is lost by continuing the duty on tea and that we are supplied by the Dutch . . . yet the honour of government is supposed to forbid the repeal of the American tea duty.'[90] He therefore made no move in this matter, but before the end of 1772 the Massachusetts Council's agent William Bollan was pressing Lord Dartmouth for the removal of the duty. He obtained support from an unnamed London tea merchant, whose memorandum of reasons for repeal of the duty revived the charge that the levy was contrary to the 1767 agreement between the government and the Company, and claimed that its removal would both benefit the public revenue and enable the Company to dispose of its warehouse surpluses.

---

[87] Labaree, op. cit., pp. 331, 335. These are British export totals, and differ from the amounts arriving in America each year, given above, pp. 246–7. The 1773 total was obtained by subtracting the rejected tea shipped under the Tea Act from the gross exports.

[88] Ibid., pp. 60, 334.

[89] *Franklin Papers*, XIX, 420.   [90] Ibid.

Bollan sent this document to the American Secretary on 22 December 1772.[91]

The East India Company itself had its eye on Europe as a better potential market for its tea than America. On 7 January 1773 the Directors proposed to the Court of Proprietors that application should be made to the Treasury for permission to export tea there free of duty, and Governor Johnstone stated that the aim was to send tea 'to several markets in the continent'. Objections that such a move would produce a glut in Europe and cause consequent tea smuggling back to Britain were at once made by a William Crichton,[92] who suggested the solutions should be a lower home price and the removal of the 3d. American tax. The latter idea was promptly taken up by the Directors, and the Court of Proprietors unanimously adopted a resolution 'that it be recommended to the Court of Directors to obtain an Act of Parliament, for them to export their surplus teas to foreign markets, clear of all drawbacks and duties, as well as to take off the 3d. duty in America'.[93] The removal of the Townshend tax was still a request secondary to the main objective of a European market. Here the Company was asking not only for a complete rebate on all exports of the 25 per cent duty, such as it had enjoyed in its American trade between 1767 and 1772, but also for a change in the law. Hitherto it could only sell tea wholesale to merchants at its London auctions, and not retail on its own account.[94]

The hope of a European solution to the Company's tea problem soon faded, as the truth of Crichton's warning was revealed by soundings in Holland and elsewhere. It became clear that tea exported cheaply to the continent would be promptly smuggled back to Britain and ruin the Company's market at home. A meeting of the Court of Proprietors on 9 February heard from the Chairman, once again Sir George Colebrooke, that both the Directors and Prime Minister Lord North thought that the scheme would fail. Colebrooke also reported that North had refused to comply with the Company's request for the abolition of the Townshend tea duty, but had offered to remove the two-fifths of the British duty reimposed in 1772 on the exports to America. North had also offered to assist the Company in obtaining

[91] HMC Dartmouth MSS, II, 114.

[92] The identification has been made by Dr Huw V. Bowen; the newspaper report named only a 'Mr. Creighton'.

[93] London Evening Post, 9 Jan. 1773.

[94] Labaree, op. cit., pp. 67–8.

permission to send two ships a year directly from China to America, 'laden with teas, clear of all duties'. Colebrooke reported that the Court of Directors had adopted both of these ideas, but in the ensuing debate in the Court of Proprietors the China trade proposal was vigorously attacked by Robert Gregory, himself a Director and an MP, as providing an opportunity for smuggling that would adversely affect the Company's interests, and nothing more was heard of that idea.[95]

The proposals concerning the tea trade formed merely part of the overall plan that the East India Company was concerting with the North ministry for its salvation. During February the Court of Proprietors gave lengthy consideration to the proposals put forward by the Directors; and after a series of debates a motion to submit a petition to Parliament was approved by a ballot of the Proprietors on 1 March by 377 votes to 84.[96] Next day the petition was submitted to the House of Commons, among the requests being one 'that leave may be given to export tea, duty-free, to America'.[97] The preceding Company debates and private nego-tiations with the ministry preclude any ambiguity about this request. It was for removal of the duty reimposed in 1772 and not for abolition of the Townshend tax. The Company could see no purpose in asking what the Prime Minister had already said he would not grant.

Three legislative measures resulted from this petition. Lord North's Regulating Act, the first formal government intervention in the administration of the Company's Indian territories, was the ministerial price for the concessions of the Loan Act and the Tea Act. In neither instance did the Company obtain all that it would have liked. The loan was for £1,400,000, short by £100,000 of what had been asked. The Tea Act gave the Company only what had been formally requested in the petition. The 10 per cent duty on the colonial trade was removed, and the Company was given for America the concession it had originally sought for Europe, permission to sell direct to colonial buyers instead of indirectly through tea sales in London to British or American merchants trading with the colonies. It could thereby now fix its own price for the American market. But the political stumbling-block of the 3d. Townshend duty remained, and that matter was raised in

[95] *London Evening Post*, 11 Feb. 1773.
[96] Ibid., 13, 18, 20, 25, and 27 Feb. and 2 Mar. 1773.
[97] *CJ*, XXXIV, 164–5.

Parliament when on 26 April Lord North brought the question of tea duties before the Commons.[98]

The Prime Minister opened the debate by stating that the East India Company had nearly 17,000,000 lbs. of tea in warehouses, some three years' supply. He put forward the proposals the Company had requested, the rebate of the British duty on tea exports to America, and permission for the Company to send tea directly to the colonies. North declared that it would be in the national interest as well as for the benefit of the Company if the American tea market could be gained by these concessions. Rockinghamite spokesman William Dowdeswell at once pointed out that North had said nothing about the Townshend duty. 'I tell the noble lord now, if he doesn't take off the duty, they won't take the tea.' He estimated that if this was done the annual sale of tea to America would rise to 2,000,000 lbs. North replied that the tea sales to America during the past decade showed that the 1767 duty had made little difference, and later in the debate there was a dispute between the two men over this point, with Dowdeswell claiming lower sales after 1767 than before and North denying this. The Prime Minister emphasized that he expected the East India Company to be willing to sell tea in America at a loss, to ease the financial burden of maintaining such an enormous stock. He then provided a political motive for retaining the tea duty.

I am unwilling to give up that duty upon America upon which the [colonial salaries] are charged. If the East India Company will export tea to America, they will very much increase that duty, and consequently very much facilitate carrying on government in that part. I see no reason for taking it off. I must see very substantial reason before I part with a fund so applicable to the support of the civil [government there].

His critics sought to supply him with reasons. Dowdeswell claimed that the net revenue would be a peppercorn £400, for which an annual tea sale of 2,000,000 lbs. was being risked. When William Pulteney repeated this figure North queried the low revenue estimate, while Thomas Walpole challenged Pulteney's statement that it was based on the import of 500,000 lbs., and not unreasonably, for such a quantity would yield a gross duty of £6,250. North had in any case already stated that his aim was to increase that revenue, and he declared that he would not give up

[98] For the debate on this day see the Cavendish Diary, BL Egerton MSS 246, ff. 1–16; printed, Simmons and Thomas, op. cit., III, 487–92.

the duty until persuaded that it would be impossible to combine the tax with an American tea market for the Company.

Barlow Trecothick tried to convince him, declaring, as an American merchant, that removal of the duty was the only way to restore the colonial tea trade. Such a step would drive other European countries out of the American market. Charles Jenkinson, late of the Treasury Board and one of the administration's key men of business, had an easy answer to this line of argument, one that revealed the assumption underlying the ministry's policy. The Americans would buy the cheapest tea, he said, and since tea was currently cheaper in Britain than in Holland and other foreign markets the East India Company should be able to recover the American trade. When merchant George Prescott challenged Jenkinson's claim that tea was more expensive in Europe than in Britain, he was answered by banker Thomas Walpole. A member of the Commons' Secret Committee of Inquiry on the East India Company, Walpole retorted that the evidence of tea dealers to that Committee had been unanimous on that point.

William Pulteney took up another line of attack, doubting whether the Company could afford to sell its tea at a loss, as North had suggested. Jeremiah Dyson replied that the Company faced the question of what would be the greater loss, and the Company's new Chairman and most experienced Director, Henry Crabb Boulton, gave what amounted to the Company's official response. He said that since tea held in store would deteriorate in quality and value, and a great deal of money was being tied up by the existence of huge stocks, he was in favour of selling it to America at a slight loss.

Dowdeswell then made the counter-proposal that the ministry should cancel the rebate of duty and repeal the tea tax instead. Charles Cornwall supported this idea, pointing out that the money from the British duty could be appropriated for the payment of colonial salaries. Thomas Walpole rejoined that the current sales of taxed tea to America showed that the problem was not the Townshend duty but the competition of foreign smugglers. Dowdeswell's idea was backed by three Company stockholders, Herbert Mackworth and the brothers George Johnstone and William Pulteney, both men much concerned with Company matters. Pulteney, estimating that the 3d. tea duty would yield £5,000, alternatively suggested that it should be given up for three years as an experiment.[99] It would be worth sacrificing £15,000 to

[99] Pulteney's estimate was fairly accurate. The tea tax, calculated on

ascertain the total tea consumption in America. Lord North was impervious to all suggestions. Making his seventh speech of the day he closed the debate by refusing to give up the tea tax for 'political reasons. . . . I know the temper of the people there is so little deserving favour from hence.' What North meant by this remark, so he was to tell the Commons in a debate of 19 April 1774, was the Massachusetts denial of Parliament's right of legislation.[100] Knowledge of that may have stiffened his determination to continue the tea tax, but his chief motive was to retain a revenue for the payment of colonial salaries, and not merely 'to keep up the right', as Benjamin Franklin stated in an oft-quoted remark of 4 June.[101]

The subject of the tea tax had been well ventilated, but there had not been any vigorous opposition attack on ministerial policy. The followers of Chatham and Shelburne had been silent or absent, and Dowdeswell had not been supported by Rockinghamite colleagues, not even Edmund Burke, the agent for New York; and Burke failed to mention the Tea Act in his next report to that colony.[102] Criticism of government had come less from its political opponents than from Company stockholders and other spokesmen of the mercantile community. The issue was not pressed to a vote, and the consequent legislation passed without further debate in either Commons or Lords.[103] This lack of attention in Parliament mirrored the absence of interest outside. The last chance to alter ministerial policy on American taxation before the confrontation of the Boston Tea Party that resulted from it passed virtually without notice in contemporary correspondence and newspapers.[104]

The Duke of Richmond preferred to oppose the arrangement within the Company rather than in the House of Lords, and instigated a move to block any tea sales to America: not until mid-July did Chairman Boulton carry this policy decision in the Court of Proprietors.[105] By the end of that month the Company had

American customs returns, should have yielded a gross revenue of £5,987 in 1770, £6,562 in 1771, and £2,580 in 1772.

[100] Simmons and Thomas, op. cit., IV, 197.
[101] *Franklin Papers*, XX, 228.   [102] *Burke Corr.*, II, 439–42.
[103] Simmons and Thomas, op. cit., III, 493–5.
[104] The *London Chronicle* of 29 Apr. carried a brief report of the debate.
[105] Labaree, op. cit., p. 75, quoting a letter of 17 July, apparently by George Johnstone, that was printed in American newspapers. The *London Evening Post*, which gave extensive coverage to proceedings in the Court of Proprietors, does not report any such dispute.

worked out its price strategy. The Parliamentary argument on 26 April as to whether tea was cheaper in Britain than in Europe proved to have been an artificial one. In 1773 smugglers could purchase the most common tea, Bohea, in Holland for 1s. 9d. a lb. and were selling it in America for 2s. 7d. But if the East India Company was prepared to accept, for tea sent to America, less than its usual home price of at least 1s. 10d., then it could eliminate the financial disadvantage of the 3d. Townshend duty. This the Company proposed to do, so that its Bohea tea would sell in America at 2s. 0d. a lb., including the tax, a price the smugglers would find it virtually impossible to match.[106] During August the Company decided how much tea to send as a first consignment, 599,000 lbs. to four American ports. Only 105,000 lbs. were destined for Boston. More than double that amount was to be dispatched to both New York and Philadelphia, and a smaller cargo to Charleston.[107]

In this enterprise the Company was not to have government support. The North Ministry did not regard the Tea Act as part of its colonial policy. It was not even included among the five Acts of Parliament relating to America of which John Pownall, as Secretary to the Board of Trade, sent copies to colonial governors in a circular letter of 7 July.[108] So far was the administration from sending governors any instructions to ensure enforcement of the measure that they had not even been given details of it when confronted with the ensuing crisis. Governor Tryon of New York, when in such a predicament, wryly commented to Dartmouth on 3 November that it was 'an act I have not been honoured with from your Lordship's office'.[109] This failure to receive any official intimation of the Tea Act gave Deputy Governor John Penn of Pennsylvania the excuse to do nothing to enforce it in the other big smuggling port of Philadelphia: months later he sent this explanation to the wife of Proprietor Thomas Penn in a private letter.[110]

It was believed the Ministry would not interfere in the matter. Indeed many letters came from England which said so, and a gentleman who

---

[106] Labaree, op. cit., pp. 75-7. Labaree suggests 2s. 1d. as the lowest price at which smugglers could then afford to sell. On his own evidence it is difficult to accept Labaree's general contention that in 1773 the Company would not necessarily have undersold the tea smugglers. The fall in the Dutch price in 1774 is irrelevant.

[107] Ibid., pp. 77, 335.   [108] *DAR*, IV, 348.   [109] Ibid., VI, 238.

[110] Gipson, op. cit., XII, 93.

came from thence last winter said he knew Lord Dartmouth had declared that it was entirely the affair of the East India Company and Government had nothing to do with it, and what made this more easily believed was that no instructions were sent to the Governors by the Secretary of State nor to the Collectors of Customs. No application was made to me by the captain of the ship nor the merchants to whom the tea was consigned nor the Custom House nor indeed by anybody at all.

The North ministry and the East India Company did not anticipate difficulty in the implementation of the Tea Act. That attitude was not as foolish as the universal resistance, only highlighted by the Boston Tea Party, would make it appear in retrospect. The sale of taxed tea to the colonies had never ceased. Charleston had always imported it, as the local merchants pointed out in a public debate with other inhabitants in December.[111] Boston had been the leading purchaser, with John Hancock shipping over 120,000 lbs. since 1770.[112] It was therefore in reasonable self-justification that Governor Hutchinson informed the East India Company on 19 December, just after the Tea Party, that 'as double the quantities of teas proposed to be shipped by the Company had been imported in a year and the duty paid without any disturbance I flattered myself for several months . . . that I should find no more difficulties than when teas had been shipped by private merchants'.[113]

The lack of foresight was twofold, failure to anticipate a hostile reaction from merchants who would suffer from the new arrangements compounding failure to appreciate the continuing resentment at Parliamentary taxation. Unless they could obtain appointment as consignees for the East India Company, the merchants previously engaged in the legal tea trade would face ruin equally with the smugglers, although it was the latter who raised the initial outcry. New York and Philadelphia reacted before Boston. In New York William Smith, a member of the Council, noted in his diary for 13 October that since the legislation of 1767 'all tea had been smuggled from Holland, to the great detriment of the India House. And now the Sons of Liberty and the Dutch smugglers set up the cry of Liberty.'[114] There was at first uncertainty in America as to whether the Company tea would be free of the Townshend duty; but this doubt did not prevent immediate opposition when in September it became known that the Company proposed to send more than 500,000 lbs. at once. Governor Tryon informed

---

[111] Ibid., XII, 87.   [112] Stevens, op. cit., XXIV, no. 2029.
[113] Gipson, op. cit., XII, 84.   [114] Smith, *Memoirs*, I, 156.

Dartmouth on 3 November 1773 that 'if the tea comes free of duty, I understand it is then to be considered as a monopoly of the East India Company in America, a monopoly of dangerous tendency, it is said, to American liberties. . . . So that, let the tea appear free or not free of duty, those who carry on the illicit trade will raise objections.'[115]

The Tea Act was reckoned to be as dangerous to colonial trade as the Townshend duty to colonial liberty.[116] This mercantile reaction was encouraged and exploited by politicians whose anger at what seemed to be a ministerial attempt to force taxed tea on the colonies was heightened when the expectation of repeal of the tea duty was again disappointed. But examination of the variety and relative importance of the motives for the American resistance to the Tea Act that culminated in the Boston Tea Party is beyond the scope of this study.[117]

[115] *DAR*, VI, 238–9.
[116] Schlesinger, op. cit., pp. 272–3.
[117] Labaree, op. cit., pp. 80–125, has a full account.

14

Prelude to Revolution

THE Townshend Duties Crisis was never resolved. It culminated in the Boston Tea Party, that triggered off the final sequence of events leading to the War of American Independence. Much of what occurred on both sides of the Atlantic in that final eighteen months had already been anticipated in the preceding six years.

Parliamentary declarations in 1774 revealed the extent to which ministerial policies then were being determined by the recollection of those earlier events. On 7 March Solicitor-General Wedderburn, echoing as a governmental admission what his mentor Grenville had at the time stated as an opposition accusation, told the House of Commons that 'in 1769 and 1770 [you did] not enter into a general, serious, systematical consideration of the state of America. You went on from time [to] time in hopes [it would] blow over, that the evil would remove itself.'[1] That had been an unfair imputation when it was made. The policy then adopted had been deliberately calculated to produce a breakdown of the colonial opposition to taxation, and had to all outward appearance succeeded in that objective by the end of 1770.

Lord North, so much involved in the formulation of policy throughout the period, preferred another explanation when on 23 March he answered Rose Fuller's proposal that Boston should merely be fined instead of having its port closed.[2]

We had before us in 1769 and 1770 complaints against Boston. Parliament acted with lenity. The resolutions Parliament came to were resolutions of censure, were resolutions of warning. If resolutions of censure and warning could do anything they would have operated already. Resolutions of censure and warning can do nothing. Therefore we must proceed to some direct and immediate measure. Lenity can do nothing. Those who lead the people of Massachusetts Bay have undoubtedly construed all our lenity either in want of power or want of resolution.

This contention that a moderate line of policy had hitherto been adopted and had been regarded in America as weakness was the

[1] Simmons and Thomas, *Proceedings and Debates*, IV, 40.
[2] Ibid., IV, 91.

basis of the formulation of ministerial policy in 1774. The news from the colonies since 1770 had not gone unheeded. Awareness of the developing challenge to all forms of British authority there was reflected in many pronouncements by administration spokes-men in the House of Commons during 1774, as in this assertion by George Rice on 19 April.[3]

The Americans have gone upon a system to gain step by step, to clear themselves from the control of this country. . . . They have taken that strange distinction between internal and external [taxation]. . . . The next step to be taken, that you have no right to impose taxes in any case whatever. The next step to be taken is you have no right to make laws binding upon them in any case whatever. I desire to keep the stand here.

The experience of the Townshend Duties Crisis especially taught ministers to identify the town of Boston as the trouble-centre, and hence as the main target for punitive and remedial measures. On 14 March Lord North, when introducing the Boston Port Bill, recapitulated recent misdemeanours of that town.[4]

For the course of five, six or seven years the town of Boston has invariably been the ringleader of all the disorders, the discontents, and disturbances. It was at the town of Boston that this violent riot happened which occasioned the proceedings in this House in 1769. It was at the town of Boston that the Convention was assembled at that time to make laws for the province to govern, to make laws because the Governor could not hold an Assembly. They certainly were the first promoters of the association for not importing British goods. I think it appears then, that there were only six or seven who did not assent to that association. They, Sir, at the latter end of 1772 began this measure which gave rise [text has 'source'] to those last troubles. They, Sir, began to hold town meetings to consider the rights, and of their grievances. They established correspondence with the country towns in the province, in order to revive and re-kindle that flame which appeared to them at that time never extinguished. From thence there has been nothing but disorder and confusion, almost all originating, all at last prevailing without opposition in the town of Boston.

This ministerial interpretation shaped the American policy of 1774. What the measures would be had to a large extent already been anticipated during the previous few years. Two main courses of action had then been contemplated but never implemented, alteration of the Massachusetts constitution and effective legal retribution for colonial violence. Both formed antecedents of 1774 legislation. The Massachusetts Government Act was a develop-

[3] Ibid., IV, 182–3.   [4] Ibid., IV, 58.

ment of the former plan, considered by ministers in 1769, 1770, and 1773. The latter scheme had always been conceived in terms of the need to take political offenders out of their own colony and even across the Atlantic, on the argument that justice could not be secured in colonial courts. Such a course of action had been threatened without being seriously intended in the Parliamentary session of 1768–9, and in 1772 had actually formed part of the abortive ministerial strategy devised after the *Gaspée* outrage. Now, as contingency planning, it formed an essential part of the Massachusetts Justice Act. Some such procedure, in many British eyes, afforded the only solution to the problem of maintaining law and order in America. Even Edmund Burke commented to the Speaker of the New York Assembly in 1773, with reference to the *Gaspée* episode, that 'such a very improper mode of proceeding' had a 'plausible pretext' in 'a certain carelessness (that looks almost like a countenance to such acts) in bringing delinquents to punishment in the ordinary and proper way' in the colonies.[5]

The formulation of British government policy towards America during the ministries of Chatham, Grafton, and North was handicapped by too many distractions. The Middlesex elections case, the Falkland Islands Crisis, and the affairs of the East India Company all diverted political attention away from America at times when important decisions needed to be taken. The actual solution to the problem of control of the colonies that was attempted during these years, a colonial civil list paid by the Treasury out of taxation imposed on the colonies, was both provocative and irrelevant. Although an obvious idea to men steeped in recent British history, when Parliament had deployed the power of the purse to such good effect against the Crown, it provided no answer to the physical problem of imperial control.[6] And in any case it was not necessary: even in Massachusetts the assembly had not used this weapon against the governor.

To adopt lack of adequate attention to America as the explanation of the inadequacies of British policy would be superficial and misleading. Ministerial behaviour reflected the general ambivalence of British political attitudes towards America. Refusal to accept what was fast becoming the colonial claim to parity with Britain under the Crown was combined with a reluctance to exert the

---

[5] *Burke Corr.*, II, 430.
[6] I discussed this point in *British Politics and the Stamp Act Crisis*, pp. 361–3.

military and naval strength necessary to subdue colonial resistance. It was still the general assumption that Britain did have the option of this second alternative: Benjamin Franklin on 29 July 1773 confessed his fear 'that by a premature struggle we may be crippled and kept down another age'.[7] But during these years between 1767 and 1773 Britain failed either to crush colonial resistance or to make political concessions to appease American opinion.

Neither coercion nor conciliation was a practical solution. Coercion might succeed in a limited sphere of action, as in Massachusetts in 1768–9, but Britain lacked the resources and the political will to hold down all the colonies all the time, as the War of Independence was to demonstrate. Nor, in the context of British political opinion, was there a viable solution of conciliation. By 1773 the colonies would remain in the British Empire only on their own terms. As voiced already in Massachusetts, this meant a cancellation of all British colonial measures since 1763 and no future interference by Parliament in the affairs of America. No British ministry would adopt such a reversal of attitude, nor would Parliament have endorsed it.

Behind this American attitude lay unjustified suspicions of Britain. During the late 1760s and early 1770s colonial minds wove all manner of unrelated events into a theory of potential British oppression that would be achieved by a combination of corruption and military force. The charge of corruption had little validity in the American context: the true cause of the unpopularity of many British officials in the colonies was their efficiency rather than their venality. Nor was military force ever the bond of the British Empire. The Boston Massacre might seem to be of a pattern with the St George's Fields Massacre, in that soldiers fired with fatal results on civilian mobs. But these were local incidents, not the product of any policy of military repression.

All such events were exaggerated in significance because of the colonial disillusionment with Britain that had developed since the Stamp Act Crisis. After 1768 the mother country was no longer perceived as the bastion of freedom. The Middlesex Elections case saw John Wilkes forfeit his Parliamentary seat without any compensatory victory for 'liberty' such as had occurred over general warrants. In Corsica, Britain had failed to support the cause of freedom against French aggression. In Ireland between

---

[7] *Franklin Papers*, XX, 330.

1769 and 1772 the Lord Lieutenant, Lord Townshend, coincidentally the brother of 'Townshend duties' Charles, succeeded in imposing direct British control, a model it might seem for America. Other events could be fitted into the same scenario of incipient tyranny: the payment of salaries to colonial officials; the 1771 attempt to stop Parliamentary reporting; legislation in 1773 concerning the East India Company, an encroachment on chartered rights that had implications for such chartered colonies as Massachusetts. Ideology distorted evidence to construct a picture of potential tyranny.[8]

What further darkened the picture of Britain as viewed from across the Atlantic was the absence of any prospect of change of men or measures. From 1770 the opposition groups headed by Rockingham and Chatham were obviously in the political wilderness: and in any case their attitudes towards America afforded no hope of a significant alteration of policy.[9] If they did return to office they would champion the supremacy of Parliament as much as the current ministry.

Even the hopes centred on the King had begun to fade. The submission of colonial petitions directly to George III instead of Parliament had produced no royal response, and Americans came to realize that the King approved of what was being done in his name. Public attacks on George III were as yet inhibited by motives of propriety and impolicy, but private suspicions often cast the King in a central role, as when radical Arthur Lee wrote from London to Sam Adams on 11 June 1773 of George III's 'sole wish to be the tyrant of his people'.[10]

In one sense what was occurring in America was a clarification rather than a change of attitude. A state of confrontation became apparent because the behaviour of men like Bernard and Hutchinson in America and Hillsborough and North in Britain obliged the colonists to devise logical and explicit expressions of hitherto unformulated assumptions. The counter-arguments to the supremacy of Parliament put forward by the colonists were laconically summed up by General Gage on 4 May 1772. 'There are three fundamentals on which the people in this country endeavour to establish the political doctrines they have promulgated within

[8] Maier, *Resistance to Revolution*, pp. 113–200.
[9] For an unconstructive comment on America by Chatham in 1771 see Simmons and Thomas, op. cit., III, 400.
[10] Maier, op. cit., p. 209. See ibid., pp. 200–13, for a general survey of colonial attitudes to the King.

these few years, and as they fail in producing proof from the one, have recourse to the other. They are *Charter Rights, British Constitution,* and *the Laws of God and Nature.*'[11] The same correspondent in like vein had reminded Hillsborough on 2 July 1771 that defiance of Parliament was practical as well as theoretical. 'I wish . . . that your Lordship may live to see Acts of Parliament better respected in the colonies, which I think is wishing you a long life.'[12]

When the actions of the British government and its officials challenged the existing state of affairs in the colonies the difference between British and American interpretations of the imperial system became apparent. Comparison of, for example, the Massachusetts petitions of 14 July 1772 and 6 March 1773 with Dartmouth's letter of 2 June 1773 to Franklin conveying the government's response to them reveals the gap between the American conception of the British Empire as one with the same sovereign and co-equal legislatures, and the British stand on the rights of Parliament.[13] Even Hutchinson deemed it unwise for Britain to exercise in practice rights claimed in theory, as he hinted to Dartmouth on 2 July 1773.[14]

I have never, my Lord, varied in my principles of government. I have ever asserted the supremacy of Parliament over the whole empire. I have wished for as large a share of legislation to be left to the several colonies as can consist with the maintenance of this supremacy, and I have ever endeavoured that the advantages which the kingdom was entitled to from the colonies might arise from a well regulated commerce and not from internal or external taxation.

The unhappy Massachusetts Governor evidently did not conceal his opinions from his opponents in Boston; for on 10 December, a week before the Tea Party, Speaker Thomas Cushing sent this report to agent Benjamin Franklin.[15]

The Court party themselves . . . begin to think it absolutely necessary the measures of administration with respect to America should be altered: they find that the spirit runs higher than in the time of the Stamp Act, and that the opposition is more systematical so that they fear nothing less than the repeal of the revenue acts and a radical redress of American grievances will save us from a rupture with Great Britain which may

---

[11] *Gage Corr.,* II, 604.   [12] Ibid., I, 302.
[13] Cf. *DAR,* V, 142–4; VI, 100–2, with *Franklin Papers,* XX, 223–4.
[14] *DAR,* VI, 179–80.
[15] *Franklin Papers,* XX, 496.

prove fatal to both countries. The people here are far from desiring that the connection between Great Britain and America should be broken.

The North ministry would not allow the colonists to stay in the British Empire only on their own terms. America must acknowledge the supremacy of Parliament. The moment of decision that led to the break between Britain and America came when the British government made its stand against the political pretensions of the colonies. The conventional interpretation has been that this was the legislation of 1774 in response to the Boston Tea Party; but a more subtle analysis would point to the retention of the tea duty that precipitated that act of defiance. The cabinet meeting of 1 May 1769 was the point of no return in the sequence of events leading to the American Revolution.

Select Bibliography

PRIMARY SOURCES

A. Manuscripts

(i) *British Library [cited as BL]*

Egerton MSS 215–63, 3711	The Parliamentary Diary of Henry Cavendish 1768–1774
Add[itional] MSS 32679–33201	Newcastle Papers
Add. MSS 35349–36278	Hardwicke Papers
Add. MSS 38190–38489	Liverpool Papers
Add. MSS 42083–42088	Grenville Papers
Add. MSS 51318–52254	Holland House Papers
Add. MSS 57804–57837	Grenville Papers

(ii) *Public Record Office*

Colonial Office Papers [cited as CO]
Treasury Papers [cited as T]
Chatham Papers [cited as PRO 30/8]
Granville Papers [cited as PRO 30/29]

(iii) *In other repositories and in private possession*

Dartmouth MSS	Staffordshire County Record Office (By permission of the Earl of Dartmouth)
Dowdeswell MSS	William L. Clements Library
East India Company MSS	India Office Library
Grafton MSS	Bury St Edmunds and West Suffolk Record Office (By permission of the Duke of Grafton)

Letter-Books of George Grenville, 1763–1770. Stowe MSS, 7, vols. 1 and 2. Henry E. Huntingdon Library

Harrowby MSS	In the possession of the Earl of Harrowby
Pratt MSS	Kent County Record Office
Shelburne MSS	William L. Clements Library
Strutt MSS	Essex County Record Office

Wentworth Woodhouse Muniments, Sheffield City Library (By permission of Olive, Countess Fitzwilliam's Wentworth Settlement Trustees)

B. Printed Sources

(i) *Official and Parliamentary Sources*

Acts of the Privy Council of England. Colonial Series (6 vols., 1908–12) [Cited as *Acts PC Col.*]

Calendar of Home Office Papers . . . 1760 to 1775 (4 vols., 1878–99)

Journals of the Commissioners for Trade and Plantations 1704–1782 (15 vols., 1920–38) [cited as *JCTP*]

Journals of the House of Commons [cited as *CJ*]

Journals of the House of Lords [cited as *LJ*]

Statutes at Large 1225–1800 (10 vols., 1811)

ALMON, J., *The Debates and Proceedings of the British House of Commons from 1743 to 1774* (11 vols., 1766–75) [Cited as Almon, *Debates*]

COBBETT, W., *Parliamentary History of England from . . . 1066 to . . . 1803* (36 vols., 1806–20) [Cited as Cobbett, *Parl. Hist.*]

DAVIES, K. G., ed., *Documents of the American Revolution 1770–1783* (21 vols., Shannon, 1972–1981) [Cited as *DAR*]

O'CALLAGHAN, E. B., ed., *Documents relative to the Colonial History of the State of New York* (14 vols., Albany, 1856–93) [Cited as *NYCD*]

SIMMONS, R. C. and THOMAS, P. D. G., eds., *Proceedings and Debates of the British Parliaments Respecting North America 1754–1783* (1–4, New York, 1982–5) [Cited as Simmons and Thomas, *Proceedings and Debates*]

(ii) *Contemporary Correspondence and Memoirs*

Historical Manuscripts Commission [Cited as *HMC*]

Dartmouth MSS (II, 1895)

Various MSS (VI, 1906), pp. 81–296, 440–50. *Knox MSS*

Bathurst MSS (1923)

ALMON, J., ed., *A Collection of Interesting, Authentic Papers Relative to the Dispute between Great Britain and America . . . 1764–1775* (1971 reprint, New York, of 1777 original) [Cited as Almon, *Prior Documents*]

The Barrington–Bernard Correspondence and Illustrative Matter 1760–1770 (eds. E. Channing and A. C. Coolidge, Cambridge, USA, 1912) [Cited as *Barrington–Bernard Corr.*]

'Confronting Rebellion. Private Correspondence of Lord Barrington with General Gage, 1765–1775', ed. J. Shy, *Sources of American Independence. Selected Manuscripts from the Collections of the William L. Clements Library* (ed. Howard H. Peckham, 2 vols., Chicago, 1978, I, 1–139) [Cited as *PCBG*]

Correspondence of John, Fourth Duke of Bedford, Selected from the Originals at Woburn Abbey, with an Introduction by Lord John Russell (3 vols., 1842–6) [Cited as *Bedford Papers*]

'Private Journal of John, Fourth Duke of Bedford . . . 19 October 1766 . . . to . . . 28 December 1770', *Sir Henry Cavendish's Debates of the House of Commons during the Thirteenth Parliament of Great Britain* (ed. J. Wright, 2 vols., 1841–3, I, 591–631) [Cited as *Bedford Journal*]

The Bowdoin and Temple Papers (Collections of Massachusetts Historical Society, 6th series, 9 (1897)) [Cited as *Bowdoin–Temple Papers*]

The Correspondence of Edmund Burke (I, ed. T. W. Copeland, Cambridge, 1958; II, ed. L. S. Sutherland, Cambridge, 1960) [Cited as *Burke Corr.*]

The Writings and Speeches of Edmund Burke, vol. II, *Party, Parliament and the American Crisis 1766–1774* (ed. P. Langford, Oxford, 1981)

Correspondence of William Pitt, Earl of Chatham (ed. W. S. Taylor and J. H. Pringle, 4 vols., 1838–40) [Cited as *Chatham Papers*]

Anecdotes of the Life of . . . the Right Honourable William Pitt, Earl of Chatham . . . 1736 to 1778 (ed. J. Almon, 3 vols., 1810) [Cited as *Chatham Anecdotes*]

[Sir George Colebrooke]. *Retrospection: or Reminiscences Addressed to my son Henry Thomas Colebrooke, Esq.* (2 vols., 1898–9) [Cited as *Colebrooke Reminiscences*]

'Letters of Dennys De Berdt, 1757–1770', *Transactions of the Colonial Society of Massachusetts*, 13 (1910–11), 293–416 [Cited as *De Berdt Letters*]

'Memoir of the Right Hon. William Dowdeswell . . . written by his son John Edward Dowdeswell', *Sir Henry Cavendish's Debates of the House of Commons during the Thirteenth Parliament of Great Britain* (ed. J. Wright, 2 vols., 1841–3, I, 575–90) [Cited as *Dowdeswell Memoir*]

The Papers of Benjamin Franklin, vols. 14–20 (eds. L. W. Labaree, W. B. Willcox, 1970–76) [Cited as *Franklin Papers*]

Benjamin Franklin: Letters to the Press 1758–1775 (ed. V. W. Crane, Chapel Hill, 1950).

The Correspondence of General Thomas Gage with the Secretaries of State and with the War Office and the Treasury 1763–1775 (ed. C. E. Carter, 2 vols., New Haven, 1931–3) [Cited as *Gage Corr.*]

The Correspondence of King George the Third from 1760 to December 1783 (ed. Sir John Fortescue, 6 vols., 1927–8) [Cited as *Corr. of George III*]

Autobiography and Political Correspondence of Augustus Henry, Third Duke of Grafton (ed. Sir William R. Anson, 1896) [Cited as *Grafton Autobiography*]

The Grenville Papers: being the correspondence of Richard Grenville, Earl Temple, K.G., and the Right Honourable George Grenville, their friends and contemporaries (ed. W. J. Smith, 4 vols., 1852–3) [Cited as *Grenville Papers*]

The Diary and Letters of his Excellency Thomas Hutchinson, Esq. (ed. P. O. Hutchinson, 2 vols., 1883–6) [Cited as *Hutchinson Diary*]

The Jenkinson Papers 1760–1766 (ed. N. S. Jucker, 1949)

The Papers of Sir William Johnson, vol. 7 (ed. A. C. Flick, Albany, 1931) [Cited as *Johnson Papers*]

The Letters of Junius (ed. J. Cannon, Oxford, 1978)

Memoirs and Correspondence of George, Lord Lyttelton, from 1734 to 1773 (ed. Robert Phillimore, 2 vols., 1845)

Peter Oliver's Origin and Progress of the American Rebellion. A Tory View (eds. D. Adair and J. A. Schutz, San Marino, 1963)

Memoirs of the Marquis of Rockingham and his Contemporaries (ed. George Thomas, Earl of Albemarle, 2 vols., 1852) [Cited as *Rockingham Memoirs*]

'The Parliamentary Diaries of Nathaniel Ryder 1764–1767' (ed. P. D. G. Thomas, *Camden Miscellany*, XXIII, pp. 229–351, Camden Fourth Series, VII, Royal Historical Society, 1969) [Cited as *Ryder Diary*]

Historical Memoirs from 16 March 1763 to 25 July 1778 of William Smith (ed. W. H. W. Sabine, 2 vols., New York, 1956) [Cited as *Smith Memoirs*]

Facsimiles of Manuscripts in European Archives Relating to America 1773–1783 (ed. B. F. Stevens, 25 vols., Wilmington, 1970 reprint) [Cited as Stevens, *Facsimiles*]

Trade and Politics, 1767–1769 (eds. C. W. Alvord and C. E. Carter, Illinois State Historical Library. Collections, 16 (1921)) [Cited as *Trade and Politics*]

'Letters of William Samuel Johnson to the Governors of Connecticut', *Trumbull Papers. Collections of Massachusetts Historical Society*, 5th series, 9 (1855), 211–490) [Cited as *Trumbull Papers*]

The Last Journals of Horace Walpole, during the Reign of George III from 1771–1783 (ed. A. F. Stewart, 2 vols., 1910) [Cited as H. Walpole, *Last Journals*]

The Letters of Horace Walpole, Fourth Earl of Orford (ed. Mrs Paget Toynbee, 16 vols., Oxford, 1905) [Cited as H. Walpole, *Letters*]

Horace Walpole. Memoirs of the Reign of King George the Third (ed. G. F. Russell Barker, 4 vols., 1894) [Cited as H. Walpole, *Memoirs*]

C. Contemporary Periodicals

The Annual Register

The Gazetteer

The Gentleman's Magazine

Lloyd's Evening Post

London Chronicle

London Evening Post

Middlesex Journal

Morning Chronicle

The Political Register

Public Advertiser

St. James' Chronicle

SECONDARY WORKS

A. Books

ALDEN, J. R., *John Stuart and the Southern Colonial Frontier. A Study in Indian Relations, War, Trade, and Land Problems in the Southern Wilderness 1754–1775* (Ann Arbor, 1944)
—— *General Gage in America* (Baton Rouge, 1948)
ASHTON, T. S., *Economic Fluctuations in England 1700–1800* (Oxford, 1959)
BAILYN, B., *The Ideological Origins of the American Revolution* (Cambridge, USA, 1967)
—— *The Ordeal of Thomas Hutchinson. Loyalism and the Destruction of the First British Empire* (London, 1974)
BAKER, J. H., *An Introduction to English Legal History* (London, 1979)
BARGAR, B. D., *Lord Dartmouth and the American Revolution* (Columbia, USA, 1965)
BARROW, T. C., *Trade and Empire. The British Customs Service in Colonial America 1660–1775* (Cambridge, USA, 1967)
BASYE, A. H., *The Lords Commissioners of Trade and Plantations, Commonly Known as the Board of Trade, 1748–82* (New Haven, 1925)
BELLOT, L. J., *William Knox. The Life and Thought of an Eighteenth Century Imperialist* (Austin, 1977)
BONWICK, C., *English Radicals and the American Revolution* (Chapel Hill, 1977)
BREWER, J., *Party Ideology and Popular Politics at the Accession of George III* (Cambridge, 1976)
BRIDENBAUGH, C., *Cities in Revolt. Urban Life in America 1743–1776* (New York, 1955)
BROOKE, J., *The Chatham Administration 1766–1768* (London, 1956)
—— *King George III* (London, 1972)
BROWN, P., *The Chathamites* (London, 1967)
BROWN, R. D., *Revolutionary Politics in Massachusetts. The Boston Committee of Correspondence and the Towns, 1772–1774* (Cambridge, USA, 1970)
CHRISTIE, I. R. and LABAREE, B. W., *Empire or Independence 1760–1776. A British–American Dialogue on the Coming of the American Revolution* (Oxford, 1976)
CLARK, D. M., *British Opinion and the American Revolution* (2nd edn., New York, 1966)
CURREY, C. B., *Road to Revolution. Benjamin Franklin in England 1765–1775* (New York, 1968)
DAVIDSON, P., *Propaganda and the American Revolution 1763–1783* (Chapel Hill, 1941)
DERRY, J., *English Politics and the American Revolution* (London, 1976)
DICKERSON, O. M., *The Navigation Acts and the American Revolution* (New York, 1951)
DONOUGHUE, B., *British Politics and the American Revolution. The Path to War 1773–75* (London, 1964)

ERNST, J. A., *Money and Politics in America 1755–1775. A Study in the Currency Act of 1764 and the Political Economy of Revolution* (Chapel Hill, 1973)

FITZMAURICE, LORD, *Life of William Earl of Shelburne, afterwards First Marquess of Lansdowne* (2 vols., London, 1912)

FORSTER, C. P., *The Uncontrolled Chancellor. Charles Townshend and his American Policy* (Providence, 1978)

GIPSON, L. H., *The British Empire before the American Revolution*, X–XIV (New York, 1961–9)

GOEBEL, J., *The Struggle for the Falkland Islands* (2nd edn., New Haven, 1982)

GREENE, J. P., *The Quest for Power. The Lower House of Assembly in the Southern Royal Colonies 1689–1776* (Chapel Hill, 1963)

GUTTRIDGE, G. H., *English Whiggism and the American Revolution* (Berkeley, USA, 1942)

HAIG, R. L., *The Gazetteer 1735–1797. A Study in the Eighteenth Century English Newspaper* (Carbondale, 1960)

HINKHOUSE, F. J., *The Preliminaries of the American Revolution as Seen in the English Press 1763–1775* (New York, 1926)

HOFFMAN, R. J. S., *Edmund Burke. New York Agent, with his Letters to the New York Assembly* (Philadelphia, 1956)

—— *The Marquis. A Study of Lord Rockingham 1730–1782* (New York, 1973)

KAMMEN, M. G., *A Rope of Sand. The Colonial Agents, British Politics and the American Revolution* (Ithaca, 1968)

KNOLLENBERG, B., *Growth of the American Revolution 1766–1775* (New York, 1975)

LABAREE, B. W., *The Boston Tea Party* (New York, 1964)

LABAREE, L. W., *Royal Government in America. A Study of the British Colonial System before 1783* (New Haven, 1930)

LAWSON, P., *George Grenville. A Political Life* (Oxford, 1984)

MAIER, P., *From Resistance to Revolution. Colonial Radicals and the Development of American Opposition to Britain 1765–1776* (London, 1973)

MILLER, J. C., *Sam Adams. Pioneer in Propaganda* (Stamford, 1936)

NAMIER, Sir LEWIS, and BROOKE, J., eds., *The House of Commons 1754–1790. The History of Parliament* (3 vols., London, 1964)

—— and —— *Charles Townshend* (London, 1964)

NORRIS, J., *Shelburne and Reform* (London, 1963)

O'GORMAN, F., *The Rise of Party in England. The Rockingham Whigs 1760–1782* (London, 1975)

OLSON, A. G., *The Radical Duke. Career and Correspondence of Charles Lennox third Duke of Richmond* (London, 1961)

REA, R. R., *The English Press in Politics 1760–1774* (Lincoln, USA, 1963)

RITCHESON, C. R., *British Politics and the American Revolution* (Norman, USA, 1954)

RUDÉ, G., *Wilkes and Liberty. A Social Study of 1763 to 1774* (Oxford, 1962)

SCHLESINGER, A. M., *The Colonial Merchants and the American Revolution 1763–1776* (New York, 1964 reprint of 1917 publication)

SCHUMPETER, E. B., *English Overseas Trade Statistics 1697–1808* (Oxford, 1960)

SHY, J., *Towards Lexington. The Role of the British Army in the Coming of the American Revolution* (Princeton, 1965)

SMITH, C. D., *The Early Career of Lord North the Prime Minister* (Cranbury, USA, 1979)

SOSIN, J. M., *Whitehall and the Wilderness. The Middle West in British Colonial Policy 1760–1775* (Lincoln, USA, 1961)

—— *Agents and Merchants. British Colonial Policy and the Origins of the American Revolution 1763–1775* (Lincoln, USA, 1965)

SPECTOR, M. M., *The American Department of the British Government 1768–1782* (New York, 1940)

SUTHERLAND, L. S., *The East India Company in Eighteenth Century Politics* (Oxford, 1952)

THOMAS, P. D. G., *The House of Commons in the Eighteenth Century* (Oxford, 1971)

—— *British Politics and the Stamp Act Crisis. The First Phase of the American Revolution 1763–1767* (Oxford, 1975)

—— *Lord North* (London, 1976)

—— *The American Revolution* (The English Satirical Print 1600–1832, Cambridge, 1986)

UBBELOHDE, C., *The Vice-Admiralty Courts and the American Revolution* (Chapel Hill, 1960)

WICKWIRE, F. B., *British Subministers and Colonial America 1763–1783* (Princeton, 1966)

ZOBEL, H. B., *The Boston Massacre* (New York, 1970)

B. Essays, Articles in Periodicals, and Occasional Publications

BARNWELL, J. W., ed., 'The Correspondence of Charles Garth', *South Carolina Historical and Genealogical Magazine*, 29 (1928) to 33 (1932) [Cited as *SCHGM*]

BASYE, A. H., 'The Secretary of State for the Colonies', *A[merican] H[istorical] R[eview]*, 28 (1922), 13–23

BROWN, R. D., 'Massachusetts Towns Reply to the Boston Committee of Correspondence, 1773', *W[illiam and] M[ary] Q[uarterly]*, 25 (1968), 22–39

—— 'The Massachusetts Convention of Towns, 1768', *WMQ*, 26 (1969), 94–104

CARTER, C. E., 'The Significance of the Military Office in America, 1763–1775', *AHR*, 28 (1922–3), 475–88

CHAFFIN, R. C., 'The Townshend Acts of 1767', *WMQ*, 27 (1970), 90–121

CHAMPAGNE, R., 'Family Politics versus Constitutional Principles: the New York Assembly Elections of 1768 and 1769', WMQ, 20 (1963), 57–79

CLARK, D. M., 'American Board of Customs 1767–1785', AHR, 45 (1939–40), 777–806

DAVIES, K. G., 'The End of British Administration in the North American Colonies', Proceedings of the British Academy, 61 (1975), 1–24

DICKERSON, O. M., 'Writs of Assistance as a Cause of the Revolution', The Era of the American Revolution (ed. R. B. Morris, New York, 1939), pp. 40–75

—— 'Use made of the Revenue from the Tax upon Tea', N[ew] E[ngland] Q[uarterly], 31 (1958), 232–43

FENNELLY, C., 'William Franklin of New Jersey', WMQ, 6 (1949), 361–82

GREENE, J. P., 'Bridge to Revolution: The Wilkes Fund Controversy in South Carolina 1769–1775', J[ournal of] S[outhern] H[istory], 29 (1963), 19–52

HUGHES, E., 'Lord North's Correspondence 1766–83', E[nglish] H[istorical] R[eview], 72 (1947), 218–38

HUMPHREYS, R. A., 'Lord Shelburne and British Colonial Policy 1766–1768', EHR, 50 (1935), 257–77

LANGFORD, P., 'The Rockingham Whigs and America, 1767–1773', Statesmen, Scholars and Merchants. Essays in Eighteenth Century History presented to Dame Lucy Sutherland (eds. A. Whiteman, J. S. Bromley, and P. G. M. Dickson, Oxford, 1973), pp. 135–152

—— 'Old Whigs, Old Tories, and the American Revolution', Journal of Imperial and Commonwealth History, 8 (1980), 106–30

LAWSON, P., 'George Grenville and America: The Years of Opposition, 1765–1770', WMQ, 37 (1980), 562–76

LESLIE, W. R., 'The Gaspée Affair: A Study of its Constitutional Significance', M[ississippi] V[alley] H[istorical] R[eview], 39 (1952), 233–56

LORD, D. C. and CALHOUN, R. M., 'The removal of the Massachusetts General Court from Boston 1769–1772', J[ournal of] A[merican] H[istory], 55 (1969), 735–55

LOVEJOY, D. S., 'Rights Imply Equality: The Case against Admiralty Jurisdiction in America 1764–1776', WMQ, 16 (1959), 457–84

MAIER, P., 'John Wilkes and American Disillusionment with Britain', WMQ, 20 (1963), 373–95

MARSHALL, P., 'Lord Hillsborough, Samuel Wharton and the Ohio Grant, 1769–1775', EHR, 80 (1965), 717–39

—— 'Sir William Johnson and the Treaty of Fort Stanwix. 1768', J[ournal of] A[merican] S[tudies], 1 (1967), 149–79

—— 'Colonial Protest and Imperial Retrenchment: Indian Policy 1764–1768', JAS, 5 (1971), 1–17

MARTIN, A. S., 'The King's Customs: Philadelphia 1763–1774', WMQ, 5 (1948), 201–16

MILLER, J. C., 'The Massachusetts Convention, 1768', *NEQ*, 6 (1934), 445–74

REA, R. R., 'The Impact of Party Journalism in the Political Register', *The Historian*, 17 (1954), 1–17

ROGERSON, R. A., 'Political Mobilisation and the American Revolution: The Resistance Movement in Philadelphia 1765 to 1776', *WMQ*, 31 (1974), 565–88

SAINSBURY, J., 'The Pro-Americans of London, 1769 to 1782', *WMQ*, 35 (1978), 423–54

SHERIDAN, R. B., 'The British Credit Crisis of 1772 and the American Colonies', *J[ournal of] E[conomic] H[istory]*, 20 (1960), 161–86

SLAUGHTER, T. P., 'The Tax Man Cometh: Ideological Opposition to Internal Taxes 1760–90', *WMQ*, 41 (1984), 556–91

THOMAS, P. D. G., 'The Beginning of Parliamentary Reporting in Newspapers 1768–1774', *EHR*, 74 (1959), 623–36

—— *Sources for Debates of the House of Commons 1768–1774*, *B[ulletin of the] I[nstitute of] H[istorical] R[esearch]*, Special Supplement no. 4. (1959)

—— 'John Wilkes and the Freedom of the Press (1771)', *BIHR*, 33 (1960), 86–98

—— 'Charles Townshend and American Taxation in 1767', *EHR*, 83 (1968), 33–51

—— 'The St. George's Fields "Massacre" of 10 May 1768: An Eye-witness Report', *London Journal*, 4 (1978), 221–6

—— 'New Light on the Commons Debate of 1763 on the American Army', *WMQ*, 38 (1981), 110–12

—— 'George III and the American Revolution', *History*, 70 (1985), 16–31

THOMPSON, M. E., 'The Ward-Hopkins Controversy and the American Revolution in Rhode Island', *WMQ*, 16 (1959), 363–75

VARGA, N., 'The New York Restraining Act: Its Passage and Some Effects', *New York History*, 37 (1956), 233–58

—— 'Robert Charles: New York Agent 1748–1770', *WMQ*, 18 (1961), 21–35

WALETT, F. G., 'The Massachusetts Council, 1766–1774: The Transformation of a Conservative Institution', *WMQ*, 6 (1949), 605–27

—— 'Governor Bernard's Undoing: An Earlier Hutchinson Letters Affair', *NEQ*, 37 (1965), 217–26

WATSON, D. H., 'Joseph Harrison and the Liberty Incident', *WMQ*, 20 (1963), 585–95

—— 'The Rockingham Whigs and the Townshend Duties', *EHR*, 84 (1969), 561–5

WICKWIRE, F. B., 'John Pownall and British Colonial Policy', *WMQ*, 20 (1963), 543–54

C. Unpublished University Theses

BOWEN, H. V., 'British Politics and the East India Company 1766–1773' (Ph.D. Wales, 1986)

DURRANT, P., 'A Political Life of Augustus Henry Fitzroy Third Duke of Grafton 1735–1811' (Ph.D. Manchester, 1978)

HAMER, M. T., 'From the Grafton Administration to the Ministry of North 1768–1772' (Ph.D. Cambridge, 1970)

LAWSON, P., 'Faction in Politics: George Grenville and his Followers 1765–70' (Ph.D. Wales, 1980)

LOWE, W. C., 'Politics in the House of Lords 1760–1775' (Ph.D. Emory, 1975)

MARSHALL, P., 'Imperial Regulation of American Indian Affairs 1763–1774' (Ph.D. Yale, 1959)

REES, S. E., 'The Political Career of Wills Hill, Earl of Hillsborough (1718–1793): With Particular Reference to his American Policy (Ph.D. Wales, 1977)

THOMAS, J. P., 'The British Empire and the Press 1763–1774' (D.Phil. Oxford, 1982)

Index